AUTOBIOGRAPHY

BOOK 5

ROSE AND CROWN

Each volume in the evocative and richly entertaining autobiography of Sean O'Casey is essential reading for a proper appreciation of this major Irish dramatist whose plays were among the most exciting developments in modern drama.

Born in the back streets of Dublin, suffering from weak and diseased eyes, he lived in poverty and physical hardship for many years. In his late teens he became a manual labourer and, after working on the roads or in the docks from five in the morning to six at night, he would spend his evenings helping the cause of the Gaelic League and Sinn Fein. He became Secretary of the Irish Citizen Army and a founder member of the Irish Labour Party. Although his first published work was in 1907, not until the success of *Juno and the Paycock* in 1925 did he give up manual work and become a full-time writer.

In 1926 O'Casey came to London to receive the Hawthornden Prize for *Juno and the Paycock*, and never returned to Ireland. The crowded years that followed saw his marriage to the lovely young actress, Eileen Carey, the mounting controversy over *The Silver Tassie*, and his eventful visit to America for the staging of *Within the Gates*.

By the same author in Pan Books

AUTOBIOGRAPHY (BOOK 1):
I KNOCK AT THE DOOR
AUTOBIOGRAPHY (BOOK 2):
PICTURES IN THE HALLWAY
AUTOBIOGRAPHY (BOOK 3):
DRUMS UNDER THE WINDOWS
AUTOBIOGRAPHY (BOOK 4):
INISHFALLEN, FARE THEE WELL
AUTOBIOGRAPHY (BOOK 6):
SUNSET AND EVENING STAR

AUTOBIOGRAPHY
BOOK 5

ROSE AND CROWN

SEAN O'CASEY

UNABRIDGED

PAN BOOKS LTD : LONDON

First published 1952
by Macmillan and Company Ltd.
This edition published 1973 by Pan Books Ltd,
33 Tothill Street, London, SW1.

ISBN 0 330 23498 6

*Printed in Great Britain by
Richard Clay (The Chaucer Press), Ltd, Bungay, Suffolk*

CONTENTS

This is the porcelain clay of humankind

LONDON APPRENTICE

HERE he was now, planting a foot for the first time on the pavement of London; planting it firmly, with a confident air and a fluttering heart. Sliding with the hiss of steam and the throb of pistons into the heart of the

> Great flower that opens but at night,
> Great city of the midnight sun,
> Whose day begins when day is done.

A London apprentice now. Listen!

> Oranges and lemons, say the bells of St Clement's.
> When will you pay me? say the bells at Old Bailey.
> When I grow rich, say the bells at Shoreditch.

How different was the view now from that of the lovely coast of Wales, lacing the land's edge from Holyhead to Chester. Coming within the grip of the city, he had been wondering through miles of the journey at the dismal wretchedness of the houses, apparently trotting away from him as the train ambled to the end of its journey; trotting away from him so that he mightn't fully see the abject royalty of their miserable appearance. The train had run through a long, drab gauntlet of houses, some of them fat with filth. The magnificent, wealthy city of London, with her gilded Mayor and red-robed Aldermen, was entered through long kennels of struggling poverty and disordered want. Sisters to the houses he had so often seen, slinky with shame, in the shabbiest streets of Dublin. There were the lacerated walls, the windows impudent with dirt, the poor, shrinking clothing, reluctant to be washed, hanging from poles thrust through the windows, fixed to the sills. Just like the hidden parts of Dublin. 'Faith, her privates we. One didn't land in London through a lane of roses.

Euston! Alight here as many Irish had done before him; a short visit so often extended to take the emigrant's rest of life.

England; Sasana! Euston; a sprawling untidy place, dim and dark; tormented with many sounds – the clatter of trucks, the patter of hurrying, fussy feet; babble and squeak of passengers not sure of the right train or the proper platform; the sibilant hiss of steam; the sturdy smell of smoke; the soothing, sickly scent of oil; porters hurrying, guards sauntering amid the rustle of paper and magazine, bought by people who would never read the half of them; women sitting semi-alert on benches, waiting for the hands of a big clock to tell them when to move; streams of men, women, and children, dropping from the train that had just stopped, pouring along under the grimy roof like an underground river towards an open sluice-gate, to divide into rivulets and trickles, spreading fanwise to different parts of the mammoth city. Each one an individual, a soul-body; something separate from each so like itself, conceit concealing that each one is a simulacrum of the other;

> Albert Johnson is my nayem,
> England is my nation;
> London is my dwelling-place,
> And heaven my destination.

Heaven! Meanwhile, we must be satisfied with the smoke and the grime of Euston. 'Seen at night, or through a mist, Euston Station is one of the most impressive sights in London', said Aubrey Beardsley. Well, seen by night, or through a mist, there may be many things appearing impressive, be it either man or dog or eunuch; and the picturer of his own horrible delusions added, 'Euston Station has made it unnecessary to visit Egypt'. The slimy, fruitful Nile, sun, sand, date-palm, and bedouin – none are needed. Pharaoh porters about here.

To Sean, who stared at the building before he hid himself away in a taxi, the entrance looked surlily bewildered, as if it had been set down in the wrong place, as indeed it had, for ancient Egyptian architecture does not wed itself with English life. Though it forced itself into the appearance of a temple, here was no shrine at which to pray for a safe journey from one place to another. The ponderous pillars holding up its tremendous back looked like a monster's heavy feet standing in a jungle clearance, the whole brute staring in front of itself, not knowing which way to turn.

There was James B. Fagan hurrying towards him, having caught sight of the red muffler encircling Sean's neck, the insignia Sean had written to say would reveal his advent to London. Sean's play had been transferred from the Royalty to the Fortune, a little theatre directly opposite the towering, bully-like Royal Theatre in Drury Lane – Falstaff and the little page. The play was to open itself out in the new theatre two nights from now, and Sean was to be kept hidden till then so that familiarity with others should not mar the appearance of the slum dramatist on the first night in the Fortune; enhancing publicity by standing on the stage, grinning, bowing, and saying a few sweet words to the applauding audience that had filled the house for the first performance.

Embedded in a taxi, he was bowled off to the Kenilworth Hotel, Bloomsbury; hustled up in a lift to his room, while Fagan waited below, like a warder, till Sean had freshened himself with a wash, and was ready for Fagan to take him off silently. He was to be kept like a peril in an oyster till the first night of the play had passed into time that neither he nor Fagan would ever touch again. After a light meal in Fagan's flat in Great Russell Street, Sean was again embedded into a taxi, and taken, like a prisoner out for an hour's amusement, to the Duke of York's Theatre to see Jean Forbes-Robertson playing in Chekhov's *Uncle Vanya*. The theatre he was in was no different from the big ones of Dublin. That was all he learned from this outing. Things were so different with him now, so new, so far from what he had been used to; his future was so uncertain, his mind so buoyant with jostling thoughts; and he was hushed so deeply back to the rear of the box, with Mary Grey and James Fagan in front of him, that to this day he cannot remember a single thing about the play, the acting, or the production. The one memory remaining is the name of the play and the name of the leading actress, and these were fixed in his mind by the lovely coloured lights of red, yellow, and white, flashing over the entrance of the theatre, telling out her name and the name of the Russian play she acted in. The first London play he had seen, he hadn't seen at all. A long wait in the box when the play was over to ensure that the crowd had gone, in fear anyone among it should have recognized Sean, and have shouted out the hot news that O'Casey was here. Then a quick retreat into a taxi again, and so to bed.

He was to be shown off, a new oddity, an odd wonder; a guttersnipe among the trimly educated and the richly clad; the slum dramatist, who, in the midst of a great darkness, had seen a greater light. Fagan was constantly pulling Sean away from his own thoughts, trying to listen to the part of England speaking to him, trying to see the part of England passing him by. He was pulled here, pulled there; brought, bowing, before young men and women, before elderly men, before anyone who could write about him in the daily papers and in the weekly journals, so keeping the romance of his arrival in London before the people in order that the beautiful sign of House Full should garnish the front of the theatre nightly.

He was photographed getting into a taxi and getting out of one; photographed in the theatre, and in the flat where he lived; photographed talking to policemen; brought face to face with those whose pencils could dash down a swift impression to appear fresh and full-blown in some paper the following day, or in some periodical at the end of the week; some, grinning and ghastly, showing themselves in a paper on the Lord's day. Coriolanus O'Casside hurried here and there by Menenius Fagan, to show himself, to say what a good fellow he was. He was tired of it before it had well begun. Very boring, for Sean in his heart didn't care a damn what anyone thought of him. Once, when a photographer handed him a huge, green, cardboard shamrock, telling him to fix it in his coat, and look gay, Sean let loose on him; and James Fagan, going white, heard for the first time the savage and profane vernacular of the Dublin navvy.

Having written the play, he was now busily employed selling the tickets for the show – or so it seemed to Sean. Once, after a smiling interlude of an introduction by Fagan, Sean was led to a teashop by the eager and delicately mannered Beverley Nichols, young, oh, so young, and, oh, so ambitious, whose white hand was already fidgeting with the latch on the doorway to fame; trying to lift the heavy iron without hurting his fingers. Sean hoped some day he wouldn't mind hurting his fingers, for it was on lads like this one that England's literary life depended. The teashop was filled with young men and women, weary-looking and pale-faced, seeking whatever nourishment cakes and buns could give them, adding the stimulant of tea to roughly orchestrated cymbal-clash of

crockery, toned down by the bass of shuffling people, some
rising to end a meal, others sitting down to begin one.

Sean flung off a heavy sky-blue overcoat, reinforced within
by a warm, brilliant lining of black-lined red squares, bought in
Moss Brothers, second-hand for four pounds, through the advice and bargaining of Fagan, who was afraid the east wind
would do Sean harm – for Fagan had a fine kindliness deep in
his heart under his anxiety for the prosperity of the box-office.

Sean looked at the figure sitting at the other side of the table,
and wondered what was really beneath the nicely pressed suit,
the handsome shirt set off by a handsome tie. He noticed the
figure carefully placing a pair of soft, quietly yellow kid gloves
on the chair beside him, taking no notice of the turmoil around
him. He looks, thought Sean, like a canary among a flock of
quails;. or a daffodil on a morning without any of the March
winds about. Never saw a hobnailed boot in his life, not even in
a shop window. Mignonette among the nettles.

A toff! Still, such signs were deceptive. Sean had known
friends in Ireland, customarily as dapper as this lad, who had
turned into hurlers and footballers as fierce and gallant as any
who had raced around a Gaelic playing-field. Deep down, un-
tidiness was often envious of a satisfying neatness.

Be nice to him, for his articles are widely read, Fagan had
advised. Rather good-looking youth, Sean thought, but ne'er
the sign of a furrow from thought on his soft-complexioned
face. Intelligence without the practice of deeper and dangerous
thought. Too young yet. *Nichols was educated at Marlborough
School and Oxford University*, Fagan had whispered, but this
only put Sean wondering now if Oxford created souls; God
made a start, and Oxford finished and polished the job. Not
God nor Oxford, but only man himself could develop his own
soul. He had but the haziest notion of what Oxford was or
what Oxford meant, and he was too full of his own thoughts
to care what the name of Oxford meant when it was added to
the name of Man. (Later on, Sean came to know that great
men of his own day came out of Oxford and Cambridge; men
like Trevelyan with his History under an arm; the warrior,
Coulton, leading a vivid word-pageant of Five Centuries of
Religion; Rutherford with the atom an ornament on his watch-
chain; gentle-soul'd Gore, of Oxford, holding high his lantern
of Lux Mundi, to lighten men's feet along the narrow way;

and Frazer marching into the kingdom of the knowledge of
good and evil waving his lovely Golden Bough. But no man
has a reason or right to be proud of any Institution, though
many an Institution has a reason and a right to be proud of
many a man.)

The handsome lad began to question Sean as to what he
thought of the painted ladies, bright young things whose outlook on life was a squealing, giggling contempt for it all, bar
what they lived of it themselves; what he 'thought of the
crimped young men, the poisoned critics'; all the wilting,
hectic generation which many had come to take for granted –
as if this generation of gaudy gomerils had come from first
creation, and would extend to the end of time – though some
of them weren't aware even of the way to breed. Nichols asked
Sean what he thought of the 'brilliant young dramatist, Noel
Coward, who had specialized in the portrayal of this particular
stratum of life. What did he think of this utterly, absolutely
artificial crowd?'

Wasting his time and mine talking of things that didn't
matter much, thought Sean. Aloud, he said: They couldn't be
absolutely artificial, for even the worst of them are of human
flesh and blood subsisting. They may not laugh as others do, or
ponder as others do; but none of them can evade the pinch of
human pain, and, sooner or later, sorrow will singe their souls,
and then they become as others are – splendidly mortal. Careless conduct, high-handed hysterical laughter, and devil-may-
care devotion to their own flighty flock can never cover them
completely from the searching hand of life.

These, thought Sean, of whom Nichols speaks so inquisi-
tively, who dazzle his thoughts so that he can think of none
else; these are but a few false notes in the sad, sweet, silent
music of humanity. They think they dance through life, but the
dance denies its own merriment. With all their sour fragrance,
their hiccuping laughter, their contraband carelessness, their
jigging on the tomb of their own dead endeavours, they will
descend one day soon into as much dust as a new-born baby's
hand can hold.

A story of grand school and grander college was tailed on to
this sparkling young man, yet Sean thought it strange that this
son of Lady Beaufort's bounty never mentioned a name to him
that was known in any art or any science. Not a word from

this gem-like lad about England's greater children; Shakespeare unmentioned; Shelley apparently forgotten; Milton ignored; neither could Sean see a sign of a scene from a Constable or a Cotman livening the iris of his boyish eye. Not even a word for the working millions of England's men and women, whose labour made it possible for his cleverness to live and go about gay. He didn't know. Sean wondered if he cared. Refusing to brave the rougher airs of life, he had left the elegant airs of the colleges behind him. He brought with him neither airs from heaven nor blasts from hell.

What was this young fellow's England, and who lived there? From his own unjointed chat, slyly inserted between questions, it was a small part of London inhabited and inhibited by a bunch of frolicking fools, who slapped Time in the face and spit on his beard in an effort to frighten age away, not knowing that age was but crossing the crest of the hill to go down the other side of life, where new flowers grew, and charm abounded as rich and delightful as those loved and handled on the younger slope left behind for ever. These frightened young people, afraid to fight fear with courage, fought fear with fear. Well dressed, extremely well dressed, clever, with fair homes, some of them gaudy with goods, idle, yet knowing no want, these youngsters were already of life's down and out. These young, desperate things had abandoned life before even they had learned how to fight for it.

We are all artificial at times, thought Sean, edging thoughts into his mind between the mechanical answering of the questions put to him by Beverley Nichols. I am being artificial now, for two currents of thought run through my mind, mingling in orderly confusion, and betraying each other: the one bidding him, for the sake of his play, to go easy, and be nice to Nichols whose articles were so widely read; the other prompting him to tell this lad that to work for a few years in a factory; to work, too cold, too wet, too warm, in a field-farm; on a railway platform or permanent way; to come to this hot, hasty restaurant even, and take whatever meals he could get for a year and a day, would give him a good chance of receiving a revelation from God informing him that life, even the life of London, wasn't accounted for by a flippant generation whose members wouldn't crowd two streets of a tiny town.

But Sean held his peace, till the fine figure had jotted down in a note-book all that Sean had ventured to say; had carefully placed the delicately yellow gloves on the confident hands; had settled the dignified trilby on the confident head, and they had risen to take body and mind away from the centre of the tired hurry of the restaurant, the pale faces, and the walls ribbed thick with hanging overcoats and dangling hats.

—Goodbye, murmured Beverley Nichols, as they stood on the path outside, while red buses reared and roared by them; I hope we may soon meet again; and a carefully-gloved hand touched Sean's bare one for a moment. Then the young man departed, carrying himself nicely within a top-coat cleverly caught in at the waist, and flowing from the waist around the slender legs; walking along the rumbling, rancorous street as if he were sauntering down a gilt-edged garden path.

Then Sean said, Jasus! And thought, what a world without there is for this lad, but he stays at home!

The plays proved to be a passport for Sean into the big, big houses. Houses that were big-doored, with many wonderful windows opening on to fairylands of blossom and of tree; houses with wide stairways, smooth floors coddled with cosy carpets; gleaming wood of chair, table, and bureau of Louis Quatorze's fancy and Louis Quinze; Georgian make of Shera-ton, Chippendale, and Hepplewhite, that fair dazzled the eye. Houses that were patrolled by men free to wear jewelled orders dangling from their coats; and women, coarsely created or finely formed, clad in all the arrogance clever and imaginative minds could weave around them, moved hither and thither over the accommodating carpets with indolent energy, gems nodding drowsily to life on the yellowing and crinkled skin of the old, or sparkling saucily and invitingly on the bosoms of those presented with the ardour and audacity of youth, their beauty often blurred by the sparkle of a white and saucy breast.

Precious stones; precious, but still stones; lovely to look at, to handle, even to wear; but not good enough to honour, wor-ship, and obey. With all their sparkle and beauty, they were dying things, and the people who honoured, worshipped, and obeyed them, were dying too. *The fire-born moods have fallen away.* Mighty baubles, alight with smiles underneath the glow of electricity and candelabra; and, yet, with all their luminous gallantry, like the gay girls who wore them, doomed to remain of the earth, earthy. Were they richer, any more lovely than the common stones that could be gathered from a lonely beach? Pebbles, black, mottled white, or ribbed with white lines; pebbles, white, stained with whorls of sable rondelles; pebbles, red, marked with brown, or tinged with amber; loveliness trodden under foot by the elder when the great sea sparkles, but causing children to pause at play, to stoop, to pick them up, and wonder what god had dropped his jewels. Pebbles that are coaxed into quietude by the summer sea, and tossed and tumbled by the yelling and the roaring tides driven by the winds of winter. Even in all the humility of their massed production, each is as great a miracle, each is as lovely as their costly companions, glittering vaingloriously underneath the gaudy glow of electricity and candelabra.

Sean passed by and touched with his fingers the treasured furnishings in sandalwood, teak, mahogany, rosewood, and walnut, ivoried often, and inlaid with ebony, mixed with mother-o'-pearl; bowed and shook hands among the gracious, showy assembly of silk dress and displayed jewellery; sat on a reponned red couch or a golden-ribbed chair, and eyed it all, finding it elegant, often gracious; delightful at times, dignified at times, but always sadly ridiculous because it was moving towards its end. Kindly they were, eager to share by show with him all their mighty nonsense; but no silk or satin, no sibylline shine of riches could shield him from feeling that this life was nearing its end. The twilight of the goods had come. He wondered what were the real thoughts that silk and satin bannered away out of sight, what troubled outlook on life touched the heart beneath the jewelled bodice and the lace that fringed its edge. They had great possessions. Come, sell all that thou hast, and follow me; follow us; follow the people. Follow, before the fight develops into a bloody tug of war. Already the jewels on the breasts of the beauties, the orders on the coats of the men, were looking awry now, for the little streets were hurling themselves on the great houses. Within them now but shadow shows were seen: all the miracles were happening outside. With all its costly pageantry, its jewelled assertiveness, its air of everlasting confidence, this life was losing its nerve; it was all afraid; it had begun to stumble. Even Beaconsfield's six hundred baronets (the noble six hundred) couldn't save things now. Six hundred of them in their dark-green costumes – the appropriate dress of *equites aurati*; each with his badge and his sacred collar of SS; belted and scarfed; his star glittering; his pennon flying; his hat white with a plume of white feathers; the sword and the gilt spurs; on a hand of each the thumb-ring and signet; each holding his coronet of two balls.

Noble fellows, all, but utterly ineffective now. The Egremonts and the Mitfords were sliding down the hill. Steel and cement were ousting the rococo and the ormolu; the classical portico and the gothic spire were sinking into cordial insignificance. There was no greatness that couldn't be excelled by greatness elsewhere. There could be *infinite riches in a little room*. There had been more majesty in his own one-room tenement home than all the glory in these places gathered together. Shakespeare had often come there, had sat by the fire. He had brought Mistress Quickly with him, and Doll Tearsheet leaning on the arm of the panting Falstaff. And Dickens had shared many a meal with him. Keats' Grecian Urn stood on the dusty mantelpiece with its leaf-fringed legends unfading; the young lad and younger maiden, running; one for ever loving, the other for ever fair. And Shelley's Prometheus laurelled the dim room with defiant patience, waiting for the kneebenders of the earth to pass to the dark, to the past, to the dead; till, veil by veil, evil and error fall. Hardy came, too, and sat him by the tenement fire, and sighed, mourning misunderstood Tess of the D'Urbervilles and Angel Clare's dead decisions. And there, too, on that settee, poor Jude the Obscure died disconsolate and alone, while Hardy's darkling thrush, aged, frail, and small, sang its defying song out on the sill of the window. Painters came, too, to show him dim glimpses of the glory he was yet to see – Giorgione, Constable, and Goya, telling him to look away from Irish eyes of painting, smiling into miserable vistas of yellow-roofed, white-walled cottages, with their brown piles of turf beside them, bunches of gorse by the wayside, and the skies full of Yeats' purple glow; all of one piece, one manner, one misery, destitute of colour and line and form.

No great music came sounding into Sean's ear, for the clef was to him an undecoded hieroglyphic. The chant of an odd bird, the lowing of cattle, the whistling of the wind, the patient patter of falling rain; the brave, meritorious tinkle of the Abbey Theatre orchestra, were all the sweet sounds that the ear of Sean knew. Oh, and the folk-song, the folk-song, the gay and melancholy strains of the Irish folk-song, on fiddle, on harp, and fife. And no folk-art is there but is born in the gay disregard of gain, and in the desire to add a newer beauty and a steadier charm to God's well-turned-out gifts to man; and so, out of the big love in his heart for all things comely and of good shape, the great poet Yeats exclaims:

Folk-art is indeed the oldest of the aristocracies of thought, and because it refuses what is passing and trivial, the merely clever and pretty, as certainly as the vulgar and insincere, and because it has gathered into itself the simplest and most unforgettable thoughts of the generations, it is the soil where all art is rooted. Wherever it is spoken by the fireside, or sung by the roadside, or carved upon the lintel, appreciation of the arts that a single mind gives unity and design to, spreads quickly when its hour is come.

Yeats, a vic, you never spoke a truer word.

When Sean had had time to look around and to hear what was said, he discovered that the city was packed with playwrights. He would be hard set to find a place for the sole of his foot, for, according to what he was told, the city steamed with drama-genius. And which were the greatest of the great? he had asked; but no one replied to his question. There were so many, they murmured, it would be hard to choose. So many; so great. But by listening cautiously and constantly, he found that the two names most often mentioned were those of Noel Coward, a young man, and Edgar Wallace, a middle-aged one. Top dogs. Turning plays out by the baker's dozen monthly. Came natural to them. What kind of plays? he had asked. Oh, just plays, you know, plays; assorted plays; serious plays, sunny plays, sad plays; all sorts. The finest dramatic literature (to judge from what was said) given to the world was flooding the London people with deepest emotion and best of good cheer. Managers were working overtime producing the famous plays, and book merchants tired publishing them. The garlanded playwrights were the envy of all pup upholders, for they wore the best clothes, ate the best foods, drank the best wines, travelled in the best equipages, and shook hands heartily with the best people, calling them by their pet names. How'r you, Duke Jack; hope you're well, Baroness Babs. They balanced neatly on a newer peak of Darien.

So Sean was eager to see the theatre curtain rise to reveal

the stars; to share what Nathan, in a preface to a book of plays, says is innate in all good drama – 'probity, the passionate undertone, the brave resolve, the hint of spiritual music, poetic sweep, the surgery of human emotions, and the warm golden glow'. Up, up goes the tawdry curtain, and Sean saw *Cat's Cradle, Easy Virtue, The Queen Was in the Parlour, Kid Boots, This Woman Business, Journey's End,* and *Rose Marie.* Of all he saw, of all he heard, he could remember nothing; not a word, not a gesture, save one thing only: the chorus of *Rose Marie*; the extraordinary beautiful slide and slip, shimmering with colour, of the girls in the chorus of that immensely mortal musical play. Of all the rest, he could remember nothing; not a word, not a gesture. Not a rag left of all the finery worn in the theatre of that day; nothing that memory could give a salute to; not a thing. They had left not a wrack behind. How easy it is to write a play to be staged; how hard to write one to be remembered!

And yet fanfares of welcome and praise were blown by many of the critics for these poor, pottering things. Agate, the critic of *The Sunday Times,* heralded fast and furiously a number of them – *The Combined Maze, The Old Ladies, As Others See Us,* and *Journey's End,* calling them, in much excitement, great, wonderful, exquisite, and enduring. Sean had seen them all, and had sighed, and was silent. There wasn't a human heart-beat, no, nor even a human footstep in one of them; not a knock at the door; not a sob in the silence; not a stone flung through any amiable window of thought.

Most of the playwrights were out hunting the golden will-o'-the-wisp, *Ingenium,* which, Mr Agate explains in his book, *My Theatre Talks,* means 'the power to attain success'. So there they were, running hither and thither, using all the thin nets of their talents, trying to ensnare the flying West End butterfly of *Ingenium.* A name in coloured letters of glowing lights sent shivers and exultation through the hopes and down the spine of every anxious playwright. If he could but get his name there, he could fancy, as he walked along, that his name should be called wonderful, a prince of space and light and time. A garland of glowing jewels adown the dowdy street as if a flock of gaudier toucans were roosting on the ledges of the walls. Here are the shining crests of the playwrights who have caught the elusive motheley called *Ingenium*. Look and live; without seeking ye can find me here. The lights of a playwright shining upon us, giving us pride in the greeting of a great one. His lights shine before the sons of men. Lights to the jew and the gentile. But these lights are often false flatterers, deceiving the name that dwells within them.

Surely, though, occasionally, a figure comes the way of this drab street, one from the homeland, or from far across the sea, and hangs a lantern boldly on an outer wall; and the light lights, not only this one street, but every street in every town of England; a light that does not fail; a light not lit with hands, eternal in the world's ways. This light lasts; that one shines more gaudy for a day or two, but the hand of time quenches it; it is seen no more, and is gone from the ken of man for ever.

Why is the English Theatre so low in mind, so scanty in fancy and imagination, and the play-acting so fond of fasting from manly action and a lusty voice? Let him who spoke thirty years ago, speak again. Go on, Mr Yeats – we're all listening:

All exploitation of the life of the wealthy, for the eye and ear of the poor and half poor, in plays, in musical comedy, at the cinema, in Daily Mirror *photographs, is a travesty of the life of the rich; and if it were not would all but justify some red terror; and it impoverishes and vulgarizes the imagination, showing a life that is all display and hurry, passion without emotion, emotion without intellect, and where there is nothing stern and solitary.*

You're speaking the solemn truth, Mr Yeats: go on, son of my heart, go on:

The Theatre grows more elaborate, developing the player at the expense of the poet, developing the scenery at the expense of the player, always increasing the importance of whatever has come to it out of the mere mechanism of a building or the interests of a class, doing whatever is easiest rather than what is most noble, and shaping imaginations before the footlights as behind, that are stirred to excitements that belong to it and not to life; until at last life turns to other things, content to leave specialized energy to weaklings and triflers, to those in whose body there is the least quantity of herself.

Leave your hand in mine, poet from the first, friend at the

last; you took the words out of my mouth. The people of
Ireland and the clique that hemmed you in from them never
knew the man you really were. One word more before you go,
sir:

*All the arts when young and happy are but the point of the
spear whose handle is our daily life.*

Ah, Yeats, a ray from the red star had pierced your ear,
although you didn't know it then; but you began to feel its
stirring stab before you went away and left us lonely; left the
land barren of a life anyway equal to your own.

The Committee of the Garrick Club, in British kindliness of
heart, made Sean an honorary member for a few weeks till he
had settled down. Fagan towed him into it. Full steam ahead,
Fagan went forward everywhere, while Sean followed him like
a dinghy tied to a ship's stern, till he began to feel that London
was being hidden from him by the size and shadow of Fagan's
big body. Some great man of the theatre, Bancroft by name,
Fagan told Sean, had died on the day Sean entered, and, as a
sign of grief, a great wreath of brass and silver-gilt, its brightness blasted by a big black bow, had been thrust forward for all
members to see, and seeing, honour. Sean noticed that most of
the members, when they passed by the silver and brass, gave a
grin, ornamented with no reverential nod; and it seemed plain
that the thing failed to reverently link the day of radium, of
speed, of the golden bough, with the day of Dickens' mute and
Mr Mold. Bancroft? Who was he? Sean asked one or two of
the members, but neither was eager to talk of the dead man,
one of them murmuring that he had been a great actor in the
days that were past. A dead actor down under the dusts of
years ago. Sean had never heard of him before, and had never
heard of him since. Bancroft's ghost would never appear in the
mist of memories like the ghost of Macready, or Garrick's
ghost, or Kean's either.

A big house kept the Garrick Club together; big, a little
pompous, bubbling with dignity like a percolator. Balconies
stretched their way along under the windows of the upper
storey, bulging out into a bigger one over the front door. But
no page from England's shameful and gallant story was written on its façade for Sean to read; it didn't look like a bit of
England at all. No sign here of Kelt, Saxon, Norman, or Dane.
A pile of stone, mortar, and bricks that told a visitor nothing.

No scent from Constable's cornfield; no smear of salt from England's surrounding sea; no beer-stained snatch from Bardolph or from Corporal Nym; no whiff from Hogarth's hellish Holland's gin; no wave from England's life lapped as far as even to the lowest step of the entrance of the Garrick Club.

The building was an imitation of another one, of something from another life, from another land. Not knowing much about architecture, Sean could but guess that it imitated something found in Italy. It had the look of a building taken out of a crowd of others over-populating Naples, or on the road to Rome. Latinity in the bowels of London. Latin buildings, Latin saints, Latin headings to the Psalms, Latin literature; Verjil for ever! The fountain-hid of culture. King Billy looking like a fat Caesar on a Romanly-caparisoned horse in a Dublin Street; a Latin horseman with Latin armour, sword, and shield, remembering the cavalrymen who fell in the First World War; Charles the bawdy put into Latin dress, with a Latin laurel crown shading the shocked swing of his face. The Roman finger is thicker than the Englishman's thigh. No sign anywhere here of the Trumpet Major, the Lincolnshire Poacher, or the Shropshire Lad. One would imagine that, in one way or another, every important building in London should whisper a word in every ear that this is England.

A very handsome place inside, spacious and well furnished. Attractive dining-room where a fine and well-cooked meal could be had for a very reasonable price; and well the room looked when it was serving the members, the white tablecloths half shy of coloured blossoms leaning over the rims of vases like wee fairy lassies watching from crystal windows and wondering at the life they saw around them.

Fagan introduced Sean to a number of the members. These bowed, murmuring something as loud as the tick of a watch in a leather-lined pocket; bowed and went their ways; forgotten: all but two, a playwright and a play critic – Arthur Pinero and James Agate, standing, polished and prim on the dining-room floor, with Fagan courtesying before them and waving a consecrating mitt in the direction of Sean. Before coming to England, Sean had read, with a shock at the heart and head, a book, *The Old Drama and the New*, written and composed by William Archer, the drama critic, in which he had tossed the old, the Elizabethans, into the lowest circle of hell, and had exalted the new, Robertson, Pinero, Sutro, and others, into a higher heaven. This book was the first thing that cracked open Sean's belief in the London drama critics; for of them Archer was of the highest, and he had written the worst book on the theatre ever opened under the nose of man. And here was the dramatist whom Archer had lifted into a higher heaven than the higher one, swept and garnished for his imitators. Here was the hero of drama of whom Archer had written: *I re-read Pinero's plays with renewed and increased admiration. How insignificant are the blemishes upon the splendid series of comedies and dramas with which he has enriched our literature! If we had a rational system of repertory theatres, there are at least half a dozen of Sir Arthur's works that would be constantly before the public eye. When history views things in their just proportions, he will stand out as a great master of the essentials of drama. Sir Arthur Pinero, in spite of certain weaknesses, is an original dramatic genius.*

Jasus, boys, pause, now, to take breath. Sit down, sit down, golden lads and girls, and listen:

A remarkable fact is that some of the most highly esteemed dramatic criticism in the language has been written by men who had no clear conception – or perhaps a clear misconception – of the real nature of drama. Are there, I wonder, colour-blind painters and critics of painting? One is sometimes tempted, in these days, to answer the question in the affirmative; but I am sure they are not, and can never have been, so numerous as drama-blind dramatists and critics of drama.

All this was not written in a hurry. It was included in Lectures given at King's College by invitation of the London County Council, afterwards to be published in book form. So Archer must have read all he wrote a dozen times, slowly and carefully, taking thought for what he should set down in the permanency of a book. He had not to form an opinion and pour it out to harden in the pages of a journal between the descent of a curtain at eleven and the starting of a printing-press at twelve midnight. He had had time to carve it all out in the hardest of stone. And here it is, icebound, like a fossil dead for twenty thousand years.

So this was Pinero who was standing before Sean? How old-fashioned the little figure looked in its cut-away coat and dark-grey trousers; the expansive collar and the padded tie; the

gleam of a watch-chain caressing as it crossed the neatly but-
toned waistcoat; all setting off the timid face offering a look of
pertness to the public gaze. Looking like something too long
bedded in lavender, now sharing the scent of its withering
with the figure it had tried to preserve. Another fossil, still
above ground, and faintly visible in the light of the visiting
moon.

A little aside stood James Agate, appraisement in his every
glance at Pinero. No grace in this man, in build, in face, in
raiment; no power either. Heavy, clumsy-looking, but with a
cleared brow, like a refined son of a refined Caliban. A com-
plexion like faintly-ruddied lard; smooth skull, with diminishing eyebrows, and a mouth lower at one end than the other;
small eyes, having in them neither glint of humour nor gleam
of passion. Everything heavy about the man: the head seeming to press heavily on the shoulders, the trunk on the legs, the
legs on the ground, and even the clothes he wore – more
modern than those of Pinero, and natty enough – seemed to
ruffle stiffly when he moved, like a pliable suit of armour: the
bulkiness was all.

Fagan had spoken a lot about Agate to Sean: the most
important drama critic in the theatre world; most important to
get him friendly; most important to humour him; to keep him
well on your side; to let him have his way, even when he went
against you. He could make or mar a playwright. Hannen
Swaffer was next important. Hannen Swaffer, an haitch, an ay,
an en, another en, an e, another en – Hannen. Looking at
Agate, Sean thought he'd rather be marred by this man than
made by him. If you can only get talking to Agate, went on the
most important voice, and interest him, you're secure and
settled for life. Especially if you know anything about ponies.
The Savage Club is another haunt of his.

Sean would not grapple this fellow to him with any hook of
steel, for if a good play wasn't enough for a drama critic then
to hell with him. No, he wouldn't connect by a thread a button
of his coat to any button on Agate's. A small man in spite of
his bulkiness; a small inhabitant of a smaller world. Big and all
as he was in corporal size and steaming reputation, he hadn't
an arm long enough to encircle the waist or even the neck of
life; his longer arm would but stretch round the neck of a
bottle. Talk of ponies, and he'd give a good notice. Ponies!

Sean wondered if these thick and clumsy legs had ever crossed the back of horse or mare; certainly they had never crossed the back of a Pegasus or a Pooka.

Crown the critic with cow-parsley who coolly wrote that the playwright had got to write for duffers. He had got to write down to the lowest common feeling of the crowd. The play, *The Silver King*, is the type of play best suited to a general audience. Shakespeare is only popular in the theatre because he deals with the same themes as *The Silver King*. Deals in the same themes – a fine phrase for Agate. Sign of the sunday times. As Agate was in the beginning, so he was to the end: the same today, yesterday, and tomorrow. Except for the greater plays, already half worn away from the touches of praise given through the years by others, which plays he praised because he could not else, he suited himself to those plays which caught at the hearts of the duffers and roused the lowest common feeling of the richer common crowds. He fought the bad fight, he kept his dim and dowdy faith free from any touch of a great morning or dreadful night of the drama. *De mal en pis.*

All in the Garrick Club was comfortable and some of it cosy; use was here and satisfaction. No complaints. All was attractive save one room, one room only – the library. Fagan wanted to look up dress designs for the period of his play, *And So To Bed*, so he gave warning to one of the staff that the library was to be prepared for a visit. Strange, thought Sean, that he had to warn the staff to prepare the library. Sean went with him and found that the library was kept locked till some member demanded an entry. They went in. There was a fire smouldering in the fireplace, 'to banish some of the dampness', Fagan said. 'The library isn't used a lot,' added Fagan; 'that's why it smells a little musty.' Musty – the library! It seemed to be a lovely library too, and Sean mooched around, pulling a book out here, pulling a book out there, till Fagan called him over to look at designs he had found in a book, full of the frills and furbelows decorating the boozy bodies of Charles the Second's aristocrats. What a fuss Fagan was making of his poor play. Silks, satins, velvets; specially painted scenery; viols da gamba, lutes, and harpsichords; even the very snuff-box used by Pepys himself, with Edmund Gwenn and Yvonne Arnaud to muster life from a moribund play. Mr Pepys comes out of the Garrick Club and goes into the theatre. So Fagan gets the member of the staff again, the lights are turned out, and the door is locked till at some future time another playwright may seek a remedy from a book to render first-aid to a dejected play. Gloom in the library and sweetness and light everywhere else. The playwrights separating themselves from life without and from the records of life within.

The members of the Garrick Club have shut themselves away too much, too securely, with their own beady baubles of treasure and thought; farther away from England than if they had been buried in a foreign land. Their minds are safely hidden away in their heads. A new life is needed. It will come when the doors swing open to hail the noisier entrance of Covent Garden porters, salesmen, and lorry-drivers, who will add consequence of power to the dignity of the stately rooms from the vigour in the sons of the Lincolnshire Poacher, the Trumpet Major, and the Shropshire Lad; who will shake open the musty library into lasting readiness to serve the seeker after rare things; who will, in the evening-time, or during a leisure hour, stroll in to listen to human, homely talks about how England builded her honours of song, story, picture, fane, and cosy homestead in the past, and of all, or some of, the schemes in the mind of scientist, thinker, and artist, to weave and build from these a finer form and a higher glory. Mr Churchill and Marshal Montgomery say a lot now about 'the English way of life'. Well, let it be an English way of life: the way of Purcell, Constable, Darwin, Shakespeare, the morris dance, and Johnny, My Own True Love.

Perhaps those who shell themselves within the Garrick Club belong to a different pattern of life; a different pattern, perhaps, but the same thread woven from the same loom of life; and the pattern will cease to grow if they cut themselves off from the parent thread.

The arts have always lost something of their sap when they have been cut off from the people as a whole. The old culture came to a man at his work; it was not at the expense of life, but an exaltation of life itself; it came in at the eyes as some civic ceremony sailed along the streets, or as we arrayed ourselves before the looking-glass; or it came in at the ears in a song as we bent over the plough or the anvil. It

*is possible to speak the universal truths of human nature
whether the speakers be peasants or wealthy men, for,*
Love doth sing
As sweetly in a beggar as a king.

You never spoke a truer word, Yeats. Call up now to the
tight-closed windows of the Garrick Club; call to England and
the whole world; call with a loud voice, saying that you were
often bewildered, that at times you buzzed about after vain
things; but you believed; your ear caught the sounds of the
people's cry, you heard their songs, and your heart replied
fully, and your mind replied a lot.

THE SILVER TASSIE

SEAN stood in the office of a business man in whose fancy the sombre blackness of coal glittered more than the onyx, jasper, and chrysolite of heaven's architecture. It was a big, dull, thoughtless room, deprecating any emotion other than one connected with the sale of coal.

Hush! This room is sacred to the transubstantiation of coal into the shimmer of money. In front of a big, dusty window stood a wide table-desk of the dullest brown Sean had ever seen. It stood where it was, like a rock of ages, steadfast, and, apparently, immovable. No wisp of poetry, no wistful tinkle of a folk-song had ever entertained its lonely bulk. Ink, pens, blotting-paper, a ruler, and office writing-paper, each in its proper place, were piled on its pompous top, as if invoking animation out of the stillness, saying silently, Use us, and make the big desk hum. To tinge the common hue of business with the colour of art, two pictures of a costermonger and a costerwoman, by Jack Morrow, had been hung on the wall; badly done, they went on withering, colourless and cold, pictures that must have been dying while they were being painted. In a glass-doored bookcase, handy to the great desk, were two books on the value and quality of coal, flanked on one side by a huge brass-bound, brass-buckled family Bible, intimating that with the things that belong to Caesar, the things belonging to God may be very near and very dear to the business man. Under all, a red and blue rubber carpet covered the floor, the red dull, the blue duller.

There the boss sat at his desk in a wide, leather-seated swivel-chair, a portly man as firm in his seat as the desk was on the floor. A large head, bald on the top, but sprayed at the sides and back with sturdy tufts of iron-grey hair. A broad, ruddy face like a big cheese turning rusty, with small, shrewd, beady eyes; eyes that were never dimmed for more than a moment or two by any thought of worry. A thick soft nose, and under it a broad, thick-lipped mouth, which laughed, or shouted vehemently, any reason for laughing or shouting invariably equaling the others in futility.

Knowing little of art, literature, or science; self-centred, not only in the earth, but in the very universe, he sat there, humming; yet possessing a charm and forcible personality that seemed clouded with a knowledge of all things; a friend of artists, with a charm that was irresistible in a restaurant at a luncheon, or sitting, sprawled before an intimate fire with a friend or two, or persuading a doubtful business man that his way was the best way; a volatile mind that could gather coloured thoughts round trivial things, and present them to any company ordered in the frame of a confused and hilarious picture: a molten mass of brazen energy without a hope of taking an ordered form. A great soul lost in the flood of its own hilarity.

There he sat idle in his swivel-chair, a wide-brimmed black hat slung carelessly on the desk beside him; there he sat, a big, hooked pipe dangling from his red, fleshy lips, his stout, short fingers tapping out some inconstant, uneasy tune on the top of the hardwood desk.

He had nothing to do; the miners were on strike, and no coal crept up the river in big-bottomed barges to herald the income of heartening cheques in return for the toil of writing a letter after breakfast, one after lunch, and another before the office closed for the evening. The fires of the nation were going out: the big-topped desk could do no more.

Idly, the strong, fat fingers tapped the desk-top, and the thick, fleshy lips moved moodily to the humming of an air. Then the hum changed to a whistle, then words began to trickle through it to an air Sean had never heard before. He cocked an ear to listen; the words came huskily to his ear, uttered thoughtlessly, unemotionally by the moody crooner:

> Gae fetch to me a pint o' wine,
> An' full it in a sulver tossie;
> That I may drink before I gae
> A service tae my bonnie lossie.

—Ay, Sean, me lad, it's a woefu' state o' things: th' flooers o' th' forest are a' wede awa'. There isn't as much as a bean in th' locker, th' day.

But it's no' the roar of sea or shore
Wad mak' me langer wish tae tarry;
Nor shout o' war that's heard afar –
It's leavin' thee, my bonnie lossie.

Sean was startled. Aaron's rod had budded. A riotous and romantic song had drifted up from the solid rancour of the big, impassive desk, that was to hum in his mind for many months to come. He hummed it in his tiny flat in South Kensington; he hummed it in the dead of night, strolling down the Cromwell Road. He would give the title of the song to his next play. He would set down without malice or portly platitude the shattered enterprise of life to be endured by many of those who, not understanding the bloodied melody of war, went forth to fight, to die, or to return again with tarnished bodies and complaining minds. He would show a wide expanse of war in the midst of timorous hope and overweening fear; amidst a galaxy of guns; silently show the garlanded horror of war. However bright and haughty be the burning of a town; however majestic be the snapping thunder of the cannon-fire, the consummation is the ruin of an ordered, sheltering city with the odious figure of war astride the tumbled buildings, sniffing up the evil smell of the burning ashes. The ruin, the squeal of the mangled, the softening moan of the badly rended are horrible, be the battle just or unjust; be the fighters striving for the good or manifesting faith in evil.

And he would do it in a new way. There was no importance in trying to do the same thing again, letting the second play imitate the first, and the third the second. He wanted a change from what the Irish critics had called burlesque, photographic realism, or slices of life, though the manner and method of two of the plays were as realistic as the scents stealing from a gaudy bunch of blossoms.

He was working on the last act when Mr Lennox Robinson suddenly paid a visit to his flat in South Kensington. Not to linger, he said, but just to ask about the new play. There were rumours in Dublin that the play wouldn't be given to the Abbey Theatre. The rumours aren't true? You will give the play? Oh, that will be joyful! Yeats and I were sure the rumours were false. No, I can't stay for a cup of tea. Just called because of the silly rumours in Dublin that your play would not be given to the Abbey. Mr Robinson held out an aesthetic, tentative hand. Goodbye, Sean. Sorry I can't stay; so glad you'll give your play to us; and off he went to the air, it seemed to Sean, of *Danny Boy*.

Rumours? Sean couldn't believe it. If there were, surely he would have got letters asking if they were true, and he hadn't received a line. He was puzzled. The Abbey seemed to be eager to get the play; he was eager to give it, and so all was peace. He calculated the play would run in the Abbey for at least three weeks, maybe four, and the royalties he'd get would about cover the expenses of the birth of his child. Oh, that would be joyful, too!

Later on, while a play of his was running in the London Court Theatre, and Sean was in the office chatting about the poor houses, the Commissionaire came in to say that there was a bloke called Yeats outside who wanted to see him. Before he had ended the sentence, the stately figure of the poet stepped in as if it was marching to the tune of *Old Comrades*. He would sit down only for a moment. No, wouldn't take a whiskey and soda – doctor's orders. The company in the play were good, very good. He came to ask O'Casey if he intended to give his new play to the Abbey. Rumours in Dublin said O'Casey had decided to ignore the Abbey, which would be a pity. O'Casey had come to the Abbey when he had been most needed, and a refusal of the new play would cause irritation. The rumours untrue? O'Casey will give the new play? Oh, that will be joyful! He could assure the other Directors that the Abbey would get the play. No, he couldn't stay longer. Friends were waiting. Goodbye; and the great man stepped out as if marching to the tune of *Your Tiny Hand Is Frozen*.

Sean had promised the first glimpse of the play to Sir Barry Jackson, had sent him the manuscript, and had forgotten about it. Then one day Sir Barry came bustling into the house when he and Eileen were busy trying to make the debts they owed meet and marry the money they had in hand. Sir Barry was in a hurry, a panting hurry; he sat down on a chair in a hurry, first setting down a burnished bowler hat on the table in a hurry, and arranging a pompous-looking umbrella to a stately stand in a corner in a hurry too.

—You've written a fine play, he said; a terrible play! An impossible play for me. I dare not put it on – an English audi-

ence couldn't stand it. There's the script. I'm grateful to you
for letting me read it. His hand shot out for the burnished
bowler hat. I must go now. The play would lacerate our feelings; it would be unbearable. Goodbye; and he hurried out to
his waiting car, and vanished: a plain man in a plain van
rushing from life. The next morning, the plain van slid up to
the door, and the plain man slid into the house, and hurried to
the stately umbrella still standing in the corner. My umbrella –
I forgot it yesterday; and the plain man vanished into the plain
van again, and Sean saw him no more.

With, in some ways, a difficult cast, Raymond Massey, the
producer, had a hard task with a most difficult play. He had
never seen in the theatre before a scene like the second act;
neither had Sean, so he could be of no help to the producer.
But Massey's strange patience, his skill and experience, came
to his aid, so that the second act, helped hugely by Augustus
John's serenely-coloured church window and sinister, savage
gun, stood out oddly, eerily, and effectively, throwing confusion and some panic into the minds of most of London's
drama critics. Over all and through all went C. B. Cochran's
quiet, strange, and mysterious influence. So dapper; so pomp-
ously simple in his way of walking; so unassuming in his way
of talking that few would say There goes a Man of the
Theatre. But there he was, a Man of the Theatre from the sole
of his small foot to the dignified crown of his bowler hat.
Every glance of his discerning eye; every sound in his eager
ear; every word from his firm mouth; every gesture of his
hand, had something to do with the theatre; the greatest super-
visor, most imaginative and courageous man, of things low
and things high in the English theatre. An England consciously thinking the theatre more than the life or death of a
sparrow would have made Cochran independent of the Backer.
Had this man had a theatre and no necessity to coax the coming of coins into the box-office, out of a few mistakes would
have risen pride, elegance, and fun, making the English theatre
of today share the glory and gusto of the theatre in the
generous days of Shakespeare and his comrades. The Clowns
were always on one side of Cochran, the Tragedians on the
other, and he had the imaginative eye and cunning hand to
weave lovely patterns round the pair of them.

On account of the child's size, the doctor in charge of Sean's

wife decided, after consultation with a colleague, by an opera-
tion to make the birth immediate; so, to be out of the way,
Sean was packed off to spend the night with a friend. The next
morning, a telephone call told him a big boy had been born,
and that Eileen was eager to show it to him. He hurried off,
opened the door of the house in Woronzow Road, entered the
hall, and saw a large envelope from the Abbey Theatre lying
solus on a table; too big to hold an advisal of a coming production. He opened it, and read the letter from Lady Gregory and
the letter of condemnation, peppered with pompous advice,
from Yeats. Curse o' God on them! His anger grew at every
line he read.

He went upstairs, saw his wife, congratulated her on the
birth of her big boy, looked at the laddo, touched his cheek,
and said nothing about the play's rejection. He would have to
wait till she was safe; till she was up and about; and then he
would send a salvo of words that would shake the doors of the
Abbey and rattle the windows.

He read the letters again: the one from Yeats was the one
to be answered. Sean could not but believe that the play's rejection had been decided upon before the play had been sent. To
answer Yeats would be a dangerous thing to do. Yeats in his
greatness had influence everywhere, and the world of literature
bowed before him. But answered he must be, and answered he
would be, even though the strife meant the end of Sean. His
mind tore through the letter again.

*The most considerate thing for us to do is to suggest that he
withdraw the play. My letter gives an opinion, doesn't absolutely reject. He could withdraw the play 'for revision' and let
that be known to the Press. He should say that he himself had
become dissatisfied and had written to ask it back. If he dis-
agrees with our opinions as to its merits, he can wait a little,
and offer it to some London Manager. If the London Manager
accepts, then our opinion of the play won't matter to him at
all. Or, on the other hand, if no Manager accepts, or if he
doesn't offer it there, he can keep it by him, revising, or not
revising, as he pleases. I want to get out of the difficulty of the
paragraphs in the Press saying that the play has been offered to
us* (and hard both you and Mr Lennox Robinson asked that it
should be offered to you. S. O'C.). *I have not told anyone what
I think of the play, and I will get Lennox not to give his*

opinion. You have, perhaps, already written to Casey [sic], but even if you have, I should like you to write making this suggestion.

This to Lady Gregory and then to Sean. Obviously, Yeats was sure Sean would shake at the knees when he got this opinion; would hasten to sit down and write for the play back; would light a fire with it the first thing the following morning. Would he? He thought and thought it out: He was fenced in with money anxieties; he had now a wife and a child to guard and keep, and a rented house which needed many things more before it could become a home. Indeed, but for what his wife had brought into it from her own flat, there would have been barely enough in it to suit himself. Before they were married, she had sub-let her flat; had got no rent from the tenants; and only by last-minute efforts did she manage to get her belongings back again. When he and she had come to the house they were in now, the sitting-room had had but a carpet on the centre of the floor, with a broad border around it varnished by Eileen herself; one chair, John's pictures, one of a Gitana, the other of Sean himself; a coal-scuttle and fire-irons; so that, while he sat on the floor before the fire, she sat on the chair, and wept. But not for long: they soon saw the grim humour of it, and laughed merrily over the barren way the room looked. The little they had was oozing away; now, since the child had come, what was left would depart in a steady stream; and, if *The Silver Tassie* didn't bring in enough for a further year's life, then the nights would be full of anxiety's light and the days would be gloomy and glum. Still, he had been in worse circumstances before, and had come out of them. But then he had been alone – his mother didn't count, for she had the faculty of being able to live on air, and laugh. Yeats' rejection of the play was a blow on the heart.

Casey could write for the play, and say he wanted it for revision – that was the meanest moment in the letter of Yeats. It was a bitter suggestion, and made him live with anger for a long time to come. A fight was the one honest way out of it. Almost all the literary grandees would, naturally, be on the side of Yeats, and most of the Press that mattered would, directly or indirectly, make a bow to his decision. This was inevitable because of Yeats' reputation as a literary genius; and what made it harder for Sean was that the reputation was a suitable crown for the man's achievement. But fight he should; and fight he would.

Well, here he was surrounded by Yeats' opinions. *You are not interested in the Great War; you never stood on its battle-fields, never walked its hospitals, and so write out of your opinions. You illustrate those opinions by a series of almost unrelated scenes, as you might in a leading article.* Oh, God, here was a man who had never spoken to a Tommy in his life – bar Major Gregory; and to him only because he was an artist as well as a soldier – chattering about soldiers to one who had talked to them all; infantry, cavalry, and artillery; who knew most of the regimental marches; who, when a kid, had listened to them telling, in their halting way, stories about Canada, Hong Kong, India, Gibraltar, Malta, and the wilds of Shorn-cliffe Camp and Salisbury Plain. One who had known soldiers since he was a kid of six; whose uncle had been wounded on the field of Balaclava; whose brother had gone through the Boer War in the Dublin Fusiliers; whose elder brother had worn the khaki in the First World War; who had walked with the Tommies, had chatted with them, had sung songs with them in the hospitals of St Vincent and of Richmond; who had followed the Great War from its first declaration, through the Russian Revolution, to its final end by the surrender of Germany. And now he was being told by one who wouldn't know a Life Guard red from a Horse Guard blue, that he wasn't interested, directly or indirectly, in the Great War! *Not interested* to one who had talked and walked and smoked and sung with the blue-suited, wounded men fresh from the front; to one who had been among the armless, the legless, the blind, the gassed, and the shell-shocked!

Among the things that dramatic action must burn up are the author's opinions. Do you suppose for one moment that Shakespeare educated Hamlet and Lear by telling them what he thought and believed? As I see it, Hamlet and Lear educated Shakespeare, and I have no doubt that in the process of that education he found out that he was altogether a different man to what he thought himself, and had altogether different beliefs. D'ye tell me that, now, Mr Yeats? Well, I don't know; but one thing's certain, and that is if Shakespeare became a more educated man while writing *Hamlet*, then it wasn't Hamlet who educated him, but Shakespeare who educated himself. But what proof – beyond an opinion – has Yeats that what he says was so? As he sees it – of course; but it doesn't necessarily follow that everyone, or anyone, will see it the same way. A man altogether different, with altogether different beliefs when he'd finished the play from what he had been before he started! Here, the poet is suggesting, or trumpeting, the opinion that he was as intimate with Shakespeare as he was with the number on his own hall-door. There are as many opinions about the character of Hamlet as there are lines in the play. Even Shakespeare wasn't sure himself, for we are told: 'The variations of an early copy from the play of *Hamlet* in its improved state, are too numerous and striking to admit a doubt of the play having been subsequently revised, amplified, and altered by the poet'. Of one thing we can be certain, namely, that what Shakespeare makes Hamlet say was not what the living Prince would, or could, have said, but what Shakespeare wanted him to say; that the play is largely a biography of Shakespeare's thoughts.

Sean carried the letters of Yeats to Macmillan's. He presented them to Mr Daniel Macmillan, remarking that if the firm wished, after reading them he would allow the contract to be withdrawn. Mr Daniel read the correspondence through. He handed it back to Sean, saying, This is of course, a matter between Mr Yeats and you. It does not concern us. We do not agree with the criticism. We think the play worth publication, and we will publish it. We make our own decisions, and this controversy cannot alter our intentions.

Very kind, very manly, and very encouraging to Sean, for he had had a half-fear that the criticism from Yeats might check, might even prevent, the play's publication. This was his first victory over the potent, almost impregnable, influence of Yeats. So he hied himself off to C. B. Cochran, and put the correspondence before him. Beyond saying to Sean that he should never have given another party the option of a production while the play was under consideration by a London Manager, Cochran was undisturbed. Sean was taken aback by Cochran's indifference to the denunciation of the play by Yeats; for denunciation it was rather than a criticism. But the two decisions – Macmillan's to publish the play, Cochran's to produce it – defended the flanks of Sean's effort. Had Macmillan's withdrawn from their promise of publication; had

Cochran decided to abandon production, then Sean's defence
of the dramatist's right to experiment would have been a hard
one indeed. It was very curious, this rejection of the new play,
for Yeats had known it wouldn't be done in the old way. In the
Court Theatre, Sean had told him it would be different from
what had gone before; that the second act would be an impression of the World War, and that the play would be written
in a new manner; but Yeats had made no comments on Sean's
rapid and excited account of the new idea: he sat silent there,
listening. Yet during his stay in London, at that very time,
Yeats, speaking before the Irish Literary Society, had enthusi-
astically mentioned the receipt of a play from a young dramatist which contained the promise of a new idea in Irish drama.
The first act showed a group of young men making bombs in
an underground cellar. They had been confined to this work
and to this room for a long time, Yeats said, and the act was
an expressionistic effort to show the psychological reaction of
these young men to their peculiar circumstances. He went on
to say that this act foreshadowed a new direction in Irish
drama, and regretted that the rest of the play had been very
bad; adding that O'Casey had built the bridge across which the
coming Irish dramatists would pass to a new technique and a
new art. But the poet had, apparently, waxed faint and furious
to find that the first dramatist to cross the bridge was the
dramatist who had, according to Mr Yeats, built the bridge
himself. It was very curious. Though the play might not be
what Sean thought it, it was far above three-fourths of the
plays appearing on the Abbey stage, and it stood up, fearless
and steady, to the higher standard of the theatre.

Sean sent the letters written by Yeats, with his own replies,
to St John Ervine, who sent them to *The Observer*; and to A. E.
for publication in his *The Irish Statesman*. The first journal
published them; but a letter came sailing over the sea from the
lordly A. E. saying that he wouldn't, couldn't, and shouldn't
publish the correspondence in his journal for fear of a possible
action for breach of copyright. Brother Yeats taking an action
for breach of copyright against Brother A. E.! It didn't make
sense. The man who had sung about 'the golden heresy of
truth' was hedging. A few days later the Irish Press informed
the world and Sean that Dr Yeats declared a serious breach of
copyright had been committed by the publication of the corres-

pondence, and he was about to take legal action through the Society of Authors. So Sean got another letter from A. E. saying, Aha, I told you so! All Sean could do was to write to the Press to say that he was indifferent to the threat, even if Dr Yeats decided to lay the dispute before the League of Nations.

The dispute, fostered delightedly by most of the Irish Press, jumped over to the English Press, wafted itself across the Atlantic, and spread excitedly over American papers, big and small; while many European journals carried the story further, and tossed the names of Yeats and O'Casey into minds which had never bothered about them before, and would hardly ever bother about them again, many of the comments showing Sean that the name and reputation of Yeats were much more important than his arguments.

One dignified Irish paper opposed the coloured clamour. Spraying itself with the hood of literature over one shoulder, and that of civil law over the other, the *Irish Times*, accompanied by the Borris-in Ossory Thing at Arms, hastened first to the pinnacle of Christ Church Cathedral, and then to the entablature of the Bank of Ireland, where, after the Thing at Arms had blown a funfare, she proclaimed to the listening ears of Ireland, the following proclamation: Whereas the essential feature of the correspondence about O'Casey's play is its portentous gravity; whereas Yeats and O'Casey discuss the play as if its goodness or badness really were a matter of vast importance, showing that they are unable to grasp two facts: Nobody in this generation – certainly not O'Casey – has written, nor is likely to write, immortal literature. O'Casey's two acted plays are good and striking plays, but no better than a thousand that have been forgotten. If they survive for fifty years, they will survive not as plays but as historical documents.

So the manicured hand, in a kid glove, of the *Irish Times*, tossed the controversy in her waste-paper basket, and turned to better things – the church services, the racing lists for the Derby, the differences between De Valera and Cosgrave, and the price of fat cattle.

It was very important to Sean, touching the security of his life, his wife's, and the kid's in the cradle in the room beyond him. They were all depending on what the play would bring in to allow them to live decently for one more year. The first

honest home he had ever had, simple as it was, stood silent
and shaking. The previous ones had been dens to eat in, to
sleep in agitation, tormented with flea and bug; raucously
restive, dark, menacing, and ugly, save where the glow from
his mother's life made them bearable and good. His life pressed
more heavily on him than ever, for his anxiety was threefold
now – for himself, for his wife, newly fledged with motherhood, and the babe, newly fledged with life. The play was very
important to him.

Some months ago Lady Gregory had written to say how
glad she was to hear he had a little house and little garden of
his own; and how pleasant it would be for him there, to sit in
the sun among the flowers. The flowers! Sean hopping and
happy among the hollyhocks. The syringa tree was wearing its
bridal-robe of snowy blossoms, and the lilac her purple gown of
modest royalty; the pansies were tumbling out in groups,
brown and blue, white and speckled; and the little lawn – about
as big as the floor-space of his last tenement room – looked
green and buoyant. But there was no peace among them for
him. Even the rose of Sharon or the lily of the valley would be
no solace to him now. He could eat no pleasant bread amid
their scents, among their coloured blossoms. Their ways were
ways of pleasantness no longer.

While clenching his spirit into the fight against the Abbey
Theatre's determination to stereotype a writer's manner and
style, and, through them, to fight the wider literary influence
of those who believed that at the name of Yeats every knee
should bow, Sean received unexpected reinforcement from the
mind of Bernard Shaw. Out of Passfield, where the great man
was staying with the Webbs, came a fiery letter, saying: *My
dear Sean, what a hell of a play! I wonder how it will hit the
public. Of course the Abbey should have produced it, as Starkie
rightly says – whether it liked it or not. But the people who
knew your uncle when you were a child (so to speak) always
want to correct your exercises; and this was what disabled the
usually competent Yeats and Lady Gregory. Still it is surpris-
ing they fired so very wide, considering their marksmanship . . .*

*If Yeats had said 'It's too savage; I can't stand it', he would
have been in order . . . Yeats himself, with all his extraordinary
cleverness and subtlety, which comes out when you give him
up as a hopeless fool, and (in this case) deserts him when you*

expect him to be equal to the occasion, is not a man of this world; and when you hurl an enormous chunk of it at him, he dodges it, small blame to him. However we can talk over it when we meet. Cheerio, Titan. – G.B.S.

But although Bernard Shaw stood by his side, Mrs Shaw tried to prevail upon him to restore the sword to the scabbard. On her pressing invitation, Sean and Eileen went to Whitehall Court on June 21st, 1928, to have lunch with her and her husband, so that, Mrs Shaw wrote, 'they might talk freely (about our friends? – No – about the play!)'. Over a charming lunch Sean soon discovered that the ray of support from G. B. S. was being deflected away from his conception of the scurvy way the Abbey had handled his work to the ending of the dispute; towards the silencing of Sean; and towards soft persuasion to be used on Yeats to induce him to change his mind, and allow a production of the play in the Abbey. From doctor and saint he heard great argument about it and about: but evermore came out by the same door as in he went. Through the delicate fume of the conversation, Eileen's silvery voice suggested the compromise of Sean submitting any further letters to Shaw, who, if he disapproved of a paragraph or sentence, could edit it into a more suitable and tactful expression. Mrs Shaw vigorously applauded the idea, G. B. S. approved, and Sean sat silent. Mrs Shaw and her husband would come to lunch with the O'Caseys in a couple of days to push the plan further ahead. Some days after, a letter came from Mrs Shaw to Eileen to say they couldn't come to the O'Caseys because they were *Just starting off abroad for a holiday and have got so terribly tied up with all the silly odds and ends we have to get done before we go. We have taken our sleepers for Sunday, and are remaining in Passfield till Thursday. Then there will be an orgy of business and packing!*

I am the more sorry for this as I do feel Sean wants a lot of looking after just now. He is going to be very naughty and fierce and resentful – and he is a terribly hard hitter!

That idea of getting G. B. S. to see his letters to his 'friends' is a grand one. Do keep him up to it. Any letters addressed to 4 Whitehall Court will be forwarded at once, and I will send you an address the moment we are settled, and Sean must write about all he is doing, and G. B. S. will answer quickly and try to act as a lightning-conductor! Directly we come

*back, we will go to lunch with you, and see Breon, if you will
ask us again. Yeats didn't come to see us about the play, but
about the Irish Literary Academy they are trying to get up. He
never mentioned* The Silver Tassie. *It was I who insisted on
talking about it, and he was rattled, self-conscious, and reluctant! Our very kindest and most friendly thoughts to you both.
– C. F. Shaw.*

Well, so near, so bad. Sean couldn't welcome this kind of
help. He had no wish to have his letters edited, even by such a
man as Shaw. Yeats had hit as hard as he could, and Sean
wasn't inclined to hold his punches. He had refused the
counsel of Uncle Yeats, and he had no intention of taking the
counsel of Auntie Shaw. He would fight alone; one alone and
not a second. He would fence in his own sour way, thrust,
parry, and cut with his own blade of argument, in his own
way, not according to rules perfumed with the stale musk of
custom; but according to the measure of his own heart, the
rhythm of his own mind, logical now, savage and sudden a
moment after: in this fight, he would face any opponent, and
thrust straight at the side where the heart lay.

But Mrs Shaw, in her heart, resented Sean's independent
critical outcry, and remembered it against him.

THE FRIGGIN FROGS

WATCHED by Mrs Yeats, helped by the sun of South Europe, Yeats was spared for another spell with Time. Mrs Yeats still held death away from him; and the summer saw him again in Dublin; heard his voice in the Senate; and his hand, less vigorous now, still held the Abbey Theatre back from falling flat before the cleric and the clown. Sunning himself in his charming little house in Rathfarnham, in the midst of wife and children, the poet lingered in a quietness he had rarely known before; for even in the stilly nooks of Coole's gardens, roused only with rustling of linnets' wings, Yeats had always been agitated in the explanation of mysteries his own ruffling mind imagined, shaping them into living shadows following where he went.

Coming to Ireland for a brief visit on money gained out of New York's production of *Within the Gates*, Sean had got a kindly letter asking him to come to lunch and spend afternoon and evening with Yeats in Riversdale. He crossed a plankway, forming a bridge over a little brook, and came to the house to be received with a quiet, gracious welcome from Mrs Yeats, who left him to chat with the poet for a few minutes before lunch. Again they talked of the Abbey: how tiresome the customary Abbey play was becoming; how the Theatre needed new life through a newer type of play; and how several new Directors had been added to the Board to create a richer variety of opinion; but Sean's grouping of thoughts about the Theatre, past and present, were rudely scattered by a vehement and sudden remark from Yeats.

—O'Casey, he said, bending towards him, you've succeeded in your last play, *Within the Gates*. The coordination of mood, dialogue, and technique there is a success, where, I think, it is a failure in your *The Silver Tassie*.

—Oh, thought Sean, forcing his thoughts on to what Yeats had said so suddenly, *The Silver Tassie* is still in his mind. He's excusing the rejection of one play by his praise of another.

Aloud, he said, Do you really believe, Mr Yeats, that *Within the Gates* is a successful achievement?

—I do, he said, emphatically; I believe it to be a most successful achievement in your newer manner.

—I wish to God I could believe it too! came from Sean in a burst of frank fervency; and he was amused at the signs of hesitation, surprise, and doubt that flooded into the poet's expressive face. Sean learned then that Yeats wanted the Abbey to do *Within the Gates*. He objected. He wouldn't refuse, but set out the difficulties of production by the Abbey company, and showed the poet that the Abbey stage would never accommodate the play's action. Besides, the play was clumsy in parts, and, some day, he would try to amend it. He made it clear that never again would he send a play to the Abbey; but that the Abbey was always welcome to do any play of his they wished to do. He suggested *The Silver Tassie*, a play far easier to put on the Abbey stage; that Yeats could have the other, if he insisted; but that *The Silver Tassie* was a far easier venture. The poet was silent for a few moments, and then said he would put the question before the Directorate.

After lunch, a young and vigorous man, Captain McManus, of the Free State Army, came on an evening visit. Yeats at once proposed a game of croquet. Yeats, by far the best player, his daughter, next best player, on one side; McManus, a fair player, and Sean, no damn good at all, since he had never seen a croquet ground, much more played a match, on the other. Sean heard Yeats murmuring to McManus that he could show O'Casey how to play as the game went on; but, in spite of efforts towards tuition, O'Casey did very badly, and the poet and Anne won by a very large margin. Yeats was elated, McManus a little crestfallen, O'Casey glad to get in out of the sharp wind blowing from the Dublin Mountains, but a few feet away from the croquet pitch; though, when she had seen him shiver, Mrs Yeats had thoughtfully made him wear his overcoat. His first and last game of croquet. A game in which Yeats played like a champion. The only game of croquet Sean had ever played; the only one he would ever play, played with the poet Yeats.

Sean noticed how stiffly Yeats slid into the comfortable chair by the cosy fire. He was bright, though, and aimed at gaiety; had he nested sooner here and longer, letting restlessness ooze out of him, he'd have had a chance of a longer life. He couldn't, for there was in Yeats an irresistible leaven of childlike desire for glitter in imagination and masqued activity. He loved to *pace upon the battlements and stare on the foundations of a house.* The battlements, the battlements of a tower; the winding stair to the same battlements, with Sato's gift, a changeless sword on a table, forged before Chaucer saw the light o' day; and the poet's crook o' th' knee to an old and gallant ancestry. There he was, ailing, but in his insight still declaiming:

I declare this tower is my symbol; I declare
This winding, gyring, spiring treadmill of a stair is my ancestral stair;
That Goldsmith and the Dean, Berkeley and Burke have travelled there,
Swift beating on his breast in sibylline frenzy blind

Signs and symbols! Seeking substance from shadows, shining or shrieking. The poet had played with his toys too long. Aristocratic toys, self-fashioned; a few coloured with a wild philosophy, all tinged with beauty, some even with a gracious grandeur; but he had played with them all too long. More than half of life had passed him by while he was unsheathing and sheathing Sato's sword, staring over decaying battlements, or restamping out a dim impression of a long-forgotten ancestral crest. Young mortality. Ancestry had long since lost its handfast hold of man's mind. Man was no longer bothering to claim big house or battlemented castle, but was claiming the whole earth for his ancestry. Yeats was tired, and so the morioned head, the sword at hip, the spurred heel, had given place to the soft slipper, the comfortable chair, and the cosy fire.

But the poet, when he wished, with a light spring could jump down from the battlements to the earth again. The bold Yeats! Here he was now, talking laughingly about the censorship. In the beginning when Yeats and the intellectuals saw censorship was bound to come, they planned how to make it ineffective. Before a book could be banned, the Censorship Board had to come to a unanimous decision that the bloody book deserved it. The cunning mind of Yeats moved that a protestant clergyman be included on the Board, Yeats and the intellectuals feeling certain that a protestant divine would, *pro natura antagonisticeomnibus,* oppose any opinion expressed by the catholic members of the Board. They were wrong: any incautious mention of a girl's gown, or any whisper of a crack in the concrete solidarity of a creed, caused the reverend gent to close his eyes, tap the table, and cry hem! He was worse than any of the others.

—An odd man, thought Sean. No; let Yeats try ever so hard, he could never have been an aristocrat. With his castle, his crested spoons, his sword of Sato, he was no more an ancestral aristocrat than James Joyce; or even than Fluther Good when Fluther was singing his song about *The Wedding o' Glencree.* The poet was too passionate. Too dispersed in thought. The bigger weakness of Yeats was that he could never hammer his thoughts into any harmony of unity. Joyce did; Yeats couldn't. Image after image did a ballet-dance in his mind; when he chose one as perfection, he lost it among the other dancing images, and when he found it again, he saw that it had changed into another form and a different fantasy. And yet he could stamp on the earth as firmly and as rudely as any Joyce could. He was one who could sail for a year and a day in an argosy, and then go for a voyage of a week in a tramp-steamer. Born into the proletariat, Yeats would have made a magnificent docker.

When the evening had dwindled into a darkening dusk, Sean bade farewell to the poet; an affectionate farewell, with a tight grip of clasped hands.

Some time after Sean's return to London, the Abbey Theatre produced his *The Silver Tassie,* seven years after it had seen the lights o' London. When it appeared, Joyce's terrible clap of thunder, that frightened the primitive man into frenzy, shot into the startled ears of Eireann; and all Eire's sacred frogs began to croak, Brékkek Kékkek Kékkek Kékkek Kóax Kóax Kóax! A reverend member of the Dominican Order had issued a premature warning in a semi-canonical proclamation, saying: *There have been tentative announcements in the Press recently of the forthcoming production of* The Silver Tassie *by the Abbey Theatre. The Abbey once rejected this play to which it now offers the hospitality of its boards. Dublin is to have the opportunity of drinking deep* (Drinking, drinking, drinkinkin, ing, inking!) *from* The Silver Tassie. *I fancy Dublin is a little too wise in nineteen hundred and thirty-five to put its lips to a cup that possibly may have been filled from a sewer.* (Guinness is good for you.) *The Play has been published, and is in our hands for cold inspection. It defies analysis. It is a vigorous medley of lust and hatred and vulgarity. I have no hope of conveying any adequate idea of its deliberate indecency and its mean mocking challenge to the Christian Faith. The fracas over* The Playboy *was but a flash in the pan, a child's cracker, in comparison with the hostility with which the Abbey is confronted if it persists in defying Catholic principle and flouting that reticence which is characteristic of our people. Plain etiquette will not tolerate horror, indecency, or blasphemy, on or off the stage.*

Sublime is the warning, so, quick! we have but a second! Here's a hot inspection for you, from a truly, ruly, reverend gentleman too. Here's one destined to drive out the indecency of poverty, the blasphemy of disease, the dull despair of dirt, the horror of war, with the midget-magical sword of Plain Etiquette. Stainless steel. Drive these things from the Abbey stage as a preliminary, and then drive them hellter-skelter out of the world: One, two, three – go! Hearseman, pass by!

But the heated hostility, desired by the cleric and sedulously prophesied by him, made no appearance to disturb the production. The Reverend Gentleman had a quiet guard; not a mouse stirring. But there was a commotion within the theatre, behind the scenes. One of the Directors got the shock of his life. He came rushing out of the theatre, horrified that such a thing could be. The ripe ribaldry of O'Casey's play was a severe shock to his finer feeling. He exclaimed to all that he felt an outrage had been committed. Two of them now fierce in the fight: the cleric and the Theatre Director, layman, – to God and Ireland true. Two true now. The Director, in a burst of holy indignation, told O'Casey where to get off, for he was keen and tempered to uphold *Catholic cleanliness and wholesome entertainment in a theatre which our Catholic Government is subsidizing. Insane admiration here, and the half-witted culture of New York, and London's admiration for O'Casey's vulgar and worthless plays, where they are always failures, filling O'Casey full of a fantastic opinion of his own importance, though he is best at his gutter level in controversy*

*with Mr Yeats, who has replied, after silently enduring years
of the foulest abuse, with this gesture which forces our audience to endure* The Silver Tassie, *even though it was only for a
week.* He sought out those in authority, and demanded that all
the impudent, naughty words be cut out of the play, for, as he
says, *The onus lay upon the other Directors and the Producer
to respect the suggestion I had made about the cutting of the
play, and act accordingly. Their duty was clear, and I did not
wish to be unduly insistent in pointing it out to them further.
At the same time, I did not altogether leave out of consideration what I felt must be the reactions of the players to the
offensive portions of the play; but since the publication of my
statement, Mr F. J. McCormick has made an explanation on
behalf of the players that these reactions were such as might
have been expected, and that he, himself, were he a free agent,
would not, as a Catholic, have appeared in the play. On Friday
last, I expressed my regrets to the players that my statement
should have involved them, and I now take the opportunity of
saying that I wholeheartedly accept Mr McCormick's explanation. I felt it necessary to explain that some steps had been
taken to mitigate the offence of the production so that it might
not be taken as a lasting disgrace to the Abbey Theatre.*

Get out the harp, Pat, and play. The catholic Harp, man.
We're all pupae in the Papal flag. Let me alone, though I know
you won't, I know you won't; let me alone, though I know you
won't, impudent Jimmy O'Dea!

But, whisper again, boys and girls, whisper: While eager to
cut things out of O'Casey's play, he didn't like the same thing
happening to his own. Oh, no, boys and girls. Earlier on, he
had complained to the Abbey Directorate that actors were leaving out the words from author's plays, as was explained by the
Theatre's Secretary reporting to the Press that 'Owing to
representations made by the Director at a Board meeting, in-
structions were issued to the Company that no word must be
left out, no sentence changed during a performance'. It is
usual, when cuts are thought to be desirable, to ask the author
about them; but here was the lad bouncing about demanding
cuts without even letting O'Casey know that such a thing was
in his mind.

Reinforcements were hurried up to the Director. The Irish
Press, secular and sacerdotal, bawled a blast on the play. *The*

Cross, magazine of the Passionists, hands on hips, declared, *It is a poisonous draught from a dirty cup. There was a time when the Dublin men had the courage of their convictions, and were not afraid to make effective protest against anything that outraged their feelings. In these good old days, as anyone familiar with the history of the Abbey Theatre can recall* (out in the dear, dead days beyond recall!), *there was a famous week when riots took place every night during an offensive performance, and five hundred police were needed to keep order in the Theatre and its vicinity. But times have changed, and O'Casey's* The Silver Tassie, *with its dreary monotony of blasphemy, vulgarity, and filth, passed off quietly without the need to call in one single officer of the law to preserve order. We have no hope of arousing the decadent Directorate of the Abbey Theatre to a sense of its public duty. But the Abbey audience that could contentedly sit through such a perform-ance is certainly worthy of examination. What witless fools are in our midst, that could sit, open-mouthed and empty-headed, and gape at the guttersnipe's rhapsody presented on the stage for their delectation! The people that could applaud such blatant blasphemy had not even enough intelligence to see that they were throwing bouquets at one who was dragging them down with him to wallow in the mire.*

Well, boys and girls, what do you think of that delectable denunciation by a Father of the Passionist Order, a Brother of St Paul of the Cross? And a Scholar too, for he is the Editor of the magnificent magazine; a learned man; a Doniel come to judgement. How genteel and reticent the comments are. Spark-ling with the divine courtliness of the St Paul of the Cross community. Deeply disappointed, too, that disorders hadn't afflicted the performances. Delicate detonations of phrase worthy to be framed and placed on the white walls of the Marian League of Art.

Here is the report from *The Irish Catholic*, full of a pure and holy purpose: *If* The Silver Tassie *withstands the test of fire to which it has been subjected within the last ten days* (ten days that shook the world), *then, though it would not thereby be proved genuine silver, the base metal of which it is com-posed is at least equivalent to asbestos. Personally we believe that the effect of the flood of correspondence will be the exclu-sion for all time from the boards of any Irish theatre of Mr*

O'Casey's precious production. Galway and the Catholic Young Men's Societies have been in the forefront in bringing about this highly desirable result. The bitterness of the atheist heart is seen by the judicious in all that Mr O'Casey has got put upon the boards – it gives its repulsive and morbid tang to whatever comes from his dramatic pen. Those who relish the rank sort of fare that Mr O'Casey provides ought to be denied by law the opportunity of indulging their debased tastes.

Let us take a thimbleful of stimulant now as a sursum cordial against the effects of these blows from Balaam, by quoting the famous American drama critic, George Jean Nathan: *If* The Silver Tassie *with all its admitted deficiencies is not one of the most honorable experiments, then I am not the man to have been engaged to write this foreword.*

Another holy snarler, *The Standard*, otherwise *The Eagle*, came out like this: *It was a revolting production in which the Church was mocked, the name of God insulted, immorality flaunted as a matter of course, and the foulest language of the gutter used before audiences overwhelmingly Catholic. As a play – though this seems beside the point now – the production is mere trash. Nothing even remotely approaching the dirtiness and stupidity of this wretched attempt at drama would be permitted to be shown on the screen. This play gives us a golden opportunity of improving our stage, and of reconsidering the value of our literary heroes who have been set up for our admiration. Mr W. B. Yeats is no literary leader for a Catholic country.* (Remember Parnell!) *No matter to what poetic heights he may soar, he will never lift us to the heights to which we aspire.* The eagle's whistle! Excelsior!

Cu Uladh, President of the Gaelic League (the one who, when the Treaty was signed, rushed out to hang a notice on the railings outside his office thanking God, in pitiable Irish, for the sake of freedom; then, when De Valera disavowed the Treaty, rushed out to bring his blessing in again), came out with *The Abbey Theatre at its worst, which seems to be at the present moment, is intolerable and must be swept aside. I have not seen, thank God, this latest horror, but I remember some years ago going to see* The Plough and the Stars, *and having to leave before the second act from a fit of nausea.* And this *item indignatio* adorned himself with the title of Ulster's Hound, the title of Cuchulann, greatest hero of the Red Branch

Knights. Sean could only murmur, as big Joe Brady, the Irish Invincible, murmured on his way to the scaffold, Poor oul' Ireland, poor oul' Ireland!

The crinolined, Roman Catholic *Tablet* ventured out with no direct opinion about the play. Sitting sage among her cushions, perfume on one side of her, smelling-salts on the other, she gracefully fluttered her fin, snowy-white, streaked with yellow, and simpered, in reply to a question put by a reader, *To this inquiry we cannot make an answer worth having; because we have neither seen O'Casey's play nor read it in print. The Silver Tassie is known to us only by what we have heard and read about it. While refusing to give a critical opinion of our own, we are at least entitled to say that Irish Catholics, both priests and laymen, for whose honesty and intelligence we have deep respect, deplore O'Casey's play, not only in itself, but as a very blatant sign of a very evil tendency in Irish dramatic circles. Mr Louis J. Walsh has a strong article about this tendency in the October number of the Irish* Rosary. *He thinks that the temptation for an author to write down to what he regards as Abbey standards is tremendous for a poor or over-ambitious man; and he believes that there is a definite malignity in the whole Abbey outlook.*

Louis J. Walsh! Well, he wasn't poor, but he was ambitious. A competent solicitor, but an incredibly bad playwright. The title of one of his plays alone sounds his requiem: *The Pope in Killybuck*. Walsh had sent it to Sean for commendation, with a letter gleefully adding that he had modified it when it went north so that it might meet a welcome in protestant Ulster. The play was too bad to bother about, so Sean sent it back, but kept the letter, which frightened Walsh because of what he had said in it, so that he demanded it back. Give me back, give me back what I wrote unto you, for what I have written I have not written. A nest of frightened people. Fear and a sly expediency are the immoral fibres spreading viciously through Ireland's soul.

A roman catholic secular paper, *The Evening Herald*, had a leading article about the production. The article was headed by the notification of The Feast of the Day – the Beheading of John the Baptist. Holy humbug hanging on to God. It said, *It is strange that the severe criticisms which appeared in the Dublin Press (before production) of this play were not sufficient*

*to satisfy the producers of the utter unsuitability of this
blasphemous and sordid play. It is time a check was put to
such productions that appeal to morbid minds.*

Brékkek Kékkek Kékkek Kékkek Kóax Kóax Kóax. Croak
away!

In the midst of the frogs, one blackbird whistled a melody
for Sean. One Roman Catholic, Robert Speaight, the prominent English actor, in a letter to the Press, denounced the
attack saying, *The play is an outcry from a passionate and
embittered mind. But it is much nearer to Christianity, because
it is nearer to life, than the complacent criticisms levelled
against it. The soul of the bourgeoisie has betrayed itself. This
surely is the essence of the bourgeois mind – that it cannot
look tragedy in the face; for O'Casey has seen into the heart of
the horror of war, and wrenched out its dreadful secret; that
the co-heirs with Christ destroy one another in the sight of the
Son of Man.*

Sean sauntered away from the frogs, getting away from
their croaking to busy himself with other work. He would
forget them for a time – the journals, the bawling priests, the
shouting members of the Catholic Young Men's Societies, the
very wise and stout-hearted defenders of decent literature, including Shakespeare, of course, Dr J. Murphy, representing
the University of Galway grey (representing the same community, oddly enough, long after and later on, when the poet
Yeats was finally laid to rest within the reach of the strong
arms of famed Ben Bulben). Let them all alone for the present.
Like Graham Greene's Father Rank, in *The Heart of the
Matter*, they didn't quite like observant men. They saw too
much, and what they saw, they saw too clearly; and when they
saw, they said. And that doesn't please the papal priest or the
papal bishop, as Dr McDonald saw so clear and said so
promptly. The day of blinkered blessedness was nearly over.
God is numbering them off on the rosary of the years. The
light of other days is light no longer.

Twelve years later, *The Silver Tassie* was performed for two
crowded weeks in the Gaiety Theatre, the largest one Dublin
has in her pocket; and, throughout the performances, not a
word was spoken, not a drum hit, not an ecclesiastical curse
was uttered by sunray, lampglow, or candlelight. The holy
hibernians were hibernating. The play could rest in peace now.

But no! Nearly two years later, Sean gets a letter from Mr Ward Costello, an airman in the last World War, now a student of drama at Yale University, Connecticut. He wrote to say that he had defended O'Casey during an attack made upon him in a lecture given by Mr Lennox Robinson to the University's students of drama, with Marc Connolly in the Chair. The young student asked Mr Robinson 'if *The Silver Tassie*, since it had not been produced by Yeats because of his prejudice, had been produced, or considered for production, since his death?' And 'Mr Robinson had answered with a flat "no", adding that it was a bad play; even though Lady Gregory had changed her mind about it'. The old lady had said Yes, when the Huntingdons brought her to see the London production of the play.

Perhaps this was the last stroke of the bell tolling for the demise of the play? But no: *The Silver Tassie* is dead, but the damned thing won't lie down. This very month of October, nineteen hundred and fifty-one, a revival of the play in the Queen's Theatre by the Abbey brought on more thunderclaps of resentment. Miles na gCopaleen, in *The Irish Times*, quotes the critic of *The Evening Herald* as saying, 'It's a poor play. The second act, set in the trenches [by the way, the scene is Not set in the trenches, but behind them; the trenches are out on the horizon, as the script plainly says: but this is but a minor part of an Irish critic's splendid critical equipment], finds O'Casey having a shot at expressionism – and in the process being weird, vague, and lamentably wide of the mark. For the majority of play-goers this act is in exceeding bad taste. The litany to the gun is the crowning piece of offensiveness.' Bring out the hackbut and battle-brand! Miles na gCopaleen, after the sermon, gives the priestly curse: 'In the Queen's Theatre, the Abbey makes its début with as loathsome and offensive a "play" that has ever disgraced the Dublin boards. The second act is a perfectly plain, straightforward travesty of Catholic Church ritual. The rest is bunkum and drool.' The toll has changed into a tocsin!

The Irish critics have made all the use they could of the Abbey's first rejection of the play, and have pursued it with curious and persistent hatred; but it still refuses to lie down. Peace, be still, heart of O'Casey: It is only Ireland that abuses the play now. Everywhere else, the play has been accepted as a fine and courageous experiment in modern drama, and only the other day the drama critic of *The Times Literary Supplement* said of this very play, this very act, 'If the voluble rapscallions of Dublin tenement life are unforgettable, so, too, is the pre-presentment in universal terms of the horror of war in the expressionistic act of *The Silver Tassie*'; an opinion oddly different from that of J. J. F. of *The Evening Herald*. For reasons too short to explain, Sean preferred to embrace the opinion of the English *Literary Supplement* rather than that of the Irish journal.

But Yeats was stretched out, alone and motionless, in a grave, thrust away in a farther corner of France. The battler was gone from the field. His bow was broken, and the scattered arrows lay where they had fallen; but

> *Here, perhaps, a hundred years away,*
> *Some hunter in day dreams or half asleep*
> *Will hear his arrows whizzing overhead,*
> *And catch the winding of a phantom horn.*

And, now, his young shield-bearer, F. R. Higgins, has followed him: the riverside is lonely, and the street where the Abbey is; the plains of Meath and the fields of Connacht lack a lover.

> *Cold, cold!*
> *Cold tonight is broad Moyburg.*
> *Higher the snow than the mountain-range,*
> *The deer cannot get at their food.*

The frogs were happier now; louder: Brékkek Kékkek Kékkek Kékkek Kóax Kóax Kóax.

FEATHERING HIS NEST

THE General Strike in 1926 had emptied the Fortune Theatre. The packed houses had given way to audiences of ten and eleven nightly; so Sean's first play was taken off, and the second one, *The Plough and the Stars*, was put into rehearsal, its first night to be given in the New Theatre. A few days before this, the young girl playing the part of Nora fell ill, and Fagan got another young Irish lass named Eileen Carey, who had been in the cast of *Rose Marie*, to take on the part. She came to settle the arrangement while Sean was in the theatre's office, talking to Fagan. In she came, neatly and delightfully dressed, and a lovely lass she was; a very lovely lass. Sean's Irish eye was as keen in the choice of a pretty lass as the American eye of George Jean Nathan, so he stood staring at her for a long time. He had rarely seen a lovelier face or figure anywhere in this world, and didn't expect to find anything better in the delectable world to come. She was nervous; Sean saw she was sensitive, for the talk about wages embarrassed her, so he helped by demanding that she get the same as had been given to the girl whose place she had taken – for Fagan had offered her five pounds a week less, reproaching Sean when she had gone for adding to the expenses of the production. But Sean was well pleased to be of service to such a delightful girl whose voice was clear and musical and whose bright eyes betrayed a natural but hidden intelligence.

The poor girl accepted an almost impossible job, for the rest of the company were now perfect in part, movement, and position, while she had to begin, teasing them and silently asking them to show her the way through the play. And scant sympathy and little help she got from them in her efforts to come level with their knowledge and experience of the play. Had Sean had then the knowledge he acquired afterwards, he would never have allowed the young lass to undertake the uncongenial and thankless task; but she bore it all patiently and doggedly, and played the part till the other young actress

was fit enough to take it on again. There was, too, an affinity
of race between Sean and her, for she was as Irish as the
heather on Howth Hill. But there was nothing in her of Harry
Lauder's Scotch Bluebell, and, indeed, Sean didn't believe there
was such a lass in Scotland either, down in the Lowlands or up
in the Highlands. He could see that she had many undeveloped
gifts; that she was a fighter, that she was of the earth, knowing
that there was a deep blue sky over it; that, though she was
nervous now, and a little shyly hesitant, she had courage and a
determined spirit, mingling with a true kindliness – gifts that
can form, and be, only what we call the kingdom of heaven
within us. And time has proved that he made a good guess.
Emerson has said that a pretty face is a great gift to a woman,
an attractive figure a greater one, and a charming manner the
greatest of all; and when one gets these in a *trio juncta in uno*,
then one has been promoted in life by the gods themselves;
especially when their grandeur is subdued by a gloriously
human sense of humour. There's nothing lovelier in life than a
lively laugh. Eileen had faults; a lot less than he had himself,
for these were many; but faults are trivial things in a nature
worthy of all men to be accepted.

During a lot of this time the General Strike had spread itself
all over England, and Sean had been amazed at its quietness.
At first, he had thought, Now is the accepted time, now is the
day of salvation; but no voice spoke, and quietness seemed to
brood all over England. Three million of men out on a militant
strike, and it looked as if they had all gone to bed. He couldn't
help comparing the dense quietude of this effort with the ex-
hilarating uproar and daring intensity engendered in Dublin by
the Lock-out of nineteen hundred and thirteen, when every
worker was a warrior and any who blenched were banished
from the fighting tribe. Everyone was in the struggle, from the
Viceroy of Ireland to the raggedest urchin of the slums who
had reached the years of talk and a prentice understanding of
events. Then every vantage-point had its machine gun, and the
Viceroy was praying to God for help.

The excitement, as far as Sean could see, was all on the side
of those who wished to maim the strike; with those who had
more than they needed, with those who depended on those
who had more than they needed, and with those who depended
on those who depended on those who had more than they

needed. The Two Nations of England were lined up for war, the one against the other. *Two Nations: between whom there was no intercourse and no sympathy; who were as ignorant of each other's habits, thoughts, and feelings, as if they were dwellers in different zones, or inhabitants of different planets; who are formed by a different breeding, are fed by a different food, are ordered by different manners, and are not governed by the same laws* – THE RICH AND THE POOR; and Sean wondered if Disraeli had meant this when he set it down, and, if he were here now, would he get a Vavasour to lead his baronets, with their coronets of two gold balls, against this menace of men out to fight for the right to live; to fight the men wearing the Mons Star who were threatening the safety of the unearned incomes.

Those who had more than they needed suddenly displayed and paraded a remarkable burst of Christian charity and kindliness. They had cars, and they insisted in placing them at the services of those who preferred to walk. They slung placards on their windscreens saying, Ask me for a Lift, and were much upset and annoyed when a lift was refused. Young aristocrats and university men, oil-spattered and smoke-grimed, helped by soldiers, stood on the footplates of engines and tried to drive them hither and thither; and rushed here, rushed there, rushed everywhere to keep the essential services going; even the younger sons, who, as Disraeli says, *Should be the natural friends of the people, though they are generally enlisted against them. The more fools they; to devote their energies to the maintenance of a system which is founded on selfishness and which leads to fraud; and of which they are the first victims.* So the eldest sons stood with the fathers and the young sons stood with their elders to oppose the menacing workers who had spread a pall of quietude very like death over the whole land; revealing to all but themselves that without labour there can be no life.

All the Unions had been called out by the Labour leaders in support of the miners; for by coming out to help a comrade, they had but come out to help themselves, and Jim Larkin's slogan flashed through Sean's mind, An injury to One is the concern of All. They silenced England that their voice might be heard and the needs of their wives and children known. As it had been, so it was still:

The golf links lie so near the mill,
That almost every day
The labouring children can look out
And see the men at play.

The strike began on May 4th and ended on May 13th, a nine days' wonder. The Trades Union leaders found fright in their hearts when the stillness began to brood over the land; they feared for the fat salaries their jobs gave them; they feared to lose the happy assimilation of friendship with those who had more than they needed; their wives had cast off the hodden grey and had put on fine linen and silk, and they had no desire to go back to the hodden grey again; and Sir John Simon, after a search through many old books of parchment, discovered that the strike was illegal. Parchment, sacramented with seal-ing-wax, declared against the workers. The leaders called the strike off; the men, all but the miners, went back beaten, and Sir John Simon put the precious parchment back into the safe again. So the homes fit for heroes to live in that had been bobbing up and down on the waves all round the coast, dis-appeared over the horizon; for it was all a mirage; and there never will be any houses fit for heroes or humans to live in till the heroes and humans build the houses themselves. The hour had not struck.

The miners held out, and Sean sent a subscription to their funds, with a message of a comrade's support of their fight, adding another to the man for Labour who stood for the workers' cause in the by-election of Leith. It was this support that first showed Sean that free thought didn't altogether go unchallenged, even in England. He received a rather indignant and advisory letter from William Blackwood, the great friend of Harry Lauder. William Blackwood was a prominent man in the Northcliffe publications, editor of *Answers*, and he had used every possible appeal to induce Sean to write an article for the periodical, but Sean wasn't interested enough in the publication to do it. An election took place in Leith, and Sean had sent a letter of courage and good hope to the Labour candidate. Some time after a letter came from Fleetway House, signed by Billy Blackwood, saying:

'What is this I hear about you? Namely, that you have been

putting your name to election literature of the most seditious kind.

'I happen to mention the other day to a well-known literateur that I had the honour and pleasure of your friendship. He thereupon went off the deep end, cursing you loudly and bitterly for taking part in the recent Leith by-election, and allowing your name to go on some pamphlets which were distributed by the tens of thousands all over that section of my beloved land affected by the election. This morning he sends me a copy of the document, along with a note urging me in impassioned language to ask you to refrain in future from lending so distinguished a name as yours to the Anti-christs and Bolsheviks of Britain! !

'Joking apart, my own idea is that probably you never saw the document in question, and, in any event, I am not sufficient of a politician to be concerned by it either way. But I think seeing your name on such a virulent Red pamphlet has been rather a jolt to some of your literary and dramatic admirers.'

And Sean, thinking over it once only, sent something like the following:

'A leterateur, a literateur – what the hell's a literateur? How does it look? What does it eat? Where does it live? I know some of these "Literateurs" – nancy boys in art whose hands will never stretch to pluck bright honour from the pale-faced moon ... And they can go to hell, and tell them that from me. I know very little about politics, but enough to save me from the stupidities of the H of Commons. As there are "tied houses" so there are tied men, and your literateur is probably one of them: a one whose humanity is as broad as the cheques he gets for the work he does. And he can go to hell, and tell him that from me. And I will probably go on jolting my literary and dramatic admirers; let them wash their own feet and comb their own hair, for they won't get me to do it.'

He had offended Fagan too. Fagan had given him the typescript of his play, *And So To Bed*, to read, and so Sean had, and had flung it aside on to a table, forgetting about it in the excitement of his lady's loveliness and the roar of London, blazoned with business; for he had become one more among the city's crowds rushing hither and thither, waiting at the crossings till the mighty surge of oncoming traffic, bullied by the big red buses, was suddenly stayed by the upraised hand,

white-gloved, of a big policeman, who stood, or moved right
and left, with a calmness astonishing in the midst of so many
impatient, panting, go-ahead, on-ahead vehicles, crouching in
alertness, waiting for the stately, white-gloved hand to come
down, to shoot forward. So Sean watched, waited for the hand
to go up, and, when it did, shot forward in the midst of the
crowd to the other side of the street, separating to this side, or
that, to allow an opposing crowd forging forward to get to the
side of the street he had just abandoned. So he forgot the
play.

The telephone rang at his flat, and Fagan's voice, a note of
reproach in it, begged him to take a taxi, and bring down the
play to his office at once. So Sean did, hurrying down with it,
slapping it into Fagan's hand, and saying, jaunty with the
sights and sounds pressing on him everywhere, and buoyant
with ignorance, There it is, Jim, and don't waste my time any
more by making me read such trivial plays. Fagan said nothing; silently told a stout, smiling man beside him who this
excited fellow was; gave the play to him, and bid him a smiling
goodbye. Then Fagan said quietly, You might have waited to
say what you thought of the play till my friend had gone: that
was Edmund Gwenn, who is to play the part of Pepys in my
play, that was. Sean was thoughtless still. He had plagued
Fagan in other ways, for Fagan had insisted on becoming his
father and friend, watching over him, telling him what to do,
where to go, whom to meet, till Sean was angry and resistant.
He got a blank invoice from a Bond Street tailor, and, disgui-
sing his handwriting, had entered thereon a bill for a plum-
coloured velvet jacket, black satin trousers, a yellow-flowered
waistcoat, the lot costing seventy-five guineas, which he told
Fagan he wanted to wear when he was going to answer evening invitations by personal presence, making the producer
shake with nervousness that Sean would put him, with his
ignorant, exhibitionist ways, to an open and a shut shame.
Again, Sean bought a gaudy little watch for three shillings, got
a plush case for it, and telling Fagan the price was twenty-five
pounds, asked him very seriously to lock it in the theatre safe
till he made up his mind as to whether or no he'd buy it. A few
days later a bill for the amount came to the theatre demanding
the twenty-five pounds without delay, or the immediate return
of the watch. This Fagan had read, for the bill came unsealed,

and he, immediately, without Sean's knowledge, returned the
watch. When Sean learned of this, he became artificially angry,
and demanded that Fagan should never interfere with his
affairs again. Afterwards, the papers recorded that the dramatist, O'Casey, had bought a baby elephant, and was taking him
out for walks in Hyde Park; so Fagan got frightened, and left
Sean alone, asking him no more to meet particular friends, or
to come to his flat for a meal. So now Sean could sit on his
own chair, and eat at his own table, and look about for a friend
or two of his own choice. Yet Jim Fagan meant well; he was
gentle – a little too gentle – and he had a very kind nature.

So, surrounded by these things and many more, Eileen and
Sean went on building a nest. They entered a little three-
storeyed house, including a basement, used as a dining-room
because it was near to the kitchen, when the streets were knee-
deep in snow. It was a simple Georgian house, one of a long
terrace, with two decent rooms, a tiny bathroom, and a huge
kitchen, with an old-fashioned range in it big enough to do as
an altar for Stonehenge. And, by God, it burned the coal as
fast as one could shovel it in, but took its time to heat the
water. There was an oven in it would roast half an ox, my ox,
your ox, his ox, her ox; but you would have to put a turkey
into it on the very first of January if you wanted it cooked for
Christmas. Going down the basement stairs, one had to hold
tight and pray fervently to prevent a broken neck. After a
short time in residence it was found that the tank holding the
household water leaked badly, and, when examined, it was
seen that the tank had been stuffed in many places with rags to
keep the bulk of the water from flooding the whole locality.
But these things took time to discover, and, first, the home had
to be furnished. They were, he and Eileen, full of the necessity
to make the home comfortable, bright, and original. It was
delightful and easy to picture it as they thought it should be.
They would search for cretonne, for prints, for chinaware, for
curtain-stuff, for chairs, tables, and divans till they saw what
their hearts desired and their minds understood to be suitable.
Life was singing a song in their hearts. They spent days in
Heal's and holidays in the print shops of Charing Cross Road.
They were for ever handling things they couldn't buy. Lifting
lovely things, then hurrying away when told the price of them.
The house had been taken on a lease which swallowed nine-

tenths of what they had had. Now they were discovering that
the house demanded more, for a new tank had to be bought,
the roof had to be repaired, a man had to be employed, according to the lease, to keep the little garden in order, the house
had to be kept insured; again, by order of the lease, old pipes
had to be stripped from the outer walls, and new ones put in
their place; and Sean began to wonder if he would have
enough money left even to buy spoons for the two of them.
Jasus, it wasn't half as easy as it had looked!

But they had to do something; so they hurried off, hurried
to Harrod's, buying there a fender, fire-irons, a polished-steel
bucket in which to put coal, an oak chest for linen, and a
hearth-brush with a brass back. Leaving the chest behind, they
carried all the other treasures back in a taxi. When they had
settled the things in the big front room, they looked around,
and saw on the floor a square of brown carpet, meeting a wide
frame of stained flooring, for their money didn't allow them to
carpet the room to the walls, the stained margins and the
empty room making the carpet shrink to a smaller size; a
single armchair by the fire and curtains on the big window, and
that was all – a bare room, looking like a native, naked but for
a loin-cloth; a room declaring an imminent departure rather
than a hurried entry; and Eileen, after a glance around,
plumped into the chair, and wept. But not for long: shortly
after, the room's repellent glare changed to a comic look of an
appeal for help, and Eileen and he laughed loud and long,
saving themselves from the folly of self-pity.

Eileen had let her flat before meeting Sean, and they were
now waiting for her furniture to set the home fair for living in,
for he had but a few things, mostly books, which wouldn't even
furnish a decent room for his own use. She had got no rent
from the tenants, and couldn't get any reply from them when
she asked them to return the furniture she needed herself so
badly now. By a lucky chance, she managed to get the key as
they were about to flit to another place; but she found the
furniture in a woeful state, for they had planked hot saucepans
on divans, carpets, and chairs; the carpets were torn and
stained, and the kitchen-ware had never been cleaned from the
day Eileen had handed over to them. It was all very vexatious
and discouraging, but a great many things were salvaged,
lovely things in mahogany, fine cutlery, much linen, and a

beautiful Bechstein piano; so Sean, in the end, found himself
in intimate touch with a few of the elegant things of life. To
this very day, he doesn't know what they'd have done had not
Eileen brought as her dowry the furniture of her four-roomed
flat. With all my worldly goods I thee endow; an easy endowment, indeed, for all he had were two pictures, a chair, a desk
kept together by the mercy of God, a cheap divan, a crowd of
books, a spoon, knife and fork, a kettle, teapot, and a few
articles of delfware. But they were kept going to supply the
bare essentials, ekeing out payments with the few royalties he
got now and again for performances of his plays. None of the
fitments of either flat, his or hers, would suit the requirements
of the house they now had. To supplement the hot-water system, they installed a gas geyser to help the panting, gurgling
pipes coming from the range, which were choked, and now
almost useless. The geyser was easy to work (so it was said), a
thing that a child could use; foolproof (so it was said). Eileen
strolled to the sparkling copper geyser to sample its first bath,
while Sean chatted by the fire with a friend, Billy McElroy,
roguish, bombastic, laughable, and a wonderful personality.
The two of them heard things hissing, the hissing changing to
a dull thump at times; but they put no pass on it. Then Eileen
came in to say she couldn't get the geyser to work. Sean
looked it over, tried to light the jets, but, after a long effort,
gave it up. He told Eileen that she must forgo the bath for that
night, and returned to his friend by the fire. Suddenly, the
whole house rocked in a foul explosion, fretted by the mocking
tinkle of breaking glass, and from the noise's centre came a
frightened scream from Eileen. She had managed to get the
geyser to work. Sean ran to the bathroom – Eileen was stagger-
ing about, moaning that the child within her had been killed.
The bathroom window, frame and all, had been lifted clean out
of the wall, and now lay shattered down in the street below.
Sean got Eileen stretched out on the bed, and, rushing to the
telephone to summon a doctor, he saw his friend tiptoeing
down the stairs, saw him placing his big-brimmed black hat
quickly on his head; saw him open the door softly and close it
quietly after him as he hurried away home. But Eileen was
none the worse for the accident, beyond a few weeks of
anxiety about her baby and unpleasant buzzing in her head; but
the restoration of the window made quite a hole in the little

pile of money remaining, for neither Eileen nor he even guessed that they might have claimed the cost of replacement and of the doctor's fee against the incompetent, and even dangerous, fixing of the geyser. Eileen had come out of it unhurt, and what claim could thankfulness have against anyone?

The little house was one of two stuck together, as if the one couldn't stand alone; so were they all on their side of the road, each a clump of two joined together with a space of little more than four feet between each clump, the back gardens hemmed into their own privacy by low walls. A small garden, its length three times that of its width; in the centre a narrow strip of grass that residents called a lawn, surrounded by a border holding flowers, dominated by a graceful white syringa, a fragrant lilac bush, and a delightful laburnum. Eileen and he had bought prints of pictures by Van Gogh, Utrillo, Renoir, Manet, and Segonzac. Eileen had framed the pictures in her own way, refusing to make use of the conventional gilt frames. She had narrow frames made to tone with the chief colours in the prints so that, when the pictures had been hung on the walls, they looked like coloured panels which formed decorative parts of the walls themselves. And she dispersed them in a new way. She didn't hang them so that a big one took the centre flanked by smaller ones at either side. A big one might be closer to one side than the other, and a smaller one would flank it far away on the opposite side, but not on the same level. Between them, not in the centre, but nearer the smaller one, would be a vase of blossoms; and well the gay simplicity looked, forming an added picture of harmony and divided lines to the coloured dignity of the pictures.

The only gilt frame in any room was the dark gold one surrounding John's beautiful *Head of a Gitana*, one of the loveliest expressions of graceful delight in paint Sean had ever seen. Taking lunch with Augustus John in a restaurant in Chelsea while the artist's exhibition was on in a gallery opposite, Sean had shyly and timidly offered John a tenth of what he had for a picture, for all of them as marked were wildly above anything Sean dare chance. Without a word, Augustus John had written a note to the manager of the exhibition directing him to give Mr O'Casey any picture he might choose; so Sean had run straight over to the gallery, had made his choice, and had been rewarded by John saying, when he saw it, You made a good choice, Sean. So he had, and the picture is still the O'Casey centred jewel hanging upon the wall. Supplementing this treasure was the royal portrait that John did of Sean himself, in blue-green coat, silver-grey sweater, with a gayer note given by an orange handkerchief flowing from the breast-pocket of the coat; the face set determinedly in contemplation of things seen and heard, the body shrinking back tight to the back of the chair, as if to get farther away to see and hear more clearly; a sensitive and severe countenance with incisive lines of humour braiding the tightly-closed mouth – a princely gift from a great artist and a most generous man.

But when all had been done, when the simple, little house had begun to look fine, like a quakeress wearing a bright bandeau round her head and a daring locket on her bosom, they discovered that the district was a very expensive one to live in. They knew nothing, or next to nothing, about marketing or about the domestic ways of life, and had to learn by rough and punishing experience. Piously and vehemently, Eileen and he, now and again, hurried off to do the marketing in Kilburn, but the strain of the journey and the burden of hiking back all they bought, impaired their ardour, and so they plunged again into the dearer market of their own district, and the flabby little bag of money at the bank became far flabbier still. Then their first baby's birth had been a costly affair, the doctor taking fifty pounds, plus the cost of a nurse who stayed with them for six weeks. When he remembered what it cost a woman to have a kid in the tenements, he realized more fully than ever the terrible difference between one birth and another. And the Income Tax Collector, a kindly man, was coming to the house on the track of fifty pounds owed to the Revenue, which sum Sean hadn't got, but which the Collector thought must be found somewhere. Sean had tried to interest the kindly man in the bees in the garden, but the Collector didn't care about bees. He said he didn't know a thing about bees; how they lived, or how they were brought up, or a ha'porth. He knew a bee could sting a man, but that was about all. He was glad to hear that they were so useful to man in the pollination of flowers, a thing he hadn't known before. He knew, of course, that bees were thrifty things, laying up a store for a rainy day, and so a lesson to us all. He had other calls to make, but hoped he'd get the fifty pounds before the weekend, for he couldn't wait indefinitely, and went his way.

He got a letter from Lady Gregory saying how glad she was to hear he had a home of his own, with a garden too, a thing he would very much enjoy. Well, though he got in this home the rejection of *The Silver Tassie*, and all the anxiety and trouble that went with it, he had spent many enjoyable hours with the bees and the flowers, the only ones, bar those enjoyed during his days in Coole, he had ever been able to handle and watch without feeling they were not for him to pluck. He had had many still and happy hours with the spiders too, covering shrubs and bushes in the autumn with their beautifully balanced webs. He had wondered at the spider's speed, at its patience, waiting, sphinxlike, for the prey to come; at its frenzied haste, whenever a huge insect like a bee became enmeshed, to envelop it completely with silken threads, lest its frantic struggles should tear the web to pieces. Sean could never understand why some hated the spider. He knew one man who hated them so that he hunted them out, plucked them from their webs, and gloatingly plunged them into water to drown, or, if he could conveniently manage it, into hot water to be boiled; and, oddly enough, this man was a rabid pacifist; a conchie who had served a long time in jail rather than stick a needle into another man. He remembered how he himself had felt grieved in his heart when September's heavy rain ruined many of the lovely webs. Now he would have to go. He'd leave these things behind him. They'd have to sell the remainder of the lease, and live on what they got for another year. Looking at his bank book, he found that expenditure was two hundred and seventy-three pounds, against three hundred and twenty-nine pounds on the credit side, so that he had fifty-six pounds left to face the roll-call of payments which would be advancing on him soon. He'd have to sell out and go.

Yeats' denunciation of *The Silver Tassie* had done Sean's name a lot of violence. The Nobel Prize winner, the Leader of English literature, was a judge against whom there was no appeal for the time being. Sean's flying start had been rudely curtailed of its fair proportions, and he would have to start over again, and fight the battle anew. He would have to hand over his little grey house in the north-west to another. The sale to a Film Company of one of his plays had stayed the inevitable away for a few years. He had got a thousand pounds for it – six hundred down and four hundred in six months' time. One night of fierce wind and heavy snow, when the house shivered in the midst of the glow from all the fires they could afford to light, a Mr Mycroft came driving up from Elstree to offer the money for the making of the film. Out of his speedy little car came Mycroft, covered with thick flaky snow, a genuine *deus ex machina* when funds were gone and hope was waning. Pressed to stay the night because of the fierce wind and the falling snow, Mycroft refused, anxious to get back to report that consent had been given, and that the Company could go on with its terrifying plunge into experimental art; so out and on Mycroft went through the fierce wind, under the falling snow, fervent as a dashing courier carrying home the news of a gallant victory against heavy odds. Hysterical vanity of film production, hasty excitement in the production of the theatre, like hungry hens rushing headlong for a handful of scattered corn. Hysteria in the production of a mediocre film, clownish excitement in the production of a mediocre play; the more mediocre the play, the greater the excitement; the more mediocre the film, the greater the hysteria.

But Sean found that a lot of the film money would have to go into preserving the sanctity of an original peppercorn lease, and keeping the house merry and bright for the present land-lord. The Estate Surveyor, a Sir Someone or other, with his clerk, and the heir to the estate, came to check up on the state of the properties, and, in due time, came to where Eileen and Sean were finding it hard to live. Outside, round about, with a man to examine the roof, like druids in modern dress, the three of them circled, the clerk jotting down items at a whisper from Sir Someone; through room after room, the three of them marched, halted, looking up, looking down, looking round, the clerk again jotting down items in a note-book at a whisper from Sir Someone. When they came to Sean's room, they gave but a faint echo to his lusty good morning; Sir Someone was quiet; the clerk quiet and deferential; the heir excited, thrusting his face forward towards Sir Someone to say, Quite a nice little property, sir, which caused the Sir Someone to quietly leave the room, possibly having caught a glimpse of Sean's sardonic grin as he watched the ritual.

Property is theft, said Proudhon, but he must have been

doting. Property must add to righteousness, for it is supported
and sanctified by bishop, priest, and deacon. Some talk of morality, and some talk of religion; but give me a snug little property, sang Maria Edgeworth; and she was right. This lad had a
snug little property, and he was beaming. And Tennyson
chorused:

> Dosn't thou 'ear my 'erse's legs,
> As they canters awaäy?
> Proputty, proputty, proputty – that's what
> I 'ears 'em saäy.

Even horses know the importance of property, so who was
Sean to question the demand to fork out what he needed for
himself and family, to plaster ceilings, pipe walls, repair roofs
so that a nice little property of another might remain a nice
little property still. But nice and all as it was, it would soon
have to see the last of Sean and of those who were his.

From this nice little nest of property, so beloved by the heir
who owned it, which had filched a lot from Sean's limited
means, he had flown to two organized meals only: one, an
Annual Dinner of the Critics' Circle; the other, a lunch given
to Jim Brady, the celebrated New York Theatre man, by C. B.
Cochran. And these two were quite enough for a lifetime. He
had been selected by the critics to respond to the Toast of the
Drama, and before the date fixed for the event he had had
three different reminders not to forget to be in his place to
respond when the toast was given. He was there all right, and,
when the time came, spoke too damn wisely and too damn
well. He criticized the critics for their jaunty adulation of
trivial plays, the actors for their devotion to, and admiration
of, their insignificant parts in these trivial plays, and the playwrights for writing down to the leading actors and actresses by
scorching out of their work any good or important element in
the secondary characters so that the part of leading lady or
leading gentleman might add perceptibly to their own importance by the lessening of the importance given originally to the
other characters circling around them. The speech didn't go
down well, though it was politely honoured by a timid and
hesitant handclap. But Sean was bucked up afterwards by the
distinguished guest of the evening, Lord Cromer, telling him
that it was easily the best speech of the evening. But the critics

weren't at all pleased at having their colours lowered, even for a time, to a half-mast flutter; and so, signs on it, Sean has never had, for over twenty years, a whisper of an invitation to come within talking range of any annual gathering of these gentlemen: they didn't like the flash of criticism within the orbit of their own united circle of comment. Had Sean been less ignorant and innocent then than he became afterwards, he wouldn't have given 'the best speech of the evening'.

There was a big crowd of chaps only at the theatrical lunch given by that great man of the theatre, Cochran – St John Ervine, Noel Coward, Archie Selwyn of New York, old Jim Brady, Branker, afterwards lost in a flaming dirigible, and many others. Sean never cared for stag parties, and it wasn't long till he was longing for the sight of a pretty face and the swish of a woman's skirt. Never to him could a place be comfortable or fully human without a woman. But here the stags, the men, felt free, and let themselves go. The silent censorship of delicate-minded woman was absent, and unfettered language flowed free from some of the mouths. It was romantic nonsense to imagine that women couldn't swear as well as a man. There was no docker of the tenements, no labourer of the slums, proficient in what is called vile talk, who couldn't find a woman his equal in the same tenement or the same slum. Old Brady made a speech that was lurid with the lightning of bad language. But it was stage lightning badly lit. The words were forced out of a pretended intimacy with profanity. They were not natural. The poor man didn't know how to use them, and so they sounded horrible in their deformed obscenity. There was no health in them. He should, before using them, have taken a long course of lessons from some lusty seaman, some ignorant navvy, some lowly docker. For the first time in his life Sean felt uncomfortable at the sound of bad language because it was unsound. The difference between it and that of a woman of the slums was that the old man's language made his blood go hot, while the language of a woman of the slums would have made his blood run cold. Neither was it the profanity which, in general circumstances, often gave off a glow, or a great humour. Cochran made a speech as neat, as orderly, and as respectable as his own appearance. A very good speech. A quiet man, Cochran. Under the neat quietness a deep well of artistic emotion. What a will he had for the theatre! But his way was blocked, turn him how he might. Had he had the way as well as the will, the last forty years of the English theatre would have been fretted with many stars. Well, these two feasts were a long way off now. The last glimpse of the luncheon which lingered in his memory was of Archie Selwyn, the New York producer, impressed mightily by the thought of Jack Buchanan and Evelyn Laye strutting majestically on a New York stage in *Bitter Sweet,* pacing up and down the room feverishly, exclaiming *Jack Buchanan and Evelyn Laye together; in the one show. My God, what a sensation!* He seemed to think that the combination would be so tremendous that God Himself would leave heaven to make a personal appearance among the audience.

Sean tried heavens hard to imagine *Bitter Sweet* to be a good and charming musical play, principally because his wife was acting a part in it, so presenting an importance to him another play of its kind could not have. The first night cost him thirty-four pounds, for Eileen sent tickets to many friends, anxious, of course, that the show should be received well, if not tumultuously. Sean went a second time with the doctor, Harold Waller, who had brought their first-born into the world, and who had become a great friend of the family. (Sean seemed to get on well with doctors. There was Dr Cummins, of course, whose friendship he would remember to his dying day; again, Dr McGuinness, who had attended him for bronchitis, and whom he met in London; Dr Waller, who gave up a West End practice to be chief of a maternity hospital in Poplar, a son of the clergyman, Waller, who had been the friend of Livingstone; and Dr Varian, of Totnes, a Dublin man and a fine fellow.) Dr Waller, who knew a lot about it, thought the music bad, and Sean, try how he might to think the contrary, thought the wording worse. There seemed to be nothing in the first week's glow to predicate a success, but wizard Cochran worked a miracle, and by lusty nursing made of this poor thing a tremendous success for himself and for Mr Coward.

They put off the day of decision, but they knew that the day was coming when they would have to leave the pleasant little house. He remembered how many good hours he had had with his boy, Breon, watching him begin to crawl on the grass, then make primitive and violent efforts to get to his feet, enacting over again man's first painful evolution from a four-footed animal; then the thrill of seeing the tiny boy plunge forward recklessly into the steps betokening the coming man who must stand alone and walk his own way through life; who had had his own birth, and would have his own development, his own sorrow and joy, his own wife and children, his own old age, and, finally, round it all off with a sleep. Many good hours had been spent in Regent's Park, but half an hour's stroll from the house, one side of the Park running round the Zoo, where wild horses could be seen in their paddock (though they looked very much like tame ones), and the wild goats jumping about on their rocky heights. At times, the air was made uneasy by the scream of a tiger or the roar of a lion.

Occasionally, halfway on to the Park, he turned into the churchyard of the parish church of St John's Wood, opposite Lord's Cricket Ground, and sat him down to watch the nurses and nannies – too tired to go the farther way to the Park – airing their bottoms on benches, a pram holding a baby beside them, and older charges, eminent in being fit to run, tearing about on scooters, or riding sedately on tricycles along the paths bordered by grass and measured by decaying tombstones that were frantically trying to keep their heads from sinking under the ground. Some of the sturdier youngsters, risking the fire of adventure, careered away on their tricycles to the uttermost ends of the churchyard, and, with toy pistol in hand, shot all who passed without the railings, and a few that ventured nearer within, returning to their nannies breathless with the risks they had taken and the difficulties they had overcome. Voyaging farther into life among the dead. Here, indeed, were the quick and the dead. Near to each other, yet wide apart, but near enough. The graves had no meaning for the youngsters within, or for the hurrying citizens without. The ardent young ones blew their toy trumpets, shot their toy guns, careless of the rebuke of the silent dead. The living dust was vivid, asparkle, bounding about; the dead dust had ceased to shine, even in the memory of man. The dead thrust down here had been forgotten; they had died too far away in time for men to bother about them, for even the dead grow old. No stone should show where the deep dead lie.

Did Yeats ever chronicle himself as sitting and sounding out thoughts in a churchyard? Sean failed to think of any reference to such crowded isolation. Death would have been too like death to him in a graveyard. And yet the explanation of it was here and it is that there is none; except that that one who has died ends his importance, while this one newly born begins it. If Yeats were passing by here now, even as those citizens hurrying along the street outside, he would act as they do, never turning a head to look within. They leave the buried dead to take care of themselves and answer their own questions. Not among the dead, but among the living, Yeats sought an answer to the riddle of death. Old mortality had no interest for the poet; he sought out the newer mortality within a room, having heavy curtains on the windows, making himself a part of a circle of clasped hands; the lights extinguished, the hymn sung, and a diamond-tipped pencil scratching out words upon a window-pane. But all he could gather from his quivering search as an answer was the echo of his own thoughts.

Sean's own sturdy lad was gallivanting about among the graves. He and his companions were making fun of Death; playing tig around him; hide-and-seek between his legs; tiring him with their tireless movements, their present laughter, and their noisy cries. Death is helpless to prevent them; unable to force the sombreness of the scene before them. Life is too busy, too gay, to be bothering about bones hidden beneath the soil. *Weep, for ye are but mortal*, Death tries to say, but he stands there mute. He is silenced by Life. He is disregarded, pushed about, dishonoured in his own domain. He is as powerless as his own dead battalions. The little bugles blow the call of life, the little drums beat the march of life, and Death has to stand still and listen.

Yet for a little while longer, till sense and regard for life come creeping into the mind of the common man, Death, getting savage and resentful, may choke a little child with croup here; sling another under a swiftly moving car there; or thrust another little one, astray from her place of safety, under the slimy waters of a city canal; but young life in street, park, and playground laugh and mock him into quietness again. So there they go, dodging in and out among the dead, the tombstones thrusting themselves despairingly up to insinuate their importance to the notice of the passer-by, an identity and presence that have long since ceased to be. No name of a chimney-sweeper on any tomb: all seemed to have lived and died in good circumstances: golden lads and lasses all. Vanity of death, for even the name-remembering stones are crumbling too. The dead disappear from view; they fade from the memory of those who knew them; from the memory of those who loved them; and when these die too, the dead, who went from life before them, go from life altogether.

What does the hurrying sun think of Yeats' eight and twenty phases of the moon, the great Yeats, with some majesty even in his medley? What do the dead here and the living beyond think of Yeats' grouping and groping of life through various incarnations? The poet, so restive against discipline concerning his own art and thinking, would bring the whole universe within a discipline of his own. He points a finger at the dead and shouts Come forth! But not a mouse stirs. The laughing secular sun, the superstition-breeding moon, the evening star, the bright and early morning star, and all the graces and the airs within the universe, declare the monstrous insignificance of the dead.

What did this old church here think of them? The old church of either St John who baptized towards repentance in the river Jordan or St John who saw in Patmos a rabble of sights surmounting all that Yeats himself saw in the room of the Golden Dawn. The church probably never thought at all; it was beyond thinking, and it looked to be ageing. It was trying to stand up and look important, but there was an air of deep decline about it. Time and thought had made it shabby. What did it stand for; what was it for; what did it do? It seemed to be a sentry guarding the dead, but looked like a sentry asleep at his post. Custom kept it standing; custom kept its door open. It looked lonely, and seemed to be aware of its loneliness. Am I nothing to all ye who pass by? Not much.

The day is long gone when what you wearily symbolize now was the power of the city, of the whole land, of the whole known world: faith unquestioned and power unchallenged were yours. When the monks were masters. Monastery, nunnery, church, college, chantry, and chapel watched over the land, and rooked it of all it had. The Pope was Lord Mayor of every city and town in merrie England. To please the people the Grey Friars came over in rags, and, on Cornhill, built themselves homes of clay and wattles made. They were living as the followers of Christ should live, and the people were delighted; but not for long: they soon moved into a monastery in Newgate Street whose church was made of dressed stone, with a nave three hundred feet long and sixty-four feet high, the friars sitting down to tables of polished pine from which they took the best the land could give, adding wine of the better vintage from the lands where the good grapes grow; while Dick Whittington filled out a fine library for them of fine books, which a few of them read. Pile the weight of wealth and power and mighty buildings on top of the grave of Jesus, driving him deeper down. All gone now, and young lads of the Blue Coat School used to run and step and leap over where the Grey Friars sleep as do the golden lads and girls in this very churchyard of St John's Wood.

England was made merrier with Austin Friars, Black Friars, Canons Minor and Canons Regular, so that a buzzing swarm of busy bedesmen turned the land into a realm of litanies and lice. And the bells tuned them into time and authority. The bells bullied the people about from the cradle to the grave. They belled the baby into the world and belled the dying man out of it; they belled the bride to her bed; they belled the workers to field and workshop, and belled the time for him to straighten his back and give over for the day, charging fees most of the time, according to the bigness of the bell and the time he took in tolling.

This old church in St John's Wood, this spare relic of a powerful, busy past – how lonely it looked, and how shame-facedly it seemed to be aware of its unlamented loneliness. Ichabod. Am I nothing to all ye who pass by? Not much now. The Christians who have more than they need, with those who depend on them, gathering crumbs, have crucified Christ afresh, and have buried him down with the dead men. You do not mean much to us now. We are busy with other things. You have no bearing on our thoughts today. You rarely had, except to frighten us with myth and legend. A meagre myth by now. We know the herald angels didn't sing, and we are not sure that Christ was born in Bethlehem. Some say he was. They say: What is there for the man of today? Let us go even unto the little town of Bethlehem. Who goes there? And what shall we find when we get there, and how many want to go? Bethlehem is little more than a little toy for Christmas now; brought into play for a little hour, and put away again. Butlin's holiday

camp is the popular rendezvous now. Yeats would sail the seas
to come to the holy city of Byzantium. His holy city. Flecker
would go the golden road to Samarkand. His holy city.
Eileen's is New York. And what was Sean's? Moscow. Not a
holy city, but an able one, a flame to light the way of all men
towards the people's ownership of the world; where revolution
stands in man's holy fire, as in the rich mosaic of a red wall.
But he would not soon forget the lot he owed to London, or
the warmth and good-fellowship of New York.

Well, for the moment, he'd have to bid goodbye to the vision
of Yeats rushing round Ireland's market-place; his quick
mounting of the political pulpit and the quicker dismounting
of it; his divining the accurate way in which the Abbey Theatre
ought to go; and his sudden rushes away from all to put an eye
and an ear to the keyhole of the ivory door of death, to try to
catch a glimpse and hear an odd sound of what was going on
behind it. He'd have to leave his spiders, some of which he
nearly knew by name, his charming little garden, and the
pleasant district of St John's Wood for some place they
couldn't think of yet; not Rapallo or Capri or the Riviera; just
some place out of London that might soften the worry of what
they were going to do to make both ends meet. All the gallant
recreation they had cadged from what they had had, was a few
weeks' stay in a boarding-house at Margate.

Came a friend of theirs, whose daughter and her husband
had held a cottage in Buckingham, and who had now abandoned it, to tell Eileen and Sean that they could have this wee
house for as long as they liked to live in it. Another grand
myth, lifting up his heart for a day, then sending it down
deeper than ever for a year.

ROSE AND CROWN

SEAN was astonished to see the moon shining just as bright over London now as he had so often seen her shining over Dublin. So clear, so elegantly, too, that he almost thought she must have left Dublin, and all Ireland was a dark night now. But the rain fell here, on the evil and the good; the sun shone out on the just and the unjust English; the same blue sky tented London as once had tented Dublin; and, now, the same moon, so beloved of him in Ireland, shone silently and grand in the English night-sky. The English were known to God! But she did not shine quite so lovingly: when the moon shone over Dublin, a reverie could easily conjure all the wider scenes and all the famous forms of old long since into the streets again. Swift's fine face, furrowed with heaven's venom against ill things done, growled indignant with the earth beneath him as he ambled through Hoey's Court, or strode through the scaling streets home to Patrick Street; Emmet came thoughtfully out from Trinity College, his mind tense with the flaming idea of revolution; and Grattan slowly mounted the wide steps of the Parliament House, bent on delivering his nation from the cut-throat casuistry of Castlereagh.

All the fame of Dublin City from the time the first worried warriors crossed the river at the Ford of the Hurdles, to the recent days when desperate Irishmen from corner, from pillar and post, sent shot after shot into the Black and Tans, can gather to pass by, or stop to talk in a corner of an Irishman's mind. But London was too barbarously outspread for the moon's magic to gather together in comfortable compass all the brave things done, and all the figures of fame that had given her high history and made the world wonder. The famous shadows in armour, in cuirass, in buff jerkin, in red coat and blue coat, in top-boots and knee-breeches, in top-hat and cut-away coat come into the glimpses of the moon, come here, come there, pause wistfully among the people, try to speak, but cannot; they remain hidden, for rare is the English-

man who has them memoried in his mind. A city set too wide
apart to assemble them from one reverie in a single mind,
linking the Roman to the Kelt, the Saxon to the Norman, the
English unifying all, from the battles of Boadicea to the time
of the flaming building, the toppling of the masonry, when the
Fascist foe came to destroy, and found death waiting for him.

The moon of England now shone over the innocent elation
of Stanley Baldwin, for the last election had proved to be a
red-letter day for the Conservatives and their commercialized
cronies. The Stock Exchange had hung out all their best banners, the Archbishop of Canterbury was quietly deleterious
with joy, and the home of every company promoter, landlord,
and tied tenant, had roses round its door. It was another
restoration. The old order had the upper hand of the new. All
right-minded persons declared that it had all been prophesied
by the sages of auld lang syne. This was confirmed by many
who had heard the lions roar round Trafalgar Square; by
others who had seen the statue of Achilles in Hyde Park wave
his sword, saying On, Stanley, on; by some who had seen and
heard the granite gun of the Hyde Park Memorial go off with
a real loud bang; and by one, a newly appointed clergyman,
who said he had distinctly heard the statue of Prince Albert
murmuring, most devoutly, Thank God, the Conservatives are
in once more; once more in the dear homeland. There were, to
be sure, Conservatives, bright in mind, young in heart, who,
though they didn't yet believe that all things should become
new, realized that a lot of old things must go; young Tories
who had possessions, but were not bound to them, body and
soul; who said God was speaking better than Baldwin; who
heard the changes of Time chiming; and who carried the gon-
falon of conscience into Conservatism's centre.

The Old Conservatives trotted into the House dancing, as
they well might, led along by the sound of music from lutes,
flutes, pandemonia, and euphoneya. All right-minded people,
all honest folk, all God-fearing persons had been safely separated for ever from Bolshevism. Scudamour, Artegall, and
Britomart were safe. Now they could light the lamps and leave
their doors open. Conservative men could see clearly, feel
fortunate, and speak freely; each Conservative lady could go
forth with the walk of a queen. The Bolshevists could be left
alone to slay themselves· to disentrail themselves; or, be left

alone, with laughter, for each to exile all, or all to exile each to bitter cold and faraway Siberia. Soon, the men of gadsir behind Stanley Baldwin would hear the fall of a self-destroying Communism.

> *As down the cliffe the wretched gyant tumbled;*
> *His battred ballaunces in peeces lay,*
> *His timbered bones all broken rudely rumbled,*
> *So was the high aspyring with huge ruine humbled.*

It was odd that this stout, stolid man, sensible soul, thought his return to power had sliced the workers of the world away from the influence of the Soviet Union; from their own needs; from their old loyalties; from evolving life itself. Strange that the mind of Baldwin thought it could stop the change in things; that it could not conceive of life outside of itself. Drumbeat and bugle-blast! The Communist Manifesto had been jailed in the thick-ribbed, everlasting ice of sad Siberia. The quietly cocky Baldwin was too short to see over the heads of his crowding Conservatives. He wouldn't even try. No tip-toes for him: he would stand flat and firm on the ground. For this relief much thanks. Now thank we all our God with hearts and hands and voices. The workers now couldn't squirm into a strike; instead they would have to whistle while they worked.

At a gathering in a great Conservative Mansion, Richer England's tapestried tavern of the Rose and Crown, where the wines were rare and the fittings gorgeous; where the vast rooms were flounced and friezed by the gorgeous gowns of many ladies, floors pattering elegantly with sandalled shoes of crimson satin or filigree of gold, the air swooning with the moist sweetness of effectionate perfumes, and all was lit up by jewelled orders looking alive on the coats of costly men; Baldwin took Sean by the arm, setting him down on a settee beside himself, to ask him what of the night of De Valera, and of Ireland. What could Sean say to this poor man who knew as much about Ireland, and cared as much about Ireland, as the Archbishop Hinsley, or a monk of Caldy Island dead for a hundred years? Sean glanced at the wide, innocent face, blandness blazoned on it, the wide-open, guileless eyes curtaining the cunning mind of policy that had been ripening to a perfection of power for seven hundred years and more, and

island where the impossible always happens; the Land of Tir nan Nogg, where the unexpected is found whenever one looks long enough.

—Ay, said Sean, and even when you don't look at all, sir. I'm pleased to see you begin to see the darkness through the light; for Ireland is the harp in the air, the murmuring messenger from the isle of the blest, the land of clouds that lifts the silver shield high to re-echo in God's ear the Irish songs of joy; the land where a star dances on every moving plough.

—Yes, yes; I know. A spiritual land, O'Casey, never engrossed with the things of the world. A wonderful people, if only agitators would leave them alone. A people ever soaring after the things of the spirit.

—Ay, sir; ever rushing on and on and ever soaring up and up and up; a people who

> Wing all their thoughts to reach the skies,
> Till earth, receding from their eyes,
> Shall vanish as they soar.

It is the Lord's doing, Mr Prime Minister, and it is marvellous in our eyes.

—Yes, yes, indeed; very marvellous. Baldwin took a few meditative puffs, then resumed his valiant chatter. Yeats, your poet, knows his people. The Selt is well outside of the world of men. That's why your heroes are so universally renowned. You do well to remember your heroes – Daniel O'Connell, T. P. O'Connor, and Timothy Healy.

Ay, and Mister McGilligan, the famous father of Dublin's wonderful Mary Anne, added Sean.

—Him, too, added Baldwin; all good Irishmen. You do well to remember them.

—Never fear, said Sean. They shall be remembered for ever.

—You certainly know a lot of Irish History, sir, said Sean, letting his eyes shine with approval.

—Not really, O'Casey, replied Baldwin; and Sean saw that the man felt flattered; a Prime Minister has little time for study. But I know some, O'Casey; I know some. I've actually heard of Tara. And the great man actually smiled.

Carson went lumbering by; a great hulk of a man, his weight

driving his polished boots well into the pile of the costly carpet.
A heavy, jowled face, cut by deep fleshy clefts, enlightened by a
scowl, dull eyes staring about him and seeming to press out
beyond the rims of the lids. This was the man who had made a
covenant with God that he would never let Ulster put her nose
across the border. He looked bulkier in his black suit, with its
tails swinging awkwardly, and his wide, firmly pressed black
trousers. He paused on his way to stand before a huge portrait
by Lawrence, blotting the picture out, and framing himself between gilt borders half a foot wide: sable and gold. The man
who had wilfully separated the orange from the green. Ulster's
king of harms. The one who slammed protestantism into a
corner and made little jack horners of militant Ulstermen.

How dissimilar, yet how like, was this man of the Nassau
orange and blue, who had never been an orange-man, to his
comrade King's Counsel, Timothy Healy, who was never an
Irish Irelander. Both bullies, both men of a loud mouth, both
using parties for their own ends; both wrapping themselves in
the power of their several religions; both loyal to a king because it was expedient and profitable to be so; both determined
to take no risk that would dim the polish on the knockers on
their trim hall-doors. The one of Dublin or of Cork who had
never sung a Gaelic ballad; the other of Belfast who had never
sung an Orange song; both were often busied calling on God to
witness to the sincerity of their ingenuity of looking after
themselves. The one whose love of country had lifted him into
a lordship, the other whose love of country had lifted him into
its governor-generalship.

Here Carson stood, embedded within the brilliant and costly
Conservative society, framed between gilt borders half a foot
wide; he stood looking down towards Baldwin and Sean,
courtly gentlemen and glittering ladies passing to and fro behind him, the music of a waltz, played by a band in the big
room opposite, saluting the ponderous, deeply carved figure-
head of Ulster's protestant totem-pole. He came nearer, keeping himself between the golden borders, and bent forward to
say, I hope he's giving you good advice, Prime Minister?

—The best that money cannot buy, responded Sean for
Baldwin; and the bulky face seemed to become bulkier with
surprise at the answer to its question; the bulky figure hesitated, then moved on without another word, and the hand-

some figure painted between the gilded borders loomed out again.

—What grieves us, said Baldwin, after a pause, is Ireland's constant refusal to be friends; her refusal to appreciate what we have done for her; her bitterness in all things and on all occasions. What makes Ireland so bitter towards us, O'Casey?

—The winds, sir.

—The winds, murmured Baldwin, bewilderment wrinkling the placid face; which winds, what winds?

—The four winds of Eireann, sir: the white wind from the south; the black wind from the north; the brown wind from the west; and the red wind from the east.

—But I don't understand – the black wind, the white wind – what do these winds mean?

—Some say, said Sean, that the black wind signifies the Dominican Order, the brown wind, the Franciscans, the white wind, the Carmelites – three powerful Orders in the Roman Church, and very powerful at present in Ireland.

—Aah! Now I understand, O'Casey. Of course, of course; the clergy. But you mentioned, I think, a red wind – that doesn't mean Socialism, does it? It couldn't, of course.

—It does, though. Since Bunker's Hill, when it blew from the west, the red wind has always blown from the east: first from France, when the Bastille was stormed; then from Russia, when the red flag was raised in Moscow and Petrograd; blew strong first, then died down; blew strong again, when De Valera's Party sent delegates to the USSR to win support for the Irish Republic; died down when De Valera, raised to power, peered out at the world through a bishop's ring. You may remember, Mr Prime Minister, that Yeats in the midst of dream-dances and dream-kisses, stared through the collar bone of a hare,

> At the old bitter world where they marry in churches,
> And laugh over the untroubled water
> At all who marry in churches,
> Through the white thin bone of a hare.

But De Valera, safe and sound man, prosperous in the grace of God, looking through the gold circle of a bishop's ring, sees life steadily and sees it holy; and so the red wind from the east has died down in Ireland to a tantalizing breeze.

—Yeats was a great poet, I'll admit, said Baldwin, somewhat dubiously, but I'm not sure that his influence on Ireland was altogether a good one. He said and wrote questionable, very questionable, things at times.

Sean granted himself a deep inner laugh as he looked at the toby-jug face of the Prime Minister. Baldwin, thought Sean, thinks that Yeats is a great poet. What a kind concession! But ne'er a ripple of satisfaction would pass through the soul of the poet if he heard him say so; for scant would be the attention given by Yeats to either praise or blame from Baldwin.

Sean laid a hand softly on Baldwin's arm, said soothingly, aloud, You must try to be indulgent with the queer and questionable things sometimes said and written by W. B. Yeats, sir. You must always remember:

> *That Yeats had been he knew not where,*
> *And Yeats had seen what he could not declare,*
> *Yeats had been where the cock never crew,*
> *Where the rain never fell and the wind never blew.*

—There is that to be remembered and considered, of course, O'Casey. Poets claim a liberty of speech denied to ordinary men like me. They have the prerogative of being whimsical, as long as they don't go too far in saying things tending to disturb, or even dismay, law and order. The poet must strictly confine himself to his particular art. It is injurious for any artist to enter into, or bother about, the world of men. You agree with me, O'Casey?

—Cordially, sir, said Sean; but they will persist in doing it in spite of the danger. Even Shakespeare does it; even he.

Baldwin looked at Sean, puzzled and a little startled to hear that Shakespeare might possibly be ranked among the rebels; but, after some hesitation, seemed to decide that the remark had better be left unchallenged. Giving his pipe a few vigorous puffs, he resumed the talk, the homely and kindly face fixing on itself a more serious look than it had before. The priests, he said, at least, are pure. They manage to keep Ireland steady; they are to be trusted – don't you agree, O'Casey?

—Yes, said Sean, they are to be trusted. They have been your good friends in the past, and will be so again in the

future. They laurel your law and order so long as they think
that may be the way to a peak of promotion. But they haven't
always managed to keep Ireland steady, sir; they thought to do
so by destroying Parnell, and succeeded in destroying the
country with him for many years; they condemned to excom-
munication the Fenians who would make Ireland one, but the
Easter Rising burned up their curses, and slapped the bishops
in the snot. There is in Ireland, sir, a political catechism as well
as the one coined by the Council of Trent.

Sean saw that Baldwin was becoming bored or getting uneasy. He was fidgeting with his pipe; looking at it as if he were
wondering was it really his. Then his gaze left the pipe to
watch the gay, commanding figures passing to and fro from
one room to another. They were easily understood, but what
was this Seltic figure sitting beside him trying to say? Sean's
belly filled out with the ecstasy of secret, mischievous laughter,
as he saw the look of quiet perplexity on the stolid, kindly face
of the Conservative leader. Discussions with an Irishman went
dodging in and out, twiningly, like the old interlacing decora-
tion in their coloured and ancient books. Like the silky mist
sprayed by a spider over a despairing prey; a rational man
would be lost in its teeming words if he didn't struggle, break
through, and run. Here was this fellow, O'Casey, snug on the
laps of the best people, handling the tapestry of riches and
power, yet he was as bad, as inattentive to sense as the rest of
them. Hadn't these Selts eyes to see and ears to hear? Couldn't
they realize that while the heavens declared the glory of God,
the earth showeth the handiwork of the Conservative Party?
Baldwin made a stir as if to rise and go.

—What we're anxious to know, O'Casey, is why isn't Ireland willing to help. But I have to go now – I want to have a
talk with Carson. We'll meet again, I hope.

—Hold on a minute more, sir, said Sean, laying a gently
detaining hand on Baldwin's arm. The night's young yet. Wait
till I tell you: If you were to put that question about help to
Ireland herself, she'd say she helped you too damned much
already, in battlefield from Crécy to Tel-el-Kebir; sowing your
potatoes, and reaping your corn; building your docks in Liverpool, carrying your railways across Canada; evangelizing the
British pagan; and giving you an example of literature in the
prose and poetry of Virgil.

—Virgil? echoed the Prime Minister, so startled that he whipped the pipe out of his mouth. Not Virgil, the Roman poet?

—The same, sir, the very same. Though a Roman citizen, like Paul, Virgil wasn't a Roman. As the one was a Jew, so the other was a Kelt. Ferghil, the shining one, and this Kelt influenced literary thought and manner till the great James Joyce came to shove him out of the way. Yes, sir – a link with Tara rather than a link with Rome.

—This is the first time I heard Virgil called a Selt, O'Casey. It amazes and amuses me. Your race seems to have left its mark on the whole world. Well, we've had a very interesting chat, and I'm sorry I have to leave you now.

—Oh, much more than a mark, sir, said Sean rapidly, forcing Baldwin to sit still and listen uneasily out of English politeness. Sure, you haven't heard the half of it. Wait till I tell you: the very broad arrow you stamp on your governmental goods and weave into your prison garments is the broad A of the Keltic Druids. We've left marks everywhere; from where we are to the faraway land of the Calmucks. Khan is the same as the Irish word for a headman; taisha is the Mogul term for the head of a tribe, and, today, De Valera is termed the taoiseach, the leader of the nation, the tribe. Ha, man, you don't know the half of it. The silent thunder of wisdom rumbles round everywhere a Kelt is walking. If he wants to, a Kelt can have the wisdom of Fearceartais; the intelligence of the bardess, Etain; the clear truths of Mor Mumhan; but he must sell to them all he can spare, and part of what he cannot spare, in time and pleasure and property, if he is to achieve these things so that they become an interwoven part of his nature. Then the word of knowledge will fashion fire in his head, so that he can foretell the ages of the moon, and reveal the spot where the sun rests. Thus it was that the Druids who taught magic to the Persians became the spiritual ancestors of Omar Khayyám.

—Really? mused the murmuring Baldwin, half crouching towards Sean, for, out of English politeness, he disdained to shake off the gently detaining hand of Sean resting on his arm; really, now? I never heard that before. The Seltic race must, indeed, have been an amazing one. It is amusing to think of them being responsible for Omar Khayyám. The Prime Minister was well bewildered now by Sean's narrative telling of the

Keltic power by influence over the solid and the fluid world. Sean's remarks had seemingly split into many sparks which were whirling around in the toby-jug mind of the Prime Minister.

—But a Prime Minister, unfortunately, went on the murmuring mind, has no time to spare for the contemplation of the flights of the spirit; but is forced to confine himself within the problems found in the world of men. The stocky, self-satisfied figure straightened up, and Sean's hand slid from the arm. I must go now, for I want to have a word or two with Carson.

—Lookat here, sir, said Sean fervently, rising to deliver the parting shot, if you want to find things hidden and know things unrevealed, you couldn't do better than study the musings of Michael Robartes with John Aherne, the twins, embodying the two minds in one person; give and take; ebb and flow. Fully embattled with the knowledge retained, you can look at the world with the eye of a saint, and when that eye gets tired, you can look at the world through the other one with the eye of a drunkard. You'll watch the

> Sun and moon that a grand hour
> Bellowed and pranced in the round tower.

And listen: when nature falls away from you, you may in recreation be a bird of song, hammered out of silver, perched upon a golden bough to sing to lords and ladies of Byzantium.

—A sober English bird would suit me better, said the Prime Minister, with a sober wave of his pipe; and it is time enough to be that same, he added, smiling contentedly at uttering what he thought was an Irish idiom. Goodbye, for the present, O'Casey; and the Toby Jug was off to set itself upon a caparisoned table for homage and admiration. A kindly man, a shrewd one, conscientious, according to his lights; but utterly deaf to the terrible drum-beat in the march of life. As it is with Labour, so it is with the warm-hearted and younger-minded Conservatives – they are barricaded behind the sleep-shod minds of their ministers who saunter slow in thought, and never risk a run.

There goes the leader of the Party that had within its circle not only the fire, the earthquake, the big wind, but the still, small voice as well. Things done had been useless; things to be done in the future would be useless, if they were not done in the world by the Conservative Party. And Baldwin led them, while the Bulldog Drummond of the Party, Churchill, sat sulking in the conservatory. God's children without the wings. A lot of rare talent was being wasted in both Parties. Tens of thousands of Irishmen had worked in their factories, toiled in their fields, sat on the benches of their judicature, taught in their universities and colleges, gone down full fathom five in their fighting ships, strewed the British battlefields with their bodies, and yet these fellows didn't know a goddamn thing about the land these tens of thousands came from. They knew a lot about every coloured ribbon save the ribbon that was green.

A word with Carson! With Carson, who had betrayed his native land into a diminished Ulster; and had betrayed Ulster for what he could get from England. Who instead of encouraging Ulstermen to come out of a corner, had frightened them into one. Carson should have led his men over the border with a bang; fifes and drums hilarious; the crimson banner of Derry to the right, the orange and blue one of Nassau to the left, and the gallant green flag, embedding the golden harp in its folds, carried high in the centre. Oh, it was cowardly to shrink back and not thrust forward. Courage the Ulstermen have, but courage they have not shown. Occasionally, by a shower of bolts and nuts, aimed at the heads of the philistinian catholics, they have fostered rowdyism, but rowdyism is nothing more than the restlessness of a cankered cowardice.

London was Carson's damasked mistress, jewelled delightedly; full of wealth, portly with good fare, and free with gifts to those who kissed her cunningly; Belfast his wife, a puritan maid, trim; jading prayer trickling from her lips rather than the ripple of a song; afraid of charm; idealizing those who go grim for God; offering fine linen indeed, but bearing no purple to go with it; and dealing even the linen out with wary eye and sparing hand. And for London's lure, Carson, instead of putting fight into Ulstermen, took all the fight out of them. In mass formation, bunched together, they could be hilariously brave, but not so confident or sure when scanty numbers were calmly coerced into melodious deportment by a contagious roman catholic crowd.

In Dublin, when on his way to work before six o'clock of a morning, Sean had seen the little Dublin contingent of a few hundred Orangemen marching through the deserted streets, men of the Orange Order, the Purple Order, and Knights of the Grand Black Chapter; all sash-clad, spangled with insignia of Bible, sword, and crown, led by a miniature fife-and-drum band, headed by the Nassau banner of orange and blue; stepping it out for the train that would hurry them to Belfast in time to join their Ulster brethren in the mad march of bigoted elation on the day of the 12th of July; through the still, deserted streets of Dublin, brawny protestantism marched, a big Ballaghaderreen policeman halting on the sidewalk to stand and stare and wonder who and what they were; the shops shut, the doors closed, the blinds down, heads up, they marched bold and blatant, through lanes of catholics in a sighing sleep or snoring, the timid souls went on with nothing to daunt them but the chilly air of a summer morning. Oh, the canting Christians of the Christian isle that God made well and man has murked with his mad religions! The isle deluged with Christian calls to charity, where no green sash could strut the streets of Belfast in the light of day, no orange sash strut the streets of Dublin – though both decorations, as folk-art, are poor and paltry, less promising or pleasant than the gaudy paper hats hailing Christmas night's hilarity; but they are sincere, however ignorant and bigoted those who wear them; and, to that extent, they are sacred.

Jesus, how these Christians love one another! Jesus said Love one another. We heard you. We do our best. Here, lads, bring them up to him so's he can have a good look; bring up the head split open, the bleeding eye, the bruised arm, the broken jaw, the limping leg, and let Jesus have a good look. All in the day's work, sirree, and we'll do better one day. All in fair fight and no favour. Knock them out and do them in's the slogan of apostolic love. Line them up so's they can be seen proper. Papist bastards on your left, sir; protestant gets on your right. Their own mothers wouldn't know them well. A sight to be seen. We offer the work done, sir, as a token of our esteem. Whoever did it to the fellow with half his face gone deserves a noble prize. Altogether, lads, now, in harmony:

Faith of our fathers, we will love
Both friend and foe in all our strife;
And preach thee, too, as love knows how,
In kindly words and virtuous life!

And so do we. The hymn shows it. Father Faber's moulder-
ing fable. Speak your mind! Jesus did, and was crucified. He
speaks it still, and still is crucified.

The ministers of the Rose and Crown have never known, and
know not now, anything about the ways and means that have
made the Ireland of today. Knew nothing, know nothing,
about her folk-art in story, song, music, legend, and dance;
know nothing about her struggles to perpetuate her life with
something else besides a potato; know nothing even about the
later things that tingle the Irish nerves, fire the Irish blood,
provoking one section into wearing an orange sash, and
another into wearing a green one. One or two of the ministers
may have a faint remembrance of having heard an echo somewhere of a melody by Moore, but why it was composed, or
what it was all about, they cared little and knew nothing;
though, by standing on a chair in their house of Downing
Street, any of them could have seen the Union Jack flying
from a tower of their castle set down tight in the centre of
Dublin City.

Yet the predecessors of these men ramped over the land for
hundreds of years; shot, hanged the leaders of the Irish who
couldn't agree with them, and jammed the jails with the rest;
when every tenant-farmer in the land lost the right to live;
when hunger rose up with them in the morning and went to
bed with them at night; when at one go, in one place, seven
hundred people were flung from their homes, poor mud-made
homes at that, but homes all the same, by an absentee landlord,
because the tenants couldn't give him enough for an extra fit of
whoring; when peasants were bound to pay six pounds an acre
rent and work for their landlords at fippence a day; when an
English earl was forced to exclaim, *If the military force had
killed half as many landlords as it had the revolting Whiteboys,
it would have contributed more effectually to restore quiet;*
when in eighty-five years eighty-six coercion acts were passed
to keep the Irish peasants toeing the landlordian Christian
line; when to have a pike, a lance, or a knitting needle consti-

tuted an offence worth a term of transportation for seven years; when everyone or anyone found walking the roads, or standing at a corner, an hour after sunset in a proclaimed district was liable to the long holiday of fifteen years' transportation; when every judge to be a judge had to be a landlordian lover, and, finally, all were made to act as jurymen as well as judges; when the catholic peasant of the south and the protestant peasant of the north of Ireland spent their lives sowing their own graves that stretched from the river Lee and the river Boyne to the shores of Lakes Ontario and Erie and far beyond them; when every government minister, every privy councillor, every magistrate, was a landlord, or a landlord's brother, or a landlord's friend; so that the threat, as recorded in the Holy Bible, made by the king of Assyria to the people of Israel that he would reduce them to eating their own dung and drinking their own piss, fell upon the catholic peasant of the south and the protestant peasant of the north; while the perfumed voice of Lord Beaconsfield applauded, and Lord Salisbury declared, with a clapping of cold hands, that very soon the Kelt in Ireland would be as scarce on the banks of the Shannon as the Red Indian on the banks of Manhattan. But these powerful boyos inserted a clause in the eviction laws which redeemed their terror, and justified their severity in the eyes of God: they declared that no eviction could take place on Good Friday or on Christmas Day, and that the roof of a house must not be sent tumbling down till the tenant and his family had had time to get out.

The sowls of the ministers of the crown were salvaged by this act of grace, and when it was first proclaimed it was said that all the red roses of England went white with the sense of their deep purity and perfection. Oh, generous genuflexion to the glory of God! No family could be thrust from its home on the day that saw Jesus born or on the day that saw Jesus die! Ballyhoojah, ballyhoojah, ballyhoojah!

Baldwin and Carson were going to and fro on the cordial carpet, walking up and down on it, as if it were the earth; and there goes Churchill astrut on the same deistic daïs, solidly set on himself, impetuous for the renewal of old, unhappy, far-off things and battles long ago; visioning himself in buff jerkin, halberd in hand, and morion set tight on his corybantic head; an officer of the king's guards, a bulky and ageing D'Artagnan of the Conservative Party, a little scornful of the officers of the regiments of foot. A man of many splendid qualities which seemed to be at ease only in thunder, lightning, and in rain, in a plunge back to an old world, rather than a step forward to the new life.

Mayfair had marooned itself by its loud victory in the last election. They had packed the House of Commons with too many clumsy bodies and too many dead heads. They were in great glee. During the progress of the election, the broadcasters had announced with ribald monotony, with voices paused and poised in exquisitely official adulation, *Conservative gain, Labour defeat, Conservative gain,* and Baldwin looked as if he had succeeded in commanding the sun to stand still in the heavens. They could pray or praise now in Westminster Abbey or St Paul's with acclamation. The Labour Party were gamins in the street again. But the leviathan of Conservative rule, of law and order, had a fatal weakness – it hadn't one representative from the workers at the desk, in the field, factory, or workshop. The skin of the Conservative fruit was shining and gay-coloured, but rotten at the core; the skin of the Labour fruit was jagged and thin, but its core was sound, and needed but another day to be perfect with vigour and sap.

Nor was there any worker in this beautiful big house either. No miner, no farm-worker, no clerk, no shop assistant, not a single railway guard, driver, signalman, or porter: no visitor from among those who kept the life of England going. Not one in this imposing residence, showing how rich the rich were, with its gilded ceiling, carpeted floors, luscious furniture, costly pictures; with a stairway up which a column could march without touching the banisters; with silver ware for the morning meal, and golden ware for the meal at night; where every woman wore a gown costing enough to keep a worker's family going for a year without privation. And in and out through the caramelic splendour went Baldwin; while Churchill walked under the figure-filled ceiling, within the aurora of the glowing chandeliers, trenchantly treading down the cringing carpet, his forensic head, sunk down between his shoulders, thrust forward, as if seeking out some policy or opponent to puck. Earlier on, Stephen Gwynn with Sean beside him had spoken, rather diffidently, as if a word or two with the great man was a sly adventure; but two Irishmen were too many or too few for the politician, for, though he slackened his step, he kept moving, sending back a few mumbled words heard by God only; then he went on to where the warriors were, disappearing behind the moving curtain of silk and satin worn by the ladies of the land. He was right to pass on quick, for there was no answer for him with O'Casey or Gwynn as to what would happen, or what was to be done.

Sean had yet to meet a government official who knew anything about Ireland; or even one who wanted to know anything. Indeed, what do they want to know about Wales, either? Only today, the Labour Prime Minister, speaking to a meeting in Llandudno, was asked to receive a Welsh National deputation to discuss the question of an independent parliament for Wales. While he was putting on his hat running to his car, the Prime Minister flipped into the face of the deputation the remark that he hadn't time to meet such a question, much more discuss it. Though the Englishman George Borrow thanked God the Welsh kept their language, the English Prime Ministers think of it as puff puff; and the lives of the Welsh people are of no more importance to any one of them than a wave of a ministerial hand from a Downing Street window. But Attlee hasn't come to walk under the gilded ceilings yet; at present, like a nice little boy, he is just squinting in through a window at the gay goings on in the big house.

Yet it would serve these portentous and prime ministers to know something of the lands, different from their own, that they govern. Had Churchill known the little he should have known about Scotland, he would never have hailed Harry Lauder, singing 'Keep richt on tae the end of the road', as Scotland's national bard at a great meeting in Dunedin, presided over by the Lord Provost of Scotland's capital. God knows there are many to choose from; but Churchill chose one who is none. Stalin would probably know better about him who had a claim to be called a national bard of Alban. Scotland's history and Scotland's art is more than a tartan tie, or the waggle of a kilt. And what have we ever been told by these governors, pastors, and masters about the Commonwealth countries perched on the rim of the world? Not a damned thing. We know the Australians and New Zealanders as great cricketers, great breeders of sheep, great exporters of wool; and there the story ends. Indeed, not to journey too far away, what

do these ministers know about the people in the counties of
their own fair land? Curse o' God on the much. They don't
appear on the stage; they don't show themselves on the films;
they are shunted on to a siding over the wireless, and tolerated
for a brief half-hour in song or story, like a child brought into
a gilded drawing-room to display a childish gift, and then hurried back to the hidden haunt of the nursery. It is hard to
believe that either Churchill or Attlee would bend away from
their business even long enough to listen to a Northumbrian
playing *The Bonny Tyneside*, or listen to one singing for the
ferryman to come and bring him to his sweetheart over the
rough waters of the river. They're too big for that diversion.
With them it was always over the sea to Paris, over the sea to
Amsterdam, but never over the sea to Skye. And yet it is these
singers and pipers, allied with the dockers of the quaysides, the
men and women of the farms, the workers in the big and lesser
cities, who made England in the past, and will remake England
in the future. The General Strike showed this, for it struck
England like lightnings from the hands of Zeus. England
within a few hours became a waste land. And remained so till
J. H. Thomas, frightened into respectability by Sir John
Simon's revelation from heaven that the Strike was illegal,
sought the counsel of the lords and ladies, becoming one with
them as a faithful butler to an old family dizzily bedizened in a
web of inherited quarterings of their coats of arms bestowed at
first-hand by Billy the Conqueror or Billy from the Boyne. He
chose the red carpet to be under his proletarian feet rather
than the red flag to fly over his head. He chose well for the
time being; putting, as he thought, the workers away in drawer
or on shelf, like little tin soldiers, leaving the rebellious and
blackened miners to fight alone a gallant rearguard action.
Though he looked hale and was excited at having done the
decent thing by the Rose and Crown, the moment he had
handed over the workers to the chill clutch of defeat, that
moment he had fallen, had died, as Courage tossed his name
out of the book of the people's life.

Here he was in grand form, tailed coat, white waistcoat and
tie, stormy with a sense of his own importance. He did not
walk about with the silent solidity of Baldwin, or the restless,
stoical step of Churchill; but came in and went out in spurts.
I'll hear no word against Thomas – he has played the game, as

a gracious and intelligent lady said tersely to Sean, in reply to
a critical remark of his. Indeed, he had, and he was playing it
still, even now; even here. It was Jimmy there and Jummy
here; a companion of honour, breathing the soiled air blown
from fans, the whole world a promise before him. The workers
out in the rain. Oh, never mind – they're used to it. But shove
as Jimmy Thomas might, he couldn't find a place in the
arustocratic frieze in which to fix himself. He could edge in
here and there sideways; but there was no niche for an eyes-
front pose. He was permitted to climb the wide-awake stairs,
lounge in the drawing-room, but not allowed to sit down at the
family fire. A useful, handy man to have about the big house.
And dream himself, if he liked, into being one of the family;
and dream it he did, in his tailed coat, his white waistcoat, his
quite right white tie. He enjoyed a lackey's privilege for pulling
the family out of a bad crisis. He was allowed to run up and
down the imposing stairway, sit down on the gilded chairs, eat
out of the finest of porcelain, and even from the gold ware once
or twice, so that he could see and handle and understand the
exquisite and kindling treasures he had saved from the mean
defacement of a rest in the proletarian pawnshops. All the
church bells are ringing, Jimmy. Ding-dong ding-dong-dell; for
you and for me and for everyone else.

They were to ring again, louder than ever, later on. A day
after, or, maybe, later, the bankers, making their rounds of the
strongrooms to count the bars of gold, got the shock of their
lives. The cupboards were bare, their hearts stood still. They
ran and hurried the Prime Minister, Ramsay MacDonald, the
Chancellor of the Exchequer, Philip Snowden, and Jimmy
Thomas to the place where the gold hath lain, nothing now but
wide and empty spaces.

—Look for yourselves, they said; you can still see the marks
on the shelves where the gold bars lay.

—Distinctly, said Philip.

—We cannot go on and on and on and down and down, said
Ramsay.

—Not bloody likely, said Jimmy Thomas.

—Listen to the bells, said the bankers.

No joy in them now. A single stroke; a long silence; another
stroke, slow, sad, shivery. Out of the deep we cry unto thee.
The bells were tolling. Britain was about to be buried. Sad

sounds. The Crown is crushed, the Rose is withering. England's golden day is going, England's golden day is going, England's golden day is gone. For whom the bell tolls. The church bells are tolling for you and for me.

And they mourned in that place which to this day is called The Place of Retrenchment; they mourned there with great and gleeful mourning, rending their garments and throwing dust over their heads and into the eyes of the people; for their souls were brought low, even to the dust; and their bellies cleaved unto the ground. It was a pitiable sight to see; all the world wondered. And the gods took pity on them, and, as a token, sent a voice roaring out of heaven, saying, Get up, get up boys, and get a move on! So they rose up, comforted, and took counsel together to end the exceptional and menacing emergency.

—We must do something to avert disaster at the earliest possible moment, said MacDonald.

—We must explore every avenue to see what can be done, said Snowden.

—We must leave no stone unturned in order to solve the problem, said Jimmy Thomas. We must balance the budgit. Let's go and have a chat with our buddies, the bankers.

And they hurried to where the bankers were gathered at the gates of the cities, in the churches, in the major manors of Mayfair, in the sanctuary, and in the courts of the lords. And they held up their hands, saying, Is it peace? And the bankers held up theirs, saying, It is peace, provided ye do what is just and lawful, following the commandments of the governors given by God to the Bank of England, true liegemen in financial verity and honour to the Rose and Crown. Honour their commandments, keep their ways, and they shall promote thee, that ye shall possess the land for ever. And the three suppliants bowed down, saying, We're only too anxious to do those things that are righteous in your eyes, to the greater glory of the Crown and the Rose.

—Expenses must be cut down by fifty millions, said the bankers. As an earnest of faith, hope, and charity the unemployment benefit must be reduced. It is costing the Rose and Crown twelve millions a week. It must be cut.

—It must be cut, echoed Ramsay; quick, said Philip; soon, said Jimmy Thomas.

—We must all make equal sacrifices, said the bankers. We must slash everything, except profits; for these be incentives, and keep the Rose fresh and the Crown sparkling. Profit is the great incentive in every Christian country, though there is patriotism, too.

—Patriotism isn't enough, said Ramsay.

—Not half enough, said Philip.

—Not worth a damn, said Jimmy.

—We must have a National Government, said the bankers.

—Representing the people, said Ramsay.

—The whole people, said Philip.

—And nothing but the people, added Jimmy.

And so for the sake of the Rose and the Crown, these three men made great sacrifices, without the murmur of a moan. Ramsay retired into the position of Prime Minister; Jimmy into the job of Minister for the Dominions; and Philip into the rich robe and coronet of a Viscount.

Sean first met Ramsay MacDonald at a lunch in the flat of Lady Gregory's daughter-in-law, where Lady Gregory was staying at the time. Among those present were the then High Commissioner for Eirinn and his pretty and clever wife, Josephine MacNeill. The company had come together as helpers in the effort to get the Lane Pictures back to Dublin. Sean turned the pictures towards the wall to demand from Mr MacDonald more revolutionary action in the policy of the Labour Government. He said that the Labour leaders had put on a Tory overall to keep their clothing clean. He urged MacDonald to advance into the fight by forcing the larger enterprises out of the hands of private ownership into the full possession of the people; but MacDonald had laughingly set the appeal aside as the wild vision of an idealist. Sean had insisted that, ideal or no, it was what the Labour Government were bound to do by their baptism, at which they had renounced all the works and pomps of Capitalism; by their faith in the workers; and by their abounding hope for the future; adding that even this achievement would be but a beginning; but the learning of the first few letters of Socialism's alphabet. But MacDonald had turned the pictures right face forward again, and lost his hearing looking at them.

MacDonald was a handsome fellow, tall as one of the old Gaels, who carried himself about with great dignity and grace.

His head was splendidly formed, his face finely-moulded, with just the touch of ruggedness that made it manly. A charming manner flowered from his nature when he was faced with friends, or with those whom he thought to be his friends. Had he had but the deep carelessness of Walt Whitman, he would have lived, he would have died, a great man. But the odd narcotic vanity unbalanced him, craving admiration and a twinge of envy from all who knew him in person or by picture. I am Ramsay MacDonald, Prime Minister of England, was the slogan of his later life.

> *He trod on silk, as if the wind*
> *Blew his own praises in his eyes.*

Lux Britannica. The title of Prime Minister was his lady-love, his Lily of Laguna. *The Conference is to be opened by the Right Honourable Ramsay MacDonald, Prime Minister of England,* was, for him, the unrolling of many flags, the beating of many drums. He sacrificed the workers, his own ease of mind, and, at the last, his life, that he might hear the title announced in public and in private, and sense it being murmured by the undulant mind of the nation. But within the man there was no fruitful force behind the thundering title. He wore the kilt without the claymore. He had handed over the claymore to the Tories the time he handed over the power lent to him by the united front of the working class. He was lost among his friends. They smothered him elegantly with their scented odours, their soothing organdies, and their sleepy silks. He escaped from the taint of coal-dust, the smell of factory oils, the decay that made agriculture fruitful; his ears slept away from the discordant clang of railway wagons clashing together; the bang of the hammer and the buzz of the saw: he shrank away from all that had moulded his life into the service of man; and with these he gave away the fierce fealty of those who go forth to work, to their labour until the evening. For a tinsel dream he gave away his glory. He shrouded himself within an iridescent bubble.

The three were rewarded: one became Prime Minister for an hour; a second was allowed to wrap himself up in the phantasy of a Viscountcy for an hour and a half; and the third became a Minister of the Crown and Rose for a day. Then they died, and their names are on no banners now. All for nothing! The incomplete revenue of the time was but a summer shower, but the three made it an excuse to scramble for shelter into the bright pavilions of the Tories where there was warmth and wine and fine feeding. But they and those were punished for taking from the workers part of their daily bread given them of God. The deluge came later, when the bright pavilions came tumbling down, to be swept away in the swirling surge of war, leaving the Tories to find political homes in barns, or slumber, bruised, on the benches in the parks.

Of the three, MacDonald was the one, despite his weakness, his corroding vanity, who preserved within his nature some of the salt of dignity which never lost its savour; and, in a limited way, he held on to the vision of colour and form. He appreciated the variegations of art, and intently watched the latest work done by the younger painters. He was a genuine patron of the drama, and could easily lean on an elbow when talking about a book; qualities that most of his comrade Cabinet ministers needed to quicken their tempered outlook with the sudden snatch of a song. Sean had a deep and distant affection for him, but could never manage to get to talk with him alone. MacDonald always protected himself with the company of others, knowing that Sean knew and deplored the way he was going. Sean wanted to warn him, to use all his feeling of affection to coax the man to keep heart-deep within the might of the masses. MacDonald was willing to see Sean in the House, on the terrace, or in the foyer of a theatre, when surrounding company kept him safe from questioning or appeal. He would never come to Sean's home for a talk and a smoke by a friendly fireside. He promised to come, but he never came. Sean wrote to him, even pretending sympathy with the Prime Minister's difficulties of governing, in an effort to entice him to where an Irishman and a Scot could sit together quiet, and talk things over. This is his reply:

CHEQUERS
PRINCES RISBOROUGH
BUCKS
February 19th, 1932

MY DEAR O'CASEY,

I was so glad to have your letter. You understand so many things which the ordinary person does not. I would like very much if you would come and see me here one weekend when I am down, and I shall write to you when I get back from my holiday. Thanks to an upbringing something like your own, I am getting better by leaps and bounds.

With kindest regards to your wife and yourself, I am

RAMSAY MACDONALD

But he would not come. *We must meet soon*, said one of his letters; but he never came. He was joined to idols, and had to be let alone. And snappy Snowden and sunny-jim Thomas valeted and worried him well on his way.

Consummatum est. Here were MacDonald and Thomas, elate and hysterically calm, above the richness of the carpet, under the starry chandeliers, with Churchill and Baldwin and a fine flock of great ones murmuring in the ears of the two men, Well done, good and faithful servants: enter ye into the joy of your lords. They were all so excited that they heard the trumpets of the workers but *as horns of elfland, faintly blowing.* So happily trimmed with triumph that they couldn't be mindful of even their own poet singing of

> *The vast republics that may grow,*
> *Titanic forces taking birth*
> *In divers seasons, divers climes.*

Yet Sean's heart knew that MacDonald's heart was not in what was done. The echo in the glory of cheering workers, lost now, lost for ever now, would dimly simulate itself and sound sad in his ears every day unto his last day, his very last hour. In an attempt to break the workers, he had but broken himself. Even Winston Churchill, guerdon of the Conservatives, hurrying along, and contemptuously shoving MacDonald aside, saw in his divided way that MacDonald's harassing of the workers served but to harrow his own soul, for he set down in a book that *MacDonald, the Prime Minister, had severed himself, with the uttermost bitterness on both sides, from the Socialist Party which it had been his life's work to create. Henceforth he brooded supinely at the head of an Administration which, though nominally National, was in fact overwhelmingly Conservative. Mr Baldwin preferred the substance to the form of power, and reigned placidly in the background.*

Supinely brooding! Churchill didn't know, probably didn't care, how a man might feel having viciously abandoned what had been his life-work to create. How pitifully a soul may suffer when it has betrayed its heart's desire. Churchill, too, was lavishly concerned with himself. He, too, had his own tormenting vanity, a belief in a Cassandrian power of prophecy that no one paused to listen to. He carried it about with him like a hump on a camel's back. Although he calls and calls upon the people, his prophecies were directed towards the white ears of those who dwelt within the porticoed houses and walked beneath the gilded ceilings; beings *who had been formed by a different breeding, were fed by a different food, are ordered by different manners, and who are not governed by the same laws*: who go about, who act and think as if they had not been born of mortals as others were, but had been carefully lowered from heaven in arks made from golden bulrushes, strengthened with precious stones, to grow up, well watched, till they had ripened enough to become the owners and guardians of the earth's domains. Specials from Providence: who parade the rich places of the earth, whose tattle in the salons, according to Beaconsfield, *Has in it something humiliating. It is not merely that it is deficient in warmth, and depth, and breadth; that it is always discussing persons instead of principles, and cloaking its want of thought in mimetic dogmas, and its want of feeling in superficial raillery; it is not merely that it has neither imagination, nor fancy, nor sentiment, nor feeling, nor knowledge to recommend it; but it appears to me, even as regards manner and expression, inferior in refinement and phraseology; in short, trivial, uninteresting, stupid, really vulgar.*

Gracious, intelligent, and even noble as some of these silk-clad chatterers were, they could not, in market or exchange, be other than the guardians of profits, rent, and interest, the frantic defenders of the cohesive power of public plunder. MacDonald and Thomas now wandered among them, not as equals, but as favoured servants allowed into the drawing-room for a period to admire its stately grandeur. This is what you have preserved, you two; have a good look, and go. MacDonald was above it all, and did what he did only out of the craving of vanity embedded in his inner nature. He was sick and ailing. He left it, and set sail in a big ship for a far country; but his heart failed him, and there on the ship, he died, never again to show off his vanished face.

When workers march, mayhap they'll pause a while where he lies low and lonely. The boy and man lie buried here: the man who left them, and the bonnie, ragged lad of Lossie-mouth. Buried here's the gallant bird that lost its comely look; the disc of gold that nearly turned to lead; the thistle's purple plume that took to rust; the Scot who dropped his claymore and his targe; the chief who in the last frenzy of the struggle sank down under the burden and heat of the fight.

Oh, workers, pause a while where lowly buried is the one who listened long to the parrot screeching 'till he was deeved to deafness; who listened too long, and left the views

> *That were peculiar to us*
> *Afore his vision narrowed*
> *And gar'd him think it time*
> *The Claith was owre the parrot.*

Oh, workers on the march, pause here awhile, and lay a wreath of part-forgiveness on the lonely grave. Bring forth a piper of his lordly clan and bid him play a brief lament for a clansman's weakness; forgetting the grey-haired man who did not stay the strife; remembering only in the minute's pause the gallant ragged lad of Lossiemouth.

BLACK OXEN PASSING BY

AFTER the threat of an action for breach of copyright, which was never carried out, Yeats fell silent. He returned to the attack no more; no longer stood on the defensive. Perhaps the comments made by Mrs Shaw when they lunched together persuaded the silence; maybe it was the letter written by Bernard Shaw to Lady Gregory, criticizing the conduct of the Abbey, shamed him into it; or a decision to ignore Casey as a contemptible item in his life. Perhaps, like Aeschylus who delighted to begin a play with an awful silence, Yeats liked to end a discussion with another awful silence. Whatever the reason, the poet decided to stay in his room with the blinds down. To Sean it seemed that the great man was determined to be interested in, to listen to, to dispute with, those only who were content to be so many coloured buttons on the poet's dinner-jacket.

Up went the London curtain on *The Silver Tassie*, and, in spite of the fact that Laughton was badly miscast, and had a bad cold, that a few others were as bad as he, in spite of a few mishaps, the play was a hit; not at all in the conventional sense, but in a moral and a complex sense: using a Joxerian expression, the play gave the patient, wondering public a terrible belt in the kisser. It caused many of the critical minds to turn their usually serene and complacent comments into a shout; for comments were so many, so angry, and so conflicting, that only a bawl of an opinion could be heard through the din; an opinion, though heard, was not listened to, for each who saw it, wanted to yell out his own. They didn't want such a play; they didn't wish for it. They wanted war with the flame died down in it, and the screaming silent. This thing was so different from the false effrontery of Sherriff's *Journey's End*, which made of war a pleasant thing to see and feel; a strife put spiritually at a great distance; a demure echo, told under candlelight, at a gentle fireside, of a fight informal; a discreet accompaniment to a strident song, done on a lute, played low;

the stench of blood hid in a mist of soft-sprayed perfume; the yells of agony modulated down to a sweet *pianissimo* of pain; surly death, or death exultant, fashioned into a smiling courtier, bringing himself in with a bow; a balmy breath of blood and guts; all the mighty, bloodied vulgarity of war foreshortened into a petty, pleasing picture. Here is shown, according to the famous G. J. Nathan, 'a ladies' war. A second view of *Journey's End*, widely acclaimed as a masterpiece, emphasizes my original conviction that there is a humorously falsetto note to the exhibit, and that the late war, as the author sees it, apparently needed only a butler to convert it into a polite drawing-room comedy.'

But this play of Sean's was a very different thing. It tried to go into the heart of war, and, to many people whom it blasted with dismay, it succeeded. The curtain fell on the last scene amid a chorus of boos. The critics were confused, one saying this, and another saying that about the play, failing to analyse it faithfully or well, which was no wonder; for, if the author had been asked to analyse it himself, he would have failed as badly. One kind and effective thing the critics did for him. Almost unanimously, their criticisms implicitly declared that the play, with all its faults, was a work well worth producing by the Abbey Theatre; and that the play, far from taking away its high fame, would have added another spot of honour to the Theatre's reputation. And Sean knew that their comments had, unintentionally, delivered him from the thickest of the dangers that had come upon him through the contemptuous rejection of the play by the Abbey Directorate. He had but to wait a few years longer.

Sean O'Faolain ran home to tell Da Russell that 'it was to be feared that before he had exhausted the possibilities of the technique he knew, O'Casey had turned to technique that proved beyond his powers. Showed in other words that this play is not good theatre as we understand the term in these islands. O'Casey and the producer found the result of this experiment in a new technique a little beyond the capacities of the modern stage. The second act suggests that Mr O'Casey finds the conventions of the modern stage insufficient for his purpose; though, as I suggest, he has written far too little to say so with any authority. The producer was clearly at a loss. The second act he must have found easy game; that sort of stuff has been done more than once before. Augustus John designed the scene, the chanting was handed over to a special man, and, anyway, there wasn't enough sensible core to the rigmarole for anything much to be obviously wrong. It was clear that neither money nor trouble was spared to fashion Mr O'Casey's noveletta into a stage play. O'Casey must not be angry with us because we do not flatter him, as his easy English critics do. His talents are undeniable, but, so far, as all agree, they have not produced a play without the stamp of the workshop on it, and this one as much as any.' The Wild Irish boy soothing O'Casey's last moments.

In the quiet domestic turmoil of living from week to week, Sean got a letter from Lady Gregory saying she was in London, and would like to come to see him, his wife, and their baby. He was greatly troubled, and wished that Lady Gregory had forgotten him. He would not let her come. He would say hard things about Yeats and Robinson that would hurt her. His wife begged him to let Lady Gregory come, for she was eager to get to know the woman of whom he had so often spoken affectionately and well. No; he would not let her come. Eileen begged him again to change his mind, saying his refusal to see her would hurt Lady Gregory more than anything he might say. But, no; he would not let her come. So Lady Gregory went back to Ireland without a word with him; without a last affectionate handshake, for he never laid eyes on her again. This refusal was one of his silly sins. He still thinks angrily of himself when he thinks of her, or hears the name of the gracious, gallant woman. He should have listened to Eileen.

Sinclair wanted to do Juno in Belfast, and Sean wanted the money that might come from the royalties. He had now no connexion with the Abbey Theatre, and so gave a hearty consent to the production. Then came a telegram from Sinclair telling him the Abbey had prohibited the performance, alleging that they alone had the licence. Sean maintained they had no claim to the play, but the Abbey solicitors pointed out, in majestically legal terms, that the contract, lasting for a year, could be extended to another one, by acquainting the author of the Theatre's wish, when the first year's contract was about to end. This, they said, they did. This, said Sean, they did not do. Sean pointed out, too, that, the year before, the Abbey had pencilled in a production of the same play in the same theatre in Belfast, which, later on, they had cancelled. Now when he had succeeded in getting the chance of a production there, they got busy to prevent it. The controversy became bitter. Sean got McCracken & McCracken of Dublin to act for him, and, with their help and Lady Gregory's interference, the Belfast production was allowed; the Abbey confining its claim to Dublin, with Sean agreeing to this permission to run for one year more. All the past things, according to Lady Gregory, 'were meant kindly, if Sean but knew'. Perhaps they were, but it seemed to him that the Abbey wasn't acting fair. According to their own admission, his plays had done a lot to help the Theatre out of financial insecurity; it had had a percentage out of the London production of his plays; but this querulous attempt to prevent him from making a little money, badly needed, didn't tend to breed within him a kindly feeling for the Abbey and its odd and wondrous ways.

But this wasn't the end of the irritation. Soon after, Sean began to realize that royalties due to him weren't arriving. Some had been due quite a time. He wrote to the Theatre politely pointing out that these royalties were due. He got no answer. Blessing a second one with a curse, he wrote again. He got no answer. The Theatre was as if it was not. He wrote the third time, and a letter came back to say that the cheques had been sent long ago, and must have gone astray; but new ones were on their way to him. Again the halt happened; again he wrote to the Abbey; again there was no reply. He wrote to Lady Gregory, and she replied to say she would write to the Abbey. But over in Dublin, on a holiday with his wife, he had to go personally to the Abbey to get the payment of royalties due for months. He began to feel more acutely than ever that the Abbey was bent on making things unpleasant for him. When he returned to London, the halt in the sending of royalties began again. After a long and irritating wait, he wrote asking for them. He got no reply. Several letters followed at decent intervals, but no notice was taken of them. At last he registered one, and sent it off, but that went into the well of silence with the others. Then he placed the matter with McCracken & McCracken, the Dublin solicitors. They questioned the Abbey, and got the old answer that the cheques had been sent, and that they must have gone astray. The solicitor asked why the registered letter had not been answered, but there was no reply to this question. Finally all was paid to the solicitors, the Abbey saving Sean the solicitors' fee by paying it themselves.

Odd things appeared in some of the English Press: 'One wonders what will happen to *The Silver Tassie*. Mr Yeats suggested some slight alterations in one or two of the scenes. These O'Casey refused to consider. "You must have it whole, or not at all", was the reply. So the play went to America after a very brief run in Dublin. Mr Yeats and I were members of a house-party in Wicklow when the play was produced in Dublin. I shall always remember him sitting by the fire on a wet Irish night, declaiming verses from his own work in that impressive and sonorous voice of his. Then he turned to *The Silver Tassie*, and recited the opening lines, which were not happy. We saw the difference.' A Peter Pan picture. They were all false statements. The play had had no run, very brief or very long, in Dublin. The play had not gone to America, for it hadn't yet been done in London; and in a letter to Sean himself, Yeats said, 'he never told anyone he suggested slight alterations in the play, or alterations of any kind; and that he could not imagine himself declaiming verses at any house-party; and that he could not recall seeing the critic on a wet Irish night in Wicklow, or anywhere else'.

Then the American *New Republic*, writing about Yeats and the Abbey Theatre, went on to say that 'The Abbey Directorate, led by Mr Yeats, was definitely changing its outlook and ideal; a change clearly shown by the quick rejection of O'Casey's play, *The Silver Tassie*, because of its continuance of the cult of naturalism'; whereas the contrary was the case, for the play was refused, not because of its naturalism, but because of the play's lack of it. By a twisted version of the controversy, O'Casey's unnaturalism was being used in defence of Yeats' continued desire for realism. And it was all very annoying.

Sean must have replied to some, or one, of these misrepresentations, for in a copy of a letter sent to Mrs Shaw, in 1931, he finds himself saying, 'I do not know how much I must read into your advice "not to be too belligerent". God be my judge that I hate fighting. If I be damned for anything, I shall be damned for keeping the two-edged sword of thought tight in its scabbard when it should be searching the bowels of knaves and fools. I assure you, I shrink from battle, and never advance into a fight unless I am driven into it. I give you a recent instance: The Abbey Theatre are going on a tour through America; notices appeared in the Press, mentioning the plays, which included *Juno*. I wrote to Mr Robinson about this, and he replied that he had asked the Chicago Lecture and Concert Association months ago to get into touch with my American agents. I left the matter there, and said no more. Then I got a letter from my agents, Samuel French, Ltd, saying that the Lecture and Concert Association were asking for *Juno*, and that they had asked for an advance of five hundred dollars; this was refused, and the demand was reduced to two hundred and fifty dollars; this, also, was refused, with the statement that all the other dramatists were satisfied to do without an advance. I rang up the Authors' Society, explained the situation, and was strongly advised to press for the advance. The intimation (that the Abbey had selected *Juno*) came so recently that I had no time to write about the matter, and so to avoid any suspicion that I wished to hurt the success of the tour, I wrote to the agents telling them not to bother about any claim to an advance of royalties. So, in face of a possible misapprehension, I shrink even from insisting on a very modest demand.

'On behalf of James Joyce, before me now, is a letter I received this morning, which tells me that someone has translated a story into German, and has had it published in a German paper over the name of this writer. Joyce declares that he never wrote the story, and that his signature is a forgery. And, worse than all, the thing is altogether beneath the genius of Joyce. Now should I sing silently in my heart of the meanness of this deception against an artist; or should I give the man the comfort of indignant sympathy from a comrade in the evil that has been brought upon him? I shall not keep silence, and the song in my heart and on my lips shall be in harmony with the indignant song of Joyce.'

It was bad enough to have the great Yeats trying to deflect him from doing what he wanted to do; bad enough to have the envenomed clergy spitting anathemas at him; and now he had the dulcet, sour assurance of Mrs Shaw piping out a tune for him to dance to. Thank you; he would do his own tap-dance, and to his own composition too. Uncle Yeats and Auntie Shaw were equally anxious that when he roared, he would roar like any sucking dove. When he turned to the right, he was to say what Uncle Yeats wished him to say; when he turned to the left, he was to say what Auntie Shaw wanted him to say. A gilt-edged security censorship. Uncle Yeats and Auntie Shaw would join hands for him to sit on them, so that they could give him a soothing, little swing swong wrong. A nursery cursery for Sean the proud. To them the things that are theirs; to Sean the things that are his; for better or worse; for richer or poorer; till death shall call out Silence.

The time swung along from one year to another, like a monkey swinging from branch to branch of the same tree. Yeats' great black oxen trod the world, pushing away older life to give space to the newcomers. Sean's next play, *Within the Gates*, hearsed within an atrocious production, had appeared on the London stage; had run home to hide in a corner of a silent room. From a home in Buckingham, Sean had set out to America to help in a production of the play in New York; crossing to Belfast first to spend a week in Mount Stewart. Sailing back from Belfast again to Liverpool; and from there away, away to the New Island, the name given by the Irish to the United States that gave a few great riches, and gave to many of them the serenity of the grave. Home he came from America, very tired and strangely thrilled, to sit and think and recover by an electric fire in a new home formed from a flat in Battersea. There one day a letter came to him from W. B. Yeats. He recognized the writing; from the poet, right enough, the great Yeats. He was bade to come to take dinner with the poet in his lodgings at Lancaster Gate. At last, Yeats had stretched out a hand of friendship; and the heart within Sean rejoiced greatly. Then here's a hand, me trusty frien', an' gi'e's a hand o' thine! Seas between us braid ha'e roared sin' auld lang syne.

At Lancaster Gate, Mrs G. Yeats was there watching over her famous husband. Pushing death away from him with all the might in her little hands. Anxious that he should not do too much. When dinner was on the table, she left the two men alone to eat it, and Sean felt the lack of her quiet charm and her good looks. Yeats was stuck in the centre of strife, selecting poems for his *Oxford Book of Modern Verse*, and shortly after dinner, he tried to win Sean into an hour's fight with him.

The room seemed to be thronged with poem-books from all
persons; while on the mantelpiece lay a pile of Western Tales
of cowboy and Indian chief, sliced here and there by a detective story, which were there, he told Sean, to ease a mind tired
and teased with a long concentration of thought on the imagination of others. Twice, he asked Sean's advice on selections,
but Sean shut his ears, saying, with finality in his voice, that he
could not suffer himself to give a judgement on a poetical
piece. Yeats desisted, sighing and saying, it was hard work, but
his ear was true, his ear was sure; the tone of his murmur
seeming to indicate that he wasn't so sure as his words declared.

They turned to talking of the Elizabethans, whom Yeats
evidently loved, and was glad that Sean shared his delight in
the careless splendour of their poets, who made even violent
death majestic in a mass of jewelled words. The stern intensity
that Tourneur and Webster showed in velveted revenge,
plumed murther, and rotten lust that ermine covered grandly.
Mighty souls decayed to shivering flesh and chattering teeth.
Two minds whose thoughts were phosphorescent lightning, to
whom the world became a great revolving skull in which life
tried to live, knocking its energy against bony walls; out of
whose eyeless sockets life looked out on nothing, to shrivel
back, to look, and see the less within. Where the Jew of Malta
bows to the Duchess of Malfi, and Vittoria Corombona stands
indecently triumphant on the pedestal of Liberty's statue.

And yet, in spite of all their weary boniness, their mire of
lacerated flesh, their spilling wildly of the shrill, sad scent of
death, a sombre rosiness lights up their caverned despair, and
simple blossoms, wild and wanton, steal and wind around their
tomby places. Brocaded butchery of power sinks to the tender:

> *Call for the robin redbreast and the wren,*
> *Since o'er shady groves they hover,*
> *And with leaves and flowers do cover*
> *The friendless bodies of unburied men.*

What better mourners could a dead man have than a robin
and a wren, decking his buried dust with animation and
broidering it with a song; fluttering over his dense, deep sleep,
disturbing gently the everlasting silence of the dead. Finer
salute to what was, and is not now, than the cold mumbling of

cardinal-bishop or cardinal-deacon, black-robed as a Jesuit or scarlet-clad as a Secularius. A quiet trumpet sounds elation in the chirruping *de profundis* of the birds, for the dead live on in their work left behind with the living.

The teeming thoughts of Yeats turned suddenly into himself as a tremulous stoppage of breath started an outburst of coughing that shook his big, protesting body, stretching his wide chest on a rack of straining effort to rid itself of congestion, or end the effort by ending life. His hands gripped the sides of his chair, his fine eyes began to stare and bulge, showing the storm within, as he leant back and bent forward to sway with the waves of stuffy contortion that were forcing resistant life from his fighting body. The whole stately dignity and courage of the poet was crinkling into a cough. He has caught an everlasting cold, thought Sean. His own black oxen are treading him down.

These Elizabethan poets pulled a bell to tell of criminals, hidden and revealed, hiding in ermine and scarlet taffeta; the horrid things they did, nagging at heaven to get rid of the lot of them; as if the slimiest and most villainous souls of Paradise Lost had come to town to be converted into duke, cardinal, and courtier. Cardinals who 'made more bad faces with their oppressions than Michael Angelo made good ones'; and lords, who, when they laughed, were 'like deadly cannons that lighten ere they smoke'. No worse than Hogarth's later gin-mad men and maids; no more mischievous than those later ones who gambled their estates away in London, Bath, and Tunbridge Wells, impoverishing their tenants, ruining the land over which they claimed an immortal, menacing ownership. And do today.

Sean longed to cross to the coughing Yeats, and lay a warm, sympathetic hand on his heaving shoulders; to say silently so that Yeats could hear, God knows, if power were mine, you would be for ever young; no cough would ever come to warn you that the body withers. But custom held him back; the fear of offending his structured dignity by resting a kindly hand on another's shoulder. Afraid of the outward and visible sign of an inward and invisible sympathy.

—I get this way at times, the creaking voice of Yeats apologized behind his curtain of coughing. I have had congestion of the lungs.

Here, in Elizabethan drama, was not one particular court of Calabria, but all courts caught in a poet's mirror, where kings and dukes, spunned in flatteries, walked; and toadies tumbled in their haste to lick the shoes more costly than their own; where

> The poor rogues
> Pay for 't which have not the means
> To present bribe in fist; the rest o' the band
> Are raz'd out of the knaves' record; or else
> My lord he winks at them with easy will;
> His man grows rich, the knaves are the knaves still ...
> While divinity, wrested by some factious blood,
> Draws swords, swells battles, and o'erthrows all good.

Ay, and you can see the same things today, if you only look out of the window.

There's a man, Sean went on thinking of Yeats, who never saw it; and, if he did, censured the crowd because they came uncultured. But his is more than a bare name; one who will never shake hands to say farewell to reputation; who sought the society of queens and kings over the hilly lands and hollow lands of thought; and thought them brave and precious; never descrying that their careless grandeur and performed manners were milled from the sludgy life the people lived; from whose satin-bound laws, but a day ago, came the decisions that he who snatched and ran, who stole two pounds from a dwelling-house, or five shillings from a shop, or picked from a pocket a coin but one farthing over a shilling, must suffer death by hanging; and when a kindlier man brought in a bill to substitute transportation for hanging in cases of theft from dwelling or shop, six bishops voted against it, led by his grace, the Lord Archbishop of Canterbury. Oh, brave old world! Here is he whose dreams of his loved one were wronged by

> The cry of a child by the roadside, the creak of a lumbering cart,
> The heavy steps of the ploughman, splashing the wintry mould;

so that he turned away that he might not hear. A buccaneer among shining shadows. So different from Lady Gregory, who would run out to see why the child cried, or why the wheel of the wagon creaked. And yet his poems belie the man, belie him badly; for there was no braver man among the men of Eireann than W. B. Yeats. In every fray of politics, in every fight for freedom in literature and art, in every effort to tempt Dublin's city into the lure of finer things, the voice of Yeats belled out a battle-cry.

Some have said that Yeats was an actor, enjoying himself posing about in trismegistic mask on a painted stage. A charming fellow, they said, wearing his cabbalistic cloak well; but genuine only in making his acting look genuine, though done in a world painted into the panels of his own deceptions. But beneath the masque, under the cloak, was the man of powerful integrity; vain and childlike, fearful of what might be a humiliation; brave before rich or poor; courteous, even to those who lingered to bore him; a truer rebel than truest politician; and eager, like the upsprung husband of Malfi's duchess, to fashion the world right.

—The scene where the echo sounds is fine, said Yeats, when the cough had loosened its grip; where the echo tells the lover-husband, out of his own words, his wife's end and his own. It is beautiful, is it not, O'Casey?

—It is very beautiful, and it is very sad.

—Yes, Webster, murmured Yeats, though not too deep for tears, is far too deep for laughter. Others may bind the brow of life with laurel; Webster binds her brow with crêpe. The incense in his temple's burning brimstone.

—But through the choking mist, said Sean, burn many coloured candles.

—We are afraid of sadness, the poet murmured; we have it in life, but we fear it in the theatre. You mustn't be afraid of it, O'Casey.

—I'm not, if it tinges, or even startles, life, like a discordant note in a lovely symphony. I'm not when it has nobility. But when it comes brazen through hunger, disease, or wretchedness, then I hate it; then I fight against it, for through that suffering there can be no purification. It is villainous, and must be destroyed. Even Webster condemns the sorrow his own imagination created. He, too, was one of those who longed to fashion the world right.

—You're a Communist, O'Casey, aren't you? His face came

closer, and his bright eyes peered and pierced, as if he would read Sean's thoughts ere any could be fashioned into words. It is astir in the world today. What is this Communism so many place their hope in, so many fight for, and so many speak about, as if it were a new *lux mundi*?

A shock to Sean. He never imagined that Yeats would smite his mind with such a question; and he wondered if the poet was really interested in any answer to his question. Was the interest in Communism, or was it but Yeatsian curiosity eager to peer into the mind of another? Even were the poet genuine in his question, what was he to say to the white-haired man who so often took up a current question to look at it for an hour, and then let it fall from him when interest faded?

—Communism's no new *lux mundi*, he said. Its bud-ray shone when first a class that had all, or most, of what was going, became opposed by a class that had little or nothing. It has grown in power and intensity till today it floods half of the world's skies. We give it the symbol of a red star. Earlier it was called the sword of light; Prometheus; Lugh of the Long Hand.

—Ah, O'Casey, these things, symbol or myth, do not belong to the crowd. There is danger here: would you set the rabble in power against the finer and fuller things common to great and gracious people?

—No, Mr Yeats, not against them; but set the rabble, as you call them, down among the finer things of life, and give them the chance and power to help create them.

Yeats shrank back into his chair; shrank into himself, and saw the little streets hurling themselves against the greater ones. So Sean thought, and so he seemed to see that Yeats didn't like the sight entrancing.

—The finer things aren't so common among your great people as you think. There are many of them who have never read a line by Yeats. Some of them know no painting but a few handed to the family hundreds of years ago, hanging on the wall still, not as a graceful glory, but merely as a rich endowment. They journey each year to the Royal Academy Exhibition, where they are rarely puzzled, and can cry Hem! before the pictures. Many of them today do not even know the clock, and are constrained to cry out with Falstaff's What time o' day is it, Hal? Most of your great people, Mr Yeats, are so ignorant of, and so indifferent to, fine things that Lady Gregory and a few more stand out as remarkable or even unique.

Yeats sat silent for quite a time, staring into the gas-fire, not altogether relishing what Sean had said. He coughed again, then the fine head moved closer towards Sean, and he said, What is this Communism: what is its divinity – if it has any; what is its philosophy? Whatever the State, there must be a governing class placed by wealth far above fear or toil.

The mind of the poet was probing again: what did that mean, now, what does this mean? Why should Sean worry this white-headed man with thoughts alien to his nature; this man who was a warrior among mere fighters, who had given to life more than he got from it? He got to his feet, laughing. Ah, Mr Yeats, he said, the divinity in our philosophy is but the things the massed energy and individual thought can do. All of us will be above the common fear of life, and work will be a desire in us as strong as hunger or love. Our leaders will be above the rest only in the measure of more vivid minds and more enduring energy; used for the fuller security and higher benefit of all. Communism isn't an invention of Marx; it is a social growth, developing through the ages, since man banded together to fight fear of the unknown, and destroy the danger from mammoth and tiger of the sabre-tooth. All things in science and art are in its ownership, since man painted the images of what he saw on the wall of his cave, and since man put on the wooden share of his plough the more piercing power of iron or of bronze.

—It isn't enough. What I've heard of it, O'Casey, doesn't satisfy me. It fails to answer the questions of What is life, What is man? What is reality? It tells us nothing of invisible things, of vision, or spiritual powers; or preternatural activities and energy beyond and above man's ordinary knowledge and contemplation.

—Aha, said Sean, what philosophy does? Even Christian theology leaves us prostrate and puzzled. You yourself have read many philosophers who failed to answer your questions; failed utterly, or you wouldn't be asking them now. Communism deals with man as man, a glory great enough to begin with. Think deep as you can, think long as you may, life depends on low reality.

—But the Catholic Church, which has a vision, however we may disagree with it, and a divinity, though we may not believe in it, has a social philosophy, O'Casey, just as Communism has.

—Well, said Sean laughingly, the Roman Church builds her social contract on the Rearum Noharmum Harum Scarum Rerum Novarum, but we build ours on the Communist Manifesto: this time it is our philosophy that is built on a rock, theirs on a hill of sand. All the glory that was Greece, the grandeur that was Rome, sprang from corn and oil and wine. We cannot safely go a day without a hug from Demeter. All the poetry of Shakespeare, Milton, Shelley, and Yeats was first embedded in the bosom of Demeter.

They talked about the Abbey and its newer plans; of the new Directors appointed on the Board to broaden its outlook, for Yeats thought the time had come for a braver display of European drama; the poet mentioning Hauptmann's *The Weavers* and Toller's *Hoppla!* He asked Sean to tell him of any new play the Abbey might do.

The cough shook the fine frame of the poet again; the breast ebbed and flowed spasmodically; and the fine hand grasped the arm of the chair with tenseness. Odd that Yeats couldn't see that no divinity, Gaelic or Christian, came with balm to refresh with health the corroding chest of the poet. Sean stood silent, watching the shock of lovely silver hair bounce up and down to the rhythm of the racking cough, and waiting for the hoarse harshness to decline into a deceitful peace. The last mask – a mask of pain.

—It hampers me, this, he said, in little gasps; comes on so often, so often.

—You mustn't let anything disturb you, said Sean, trying to put the affection he felt into his voice, and hoping Yeats would sense it; nothing but the vexing necessity of resting. We need you, sir. Your very presence, without one thing done, one word said, is a shield before us all. I have tired you. I shall go now, and leave you in peace. Goodbye. No, no; don't stir – I can easily let myself out; for the poet was rising to give three steps from the door in courtesy to his guest.

—We shall talk of this again, said Yeats, stretching out a hand in farewell. Thanks for coming to see me, O'Casey.

Sean left him staring at the gas-fire, crouching in the big

armchair. His greatness is such, thought Sean, that the Ireland which tormented him will be forced to remember him for ever; and as Sean gently closed the door behind him, he heard the poet coughing again: broken by the passing feet of his own black oxen.

A LONG ASHWEDNESDAY

SACKCLOTH and ashes, silence and anxiety everywhere, but for the indifferent gaiety of the little fellow at play. Eileen was having a hard time of it. She had married Sean knowing he hadn't much, but hardly guessed she'd walk beside him to a time when he'd have nothing. The pretty mouth was tight again, determined to fight it out. The play agents, Samuel French, Ltd, had offered three hundred pounds for the world amateur rights of his Irish plays, provided a prompt copy of each play was given to them; and Sean and Eileen, who had never seen a prompt copy of a play, were now busy in the bungalow making out three of them. He had seen the theatrical symbols of RC, and L3E, that had spotted the editions of *Dick's Standard Plays*, so often read when he was a young fellow forcing a way to his heritage of literature; but he had never paused to ask himself what they meant; and, now, busy typing, cutting, and pasting his plays into a new form, he was adding these damned symbols into the script, things that should never be admitted to the published edition of any play. It was a sickening job; worse for Eileen, for she had to preserve interest in the work for the sake of what it would earn, while he hated the task, though forced by circumstances to go through with it. In a letter to Sean, Bernard Shaw had kindly advised against the sale, but there was no way out of it. So Eileen and Sean toiled on, he cursing, she in a brave and quiet way, for Sean couldn't shake off the belief that Yeats and the Abbey Theatre were mainly responsible for the tension of his affairs: so he and Eileen toiled on. Oh, that he could forget these matters that with himself he too much discussed!

Some days before, Lady Keeble had written to him asking him to her home in Oxford where there was to be an exhibition of verse-speaking by first-class members of the English stage, and Sean had written to say he couldn't go. Then a telegram had come to say that H. G. Wells would call to bring him to Oxford, and that she would take no excuse. In the

stress of the work in hand, Sean had forgotten letter and telegram – Lord, I am not worthy of this work, Lord, I am not
worthy; may I never have the hope to know again the in-
famous glory of this positive hour. In the midst of the typing,
cutting, and pasting, a jingle came to the door-bell, and Eileen,
returning from answering it, proclaimed that a Mr H. G. Wells
was waiting to take him to Oxford, and H. G. Wells walked
into the room to face Sean in trousers, shirt, and slippers,
sleeves rolled up, sweat on his face, tackling the job of the
prompt copies for the Firm of French. And God said, Com-
plain you to the wind, to the wind only, for only the wind will
listen. In came H. G. Wells, his broad face smiling, his chubby
hand stretched out for a cordial grip. A rather stout, shortish
figure, looking like a classic undertaker whose services were
given only to the distinguished or very wealthy. He was
dressed in black from top to toe, a black tie nicely connecting
the two ears of a stiff collar, modifying the gayer note of their
white colour; black kid gloves covered the plump hands, one of
them holding firmly to a black bowler hat. So neat, so prim, so
precise in dress and manner was he that there seemed to be
almost a *noli-tangere* touch about him. A figure of evolu-
tionized respectability stood before Sean, in no way expressing
or even implying the shape of things to come. Not H. G.
Wells, but Mister H. G. Wells stood before him. Indeed, Sean
thought, God put some odd shapes around some of the greater
souls. Sean found it hard to imagine that such an insignificant-
looking torch should give out such a great flame; a flame that
had shown the way to so many tribes of thousands out of
encircling gloom, led them bravely over torrent and crag to
where they could be brave to speak, strong to climb, and where
they could see to do; so much more effectively than the gentle
Newman, leading his tribes of thousands to where angel-faces
smiled for a moment, then left him and his thousands far from
home and lost and wandering.

In came H. G. Wells to hike Sean off to Boar's Hill, Oxford,
where distinguished persons had gathered together to hear the
trained and true recite verses from poem and from play. But
Sean could not go. Why not?

—I've come out of the way to get you, said H. G. Wells,
laying a genial and encouraging hand on Sean's arm, while
Eileen stood by, silent; Lady Keeble sent me a telegram

commanding me to call here and bring you with me. So, you see, there's no escape.

—It was good of you to come out of your way, Mr Wells, and I'm sorry I can't go with you.

—Lady Keeble will be very annoyed, said the still, small voice of Wells, the hand on Sean's arm slowly sliding away from it; very much annoyed, and I shall be very disappointed. Do come; you will meet many distinguished people.

—No, said Sean, I can't go. I'm in the centre of a job I hate, and, if I broke away now, it would be almost impossible to begin again. I will stick to what I'm at till the thing's done. And why hadn't Lady Keeble asked Eileen, thought Sean, and why didn't Wells ask her now, as she stood near them, listening to what was being said? He didn't relish leaving her alone with her boy and a host of anxieties. Besides, she was as intelligent as any distinguished person on Boar's Hill, and, probably, far more lively. They must get some money somewhere, before they could comfortably listen to a voice reciting verse. No, he would not go. Through a dark cloud of fears the time redeem, the well-read vision in the lower dream; to put new money in the fading purse, the time redeem.

H. G. Wells slowly fixed the black bowler hat on his head, and murmured a cold goodbye. Sean's mind, full of the job he was doing, only half comprehended that the great man was annoyed, and paid no attention to Eileen's whispered, You ought to go. He and Eileen went with Wells down the long narrow drive to the gate where a fine, big, black car waited to bring the two of them to Oxford, Sean funnelling excuses into Wells' ear telling how he'd written to Lady Keeble, saying he couldn't come, afterwards sending a telegram that he couldn't go, emphasizing the fact that he must have some money, and to get it, he must finish the job he was at; that debts were waiting to be paid, and that he couldn't stir from where he was till things improved; but Wells walked straight on, never answering a word, never turning his head to glance at Sean, never repeating the cold goodbye, but climbed into the stately black car, motioned to the driver, and was driven off; and, though Sean and Eileen waved a sorrowful farewell, never turned his head to see it. They stood there till the car swung out of sight, Sean with a heavy heart realizing that though he hadn't made an enemy, he had lost a friend; and, though he wrote several times later on to H. G. Wells, suggesting a meeting, he got no reply, and never saw H. G. Wells again. O Lord, teach us to stare and not to care, Teach us to stand chill. Pray for us winners all the hours of our life.

Ah! A Vancouverian letter from Barry Fitzgerald, on tour with the Abbey Company throughout America. A resplendent tour as concerning the journey; into Pennsylvania, up to Montreal, from one side of Canada to the other, down southeastwards to Florida, over the Rockies, which, when Fitzgerald saw them, made him cease to 'wonder why God rested on the seventh day'; struck dumb by the vision of Manhattan, the buildings surely being 'a new wonder of the world' though he thought that some of them 'showed a disposition to go wrong at the very top'. But things weren't going too well with the Company. Another smudge of ash on Abbey foreheads. The letter said that the audiences in the Universities and Women's Clubs weren't so friendly as those in the commercial theatres. 'In Philadelphia *Professor Tim* met with a heavy reverse, and even the great McCormick was brought hurtling down by many shafts of criticism. The University papers dismissed *Juno* with an airy wave of the hand, while they submitted *Professor Tim* and the shallow Robinson comedies to a profound and respectful analysis.' Aha, Barry has his knife in the Universities! According to the letter, Fitzgerald and Maureen Delaney got the best notices, in spite of the fact that two players, Eileen Crowe and F. J. McCormick, 'had been heavily starred in the preliminary notices and handbills prepared by Robinson. In the handbills, Lennox Robinson says, "There have never been any stars in the Abbey Theatre during its long history, but if there were stars", and then follows a long and glowing description of the work done by McCormick and Crowe.' Fitzgerald adds that the rest of the players, himself included, thought it a lousy way of breaking through the traditions; but, he goes on, 'we have been secretly comforted by the fact that McCormick has failed to live up to the reputation made in Dublin'. Indeed, Fitzgerald says that, in spite of good parts and plenty of publicity, 'McCormick has been a decided flop. I'm sorry for Peter, because he feels it keenly, I think.'

Oh lord, here's a laughing between the porch and the altar, for what is actual is actual, not only for one time, but for many times, not only for one place, but for many places. This was more anxiety, for if the American audiences thought the Abbey plays poor and the acting bad, then Abbey plays – and his were among them – and Abbey acting would excite small interest in the years to come; but Sean comforted himself with the soothing assurance that these growls were fostered by the jealousy which afflicts actors, so often envious of a line of praise given to another. Fitzgerald wrote of a plan for another tour the following year – good news to Sean. A business tour, this time, confined to the commercial theatres along the eastern coast, 'leaving the universities and small towns crying in the wilderness; a strictly business tour, without cultural cod-acting pluming it'. Fitzgerald thinks that the Dublin public are 'off him', for in press-cuttings sent to him from the Irish papers commenting on the tour 'my name is never mentioned, in spite of quite good notices', and Barry wonders if there be 'some religious prejudice, for Dublin is very catholic now'. Less catholic, Barry, more clerical.

It wouldn't be long till there would be no cultural cod-acting in the Abbey itself, either, for death had pushed Lady Gregory into the bog of stars, and Yeats was now fighting hard for breath. When the subsidy was given with the demand that the new Director must be a roman catholic, the first flush of decline touched the Theatre. There was a wariness creeping into the Theatre's conception as to what plays would make a profit and what plays would not, and the episcopal crozier was tapping at the stage door. It was to thunder on it when the Theatre ventured to put on his own *The Silver Tassie* a few years ahead; break it down and loosen the bonds that had riveted the Abbey to what was brave, fantastic, and provocative in the art of the drama. But not yet, for Yeats was still to the fore to press his back against the door's yielding. But he was soon to die, and the younger poet, Higgins, stood in his place till he, too, suddenly shuddered into the grave. Then came the rush to lay down the red carpet to the box-office, which has become the chief prop of the building: the stone the builders rejected has become the head of the corner, with the Manager, Mr Blythe, within, singing his troubadour song that the successful play was the play that filled the house. Pull down the final curtain on all or any cultural cod-acting. Be fair, Sean, be fair! The Abbey was having a difficult time; playwrights were working with the keener eye on the Censor; actors and actresses, at the first chance, swept headlong down the suction-pipe of the films, and were joyously lost in the golden dust-bag of Elstree or Hollywood.

Sean worked off and on at a new play, *The Green Gates*, a title he afterwards changed to *Within the Gates*. He had written a lot of dialogue and rough drafts of themes, and now he was trying to knit the wild themes and wandering dialogue into a design of Morning, Noon, Evening, and Night, blending these in with the seasons, changing the outlook of the scenes by changing the colour of flower and tree, blending these again with the moods of the scenes. The dominant colour of Morning and Spring was to be a light, sparkling green, that of Noon crimson and gold; Autumn's crimson was to tinge itself with violet, and Winter and Night were to be violet, turning to purple, and black.

At this time, he had become a little interested in the film, and had thought of this play as a film of Hyde Park. He thought the film world was dangerously indifferent to the life of England and her people. He thought of the film as geometrical and emotional, the emotion of the living characters to be shown against their own patterns and the patterns of the Park. It was to begin at dawn with the opening of the gates and end at midnight as they closed again to the twelve chimes of Big Ben striking softly in the distance. He had written to Alfred Hitchcock to come and have dinner with them, so that they could talk it over, and Hitchcock had agreed. Hurrah! Eileen got out the handsomest tablecloth they had, and laid the table with their best dinner-set, one kept for state occasions, or for particular friends, with a bottle of wine looking like an awkward jewel in the table's centre; for Sean and Eileen had secret visions that this coming talk might bring money worries to an end for a long time.

Sean had his own ideas about films. To him the camera was the king of the kinema. It was the actor in all the film did, or tried to do. Actors however great, actresses however glamorous, were but minor correlatives of the kinema, like fancy buttons on a coat or a pretty buckle on a belt. Good acting by man or by woman could never create an art of the kinema. No power on earth could turn the shadowy figures on a screen into living men and women. By and large, the films, without a doubt, had become the lowest form of entertainment, an insult to infant and adult man, even to him who had painted pictures on the wall of his cave. Chime their church bells as they might in film after film, they'd never win a casual glance from the passing Jesus, or induce the meditating Buddha to lift a shuttering eyelid, or Mahomed to give a stir enough to cause a crease in his cloak. Let them multiply their succulent close-up kisses as they will, they'll never show off love as Shakespeare did or Rostand either; let them crowd their streets with gunning gangsters, they'll never this way show the rapidity and excitement life has within herself. All their agitated screens that flow from Hollywoods and Elstrees to flicker and flap all over the country are little else but lurid ornamentation on a great big scab.

Hitchcock was a hulk of a man, unwieldy in his gait, seeming as if he had to hoist himself into every movement. Like an over-blown seal, sidling from place to place, as if the hard earth beneath couldn't give him a grip. Seated at table, though quiet in his movements, he seemed to be continually expanding, while Mrs Hitchcock seemed to contract, a stilly mind sitting silent but attentive, registering every gesture and every word. His sober lounge suit, straining at the buttons, seemed to want to let itself go, while her gayer dress seemed to tighten round her body, imprisoning the impressions her mind formed from the experimental talk of the evening. Hitchcock liked all the suggestions made by Sean, but Sean noticed that his wife kept a dead silence, merely answering quietly an odd question or two put to her by Eileen. Hitchcock blazed up about the power of the camera – it could take into itself all in heaven, on the earth, and in the sea under the earth; there was nothing beyond its scooping eye. But Sean felt that the camera could do very little. Keep moving was its cry, like a parrot-policeman. It could not pause to take a breath as the stage did; it had to keep on the go, or perish : a still wasn't still life; it wasn't dead life; it was nothing. The film's sad moment couldn't spare a second for a sigh, its comic moment a second for a laugh. At its best, the film is something outside of man; at its best, the theatre is something within him. The film is a sword without a blade, a banner without a staff, an arrow without a head.

Hitchcock left, bubbling with excitement over what he and Sean had proposed; leaving a hearty invitation to come to dinner some day the following week, of which Mrs Hitchcock would let them know, so that the discussion might go on again; but Mrs Hitchcock departed smiling and silent, slowly silent and sure. Sean never got the invitation, never heard from Hitchcock again.

Madame Adami came to set down the score for the songs in the play, and for the plain-chant to the verses in the second act. For days before, Sean had felt a severe, continuous pain in the place where his heart was said to be, but he ignored it, and went on, singing, with his work. Halfway through the lilting of the airs for Madame Adami, the pain suddenly burst into a flame of agony, and his chest shot out and in as if the heart was going to do a high jump out of his body. Madame Adami fled from the room. Lie still, keep quiet; phone for the doctor! Lie like a dead one, while the heart pulses madly on. Having lost its rhythm it is frightened, like a little child lost rushing hither and thither for its mother. My heart's in the Highlands; my heart's bowed down. Do not say that life is waning, or that hope's sweet day is set. Maybe soon he'd be a picture without a frame; the summer's saying goodbye to the rose. Goodbye, blackbird! Oh, give me back my heart again.

Eileen's heart was a hive of buzzing fears, and Sean, though tortured with pain, was uneasy too with the desire to laugh at the sudden change in the life of the house, the common household duties suddenly flooded over with anxiety and time-consuming care. Run along, hurry up, phone him quick – the doctor! Bar the door, shut to the windows, and keep death away; hot haste everywhere in the midst of an alarmed quietness. The repressed and dread expectancy that death may be coming up the steps to the door. Knock knock knock. When lilacs last in the dooryard bloomed. Oh, Sean, oh, Eileen! Our child, our little boy. Stifle the thought. And Sean laughed at the renewed vision of Madame Adami flying out of the room.

Death! What is a death but a fading leaf falling in an infinite forest of life! It should be sad, it should be always sad, even when the old, having used up all that life could give them, sink sleepily into darkness; but death should never put uncertainty into the life it leaves behind. Why should a sad thought in a sadder mind be forced to cry out, How are we going to live now? Why should death, which is hard enough, act harder still by bringing hardship in its train? Why should it matter a damn to the widow and the orphan as to what they shall eat or wherewithal shall they clothe themselves? Why should one be dependent on another for bread? To Give us this day our daily bread, there is often no answer. The prayer doesn't travel far enough. Not here, there is not enough silence, and there is too much noise near heaven for God to hear. Not that Eileen or her boy had had much from him. What he got from his work had, as 'twere, to be dragged out of infinity. Hardly enough to keep them; never enough to free their minds from the jagged prods of anxiety. If he went tomorrow, it's little she'd have to lose, but even that little might be missed by her and her boy. There wouldn't be enough to pay the doctor looking down at him. Certainly, Eileen with him would never be like Madame de Guermantes, able to buy and wear such a red dress that made her look like a blazing ruby.

He must remain perfectly still, the doctor was saying, the cautious eyes still peering down at the outstretched Sean. For how long – an hour or two? For a fortnight; just to lie as he lies now. Only the barest and most cautious of movements. He lay for a few minutes after the doctor had left. What if his heart was as bad as they thought, it could never be much better, and the setting of the score would finish the play. Up he got, and in he went to the room where the piano stood, and where stood Madame Adami cloaked and hatted just ready to go. He lay down on a divan, and before he gave in to the battling heart-beats in his breast, he sang the songs and chanted the plain-song till all the scores had been set down for the book of the play.

An X-ray was taken in the local hospital, but the plan showed a scarred lung hiding the heart, so the heart was hidden away, and no thesis could be written about it. He must see a London specialist, but how to get there without the burden of travelling in a bus was a problem. Lady Londonderry very kindly solved it by sending down a car which carried Sean like a grandee from his own hall-door to the doorstep of the London specialist. Then the fight began, for, after a few questions, the specialist caught a grip of him, flung him on to a couch and started an all-in wrestling tour of Sean's body, thumping, twisting, and pulling him about, till Sean thought that if there hadn't been anything wrong before, there was bound to be something wrong with his heart now. He was paying dearly now for the early luxury of his life. But Bertram Nissè was evidently a specialist in spirit and in truth, for nothing happened but a few gasping laughs from Sean as he was whirled about on the couch.

Pulled out of the hurly-burly of pummelling, Sean was wired to the cardiograph and his heart-beats were measured and timed with the quietness and confidence of electrical surveillance; and the end was that while his heart was not a first-class one, it was not what he would call diseased; O'Casey had a heart of his age. When this was said, there was a long silence, for Eileen and Sean had convinced themselves over such a long time of waiting that the heart was diseased, that, when the doctor said it was not so, they couldn't suddenly adjust their minds to the declaration, causing the specialist to ejaculate, You don't seem to be glad of the good news. Then the silence was broken by a laugh from Eileen and Sean – not because of relief, but because of the extreme care they had taken to prevent Sean stretching even a finger too suddenly.

But, added the doctor, he mustn't do any kind of strenuous work; must live for a few months on green herbs and water; and must, above all, separate himself from worry. Well, the rose of life was still held in his hand, but Sean could see some of the lovely petals falling. He who loved to trundle a barrow filled with grass or weeds, to swing a hook into undergrowth, or an axe down on a sturdy log, must sit still on a deck-chair, and listen to the humming of the bees; walk between the violet and the violet, walk between the various ranks of varied green. Well, it was better than an illness changing the universe into a corner wherein we crouch; but it was one more smudge of Lenten ash on his forehead. If the wings were no longer wings to fly, they would beat the air with effort; they would never fold themselves to stay still: for ever patient and for ever active.

No worry? But he had to worry about his family, about his play, and about the way things were going in Spain. There Saint James of Compostello, shoulder to shoulder with Franco, was herding a crowd of Moroccan Mahommedans into arms to keep the Christian Faith all alive-o in Madrid and Salamanca; the Koran was now part of the Cannon Law. England's Government was doing all good men could do to ensure fair play was rampant, opening the sky for Hitler's and

Mussolini's bombing squadrons to make a bloody blot of Guernica.

Shattered a bit by his illness, Sean took thought as to how he could get his play produced. He had waited a long time, knowing that if he didn't get something from the play, the family would be in a cleft stick of poverty. It had been published, but no sign came that any commercial manager was interested in it; no lordly amateur like Barry Jackson thought even to give it a passing nod. It lay there, enbalmed in the book. The English way of life didn't go the way of experimental drama. While the leaders of English Christians were attending the Public Schools, and the mightier universities, they tensed their minds to have a drink or two with Chaucer or Shakespeare; but when they came home they swam about in the blue lagoon of musical comedy, or sat down to enjoy the tremendous thrill of watching agitated gentlemen on the stage vying with each other as to which of them would sleep with a certain lassie when night must fall.

Had C. B. Cochran had enough of money to play with, the work would have had a production of rich colour and emotional movement, for Cochran was the bravest man England's theatre has had for a century and more; the bravest and the best. Dapper from his dainty bowler hat to his spatted boots, grasping an elegant walking-stick, Cochran had all the light, glow, and colour of the theatre within him, like the kingdom of heaven in the soul of a saint. A Master of the Revels, if ever there was one; the king's revels and the revels of the people. It was he, and not Lilian Baylis, who should have had a theatre to nourish and display, for he had more courage in a new look at things and more imagination towards the projection of the drama into the minds of men, without his cloak, than Lilian Baylis had with her cloak of pretence flowing out from her shoulders, and flicking everyone in the face. Everyone bowed the head, if not the knee, at the mention of the Baylis name; and stars of the London stage, straying into a conceited generosity, would, occasionally, play a star part to emblazon the Baylis name, and give their own a limelight glow of love for drama; indifferent to the other poor actors around them giving all they had for nothing, or, indeed, paying a fee to be permitted to play. Stars asking a paltry pound a week from Baylis (Baylis was willing), would, a week later, ask a hundred from Cochran, and get it, too. A god-testing lady, this Baylis, for whenever she needed money for the Old Vic, down she flopped on her knees, saying, Dear God, now's the time for some dough; so open up the old everlasting purse, and shower it down. And down it came, clinking down to fall on her lap as the gold of the god fell into the lap of Danaë; ay, and more than enough, for she died with a tidy superfluous sum in her private back-pocket.

The Baylis Theatre, known as the Old Vic, was said to be a world-famous place, dedicated to the production of Shakespeare's plays, but chiefly maintained to beatify the name of Baylis for ever amber. Sean was guided there first by J. B. Fagan, who had charge of the London production of his play; guided there in a taxi-cab, with Mary Grey and Fagan, silent and reverential all the way from Bloomsbury to Waterloo Road. The play staged that night was *Romeo and Juliet,* and Sean was shocked at the poverty of the audience (their numbers, not their clothes), the acting, and the scenery. Beyond the fine portrayal of the Nurse and Mercutio, there was no reason to give even a cold clap of the hands. The scenery had the faint bluster of things children at play take from a rag-bag, without a child's imagination left to make them glow; colourless, though colour wasn't costly; it was just that the children playing on the Old Vic stage wouldn't be permitted to deploy a daring, or even an eager imagination (if they had had it) by the mother Baylis; for not having any herself, she repudiated it in another. The whole play was flat and flimsy (bar the part of the Nurse which stood out from the others like a tulip half hidden in a pack of chickweed), a performance that penetrated far into nullity and put Shakespeare in front of it as a beggar for the charity and goodwill of the passers-by. Several times Sean went to see Shakespeare in differing moods, but the performances were all sullen, bold with poverty and impudent in pretence, like crutched cripples playing at football. So they went on, dragging one year after another in the performing of Shakespeare's plays, spacing them out as a farmer spaces out his regular rotation of crops.

Some time near now, the television authorities asked Sean by letter and telephone and courier to write and speak a three-minute script giving short and pithy reasons for the formation in England of a National Theatre (there had been an argument

and discussion in the Press about it, and Sean had written
heatedly in favour of one in *Time and Tide*). After much hesitation (for he didn't like the idea of televising himself), after
argument about it and about, he consented, spending quite a
time in bringing together what he thought were cogent reasons
to force forward the idea of a National Theatre within the
short space of three minutes. Finally, half satisfied, he submitted the script, which was not only accepted but praised for
its brevity, and, he hoped, for its wit. Then he spent anxious
hours waiting for the time to come when he'd stand forth for a
National Theatre on the little screens of ten thousand television sets, to be, at the end, rewarded with a fee of three
guineas. The day before the event, a telegram came, saying
that mother Baylis had lodged a vicious protest against the
proposal with the television authorities, and that Sean must
now, during his appearance and speech, make it clear that the
Old Vic was England's National Theatre; or, if not, the de-
livery of Sean's ideas would have to be cancelled. Shortly after
the telegram, a motor-cyclist came snorting up to the door, the
rider hurrying in to confirm the telegram, and to beseech Mr
O'Casey to agree to the terms of mother Baylis. Sean had
never written a word against the Old Vic; he hadn't mentioned it
in his address, for his idea of a National Theatre was something wider, more responsible, more productive of colour, line,
and form than anything yet done, or yet to be done, than the
drab dramatic heraldry displayed in performance or production by the holy house in Waterloo Road. Sean told the envoy
that what he had written had in it what three minutes gave
him to say; that the television authorities had accepted it; and
that nothing could be taken therefrom or added thereto; so the
envoy departed sorrowing, saying that the address could not be
given, mother Baylis' authority thereby depriving him of a
much-needed fee of three guineas. To this day, it is inexplic-
able to Sean that mother Baylis should have been allowed to
countermand a request by the television authorities by ordering
that O'Casey should chant a paean of praise to her, or keep his
big mouth shut.

Sean knew that the more he tried to put into a play, the less
chance he'd have of a production in England, so he had to
decide whether he would model a play so as to squeeze it
towards triviality, or persist in experimental imagination, and

suffer for it. On the other hand, if he did get a production of an experimental play, he would be forced to submit to a rag-and-tag one, one that would be cheapened so much that half the life would be gutted out of it. The English critics, by and large, would measure the play by its furtive, underhand performance, so giving the play no chance of a better and deserving production in the future. Not only that, but a furtive and fidgeting production in London echoed loudly in New York, which wrapped the play in a web of failure, encouraging the American managers to falter in having anything to do with it; while the English critics, immersed up to their buttocks in love for the tawdry and trivial, are only too ready to give an imaginative play a kick down rather than a hand up.

So Sean, grubbing the infinite for a few faint pounds, was forced to risk a paltry production which brought to light all the darkness his poor heart had feared. After a struggle with Herbert Hughes, who wanted to torture simple tunes with elaborate musical decorations, Sean handed over the mystery of his playwriting to Norman McDermott, who reduced whatever lustiness there was in the play to an agitated and timid tinkle. An ugly woman was shooting an arrow into the sky. On the very first night of the production, Sean saw in the theatre's foyer the bunch of crêpe hanging there, telling him and all who came that the play was dead. After Herbert Hughes' share had been deducted from the advance, and after various expenses incurred during rehearsals had been paid, Sean had less than twenty pounds to call his own. Indeed, were it not for the kindness of Lady Astor, who gave him and Eileen a room in St James's Square, with a fine breakfast thrown in, the O'Caseys would have been in a dire condition indeed. It would be a long time before he could retire at this gait of going; before he could lay down the pen, take up the pipe, and plank himself down in a deck-chair all in a garden fair; or smoke quietly in a valley of growing stars. No; better live on lively through the burnt-out ends of fiery days. Live in the world's garden, but not rest in it, for there are things to be said and things to be done. We chat with truth and sing with truth, and act with falsehood.

> Blessed sister, holy mother, spirit of the garden,
> Suffer us not to mock ourselves with truth.

A GATE CLANGS SHUT

RUNNING from London, fleeing from poverty as aforetime
Milton fled from the plague. A man can flee from a plague, but
never from poverty. It kisses him sourly when he wakes in the
morning, and goes to bed with him at night; lies between him
and his wife if he happens to be married. Sean was in a bad
way, for little had come in since his battle with Yeats over
the play, *The Silver Tassie*, which had been rudely placed
under anathema by the poet. His work, accepted before, had
now to force another way forward. Sean had to start all over
again, separated from even the passive approval of Yeats and
his admirers. Reviewers who hadn't yet found a way of their
own copied the condescending criticism of Yeats. Even Dr
Starkie, one of the Abbey Directors, putting a hand to his
better ear, caught the Yeatsian echo of, 'O'Casey is losing his
dramatic fire by remaining in England; he is separating himself
from his roots, and is beginning to write of things in which he
has no interest'. So Dr Starkie answered the echo by sending
one of his own into the attentive air, saying, 'O'Casey has left
the scenes of his impressionable years, and has lost the power
to see intensely'.

A most unfair and cleverly-stupid statement to make. Sean
had begun to write the play before he had been a year in England, and it couldn't have been possible to lose in less than a
year the impressions of forty. Again, a good deal of this time
had been infused into the London production of his older
plays, so that maybe a lunar month remained for him to lose
his 'power to see intensely'. Again, again, both Yeats and
Starkie had spent far more than a year away from Ireland
themselves, yet no one accused them of having lost the 'power
to see intensely'; indeed, Yeats had gone to school in England
for quite a time, had lived in London as a young man for
many years, and, afterwards, had paid many visits there; yet
no one had so far accused him that because of this he had 'lost
the power to see intensely'. Again, again, again, Yeats himself

had been inspired to write the lovely lyric, *Innisfree*, by the sight of tinkling water running down a window to keep things cool in a shop on the Strand of hot and dusty London.

So Sean and Eileen and their boy fled from London, after selling what remained of the lease of their London house; fled from the frying-pan of city poverty to the furnace of poverty in the glad, green country. A friend of Sean said he'd a cottage in Chalfont St Giles, he didn't want it, and Sean could live in it as long as he liked. Live in my heart and pay no rent. So off they hurried, Eileen first, and Sean to follow as soon as the furniture was stored. Then a message came from Eileen for a quick dispatch of seven pounds; the last tenant hadn't paid his telephone bill, so the postal authorities wouldn't allow its use till the bill had been paid. Poor Eileen, in a hurry and anxious to have a talk with Sean, signed a form acknowledging responsibility, and, though Sean wrote to, and argued with, the district manager, he couldn't get a refund of the money. A bad start.

How charming the cottage looked from the road, the road that came from Amersham and went to London, with the Chiltern Hills encasing the country round, and tucking everything in nicely. Near London, too, for the great city was only nineteen miles away. So near and yet so far: the last bus from Amersham left early for London and London's last bus left early for Amersham, so one couldn't let a friend spend an evening with one, unless he was put up for the night, and a London friend had to say goodbye at seven, if he couldn't put you up, and you didn't wish to walk the nineteen miles back to the Chalfont home. Lively chat had to cease, good company break up at seven, if the one wanted to be carried back to London or the other wanted to be carried back to Chalfont. Western way of civilized life.

It was an attractive road, hedged in with hazel, hawthorn, and bramble, which, in summer, held up vast bundles of wild bryony and wild clematis, giving place, in autumn, to masses of old man's silvery beard and myriads of beady berries, green, yellow, orange, and crimson, of the woody nightshade. And on this road stood the Misbourne Cottages, two of them, looking like dolls' houses that the manor, Misbourne House, had originally built for the amusement of the children and the use of their workmen. Misbourne House, now filled with a rich, retired business man and his family, stood, important and aloof, safe from foul contact, among its gardens, lawns, and its tennis courts. Western way of civilized life.

The cottages were surrounded by a trim privet hedge, and, at the gate of the one Sean and his family were to live in, was a lovely white lilac tree. Surely, the lilac is a rich feather in the cap of God's creation. A tiny garden of grass formed a mat in front of each cottage, ornamented with a round bed in the centre holding a red geranium within a circle of dreamy petunias. To the side, separating the cottage garden from the tradesmen's and workmen's entrance to the Big House, was a brick wall, sprinkled lavishly with slimy moss, with many ferny plants jutting from the crevices. Supporting this was a grassy slope which bordered a narrow path leading to the dry closet jutting out by itself from a side gable of the cottage. A towering, gaunt pine tree stood uneasy in a corner of the little garden, looking as if it had been kidnapped when young, and was now trying to break through the hedge and join its companions in a wood. The front door opened into a space, half hall, half room, forming a dining-room, and from this room all the other places sprang. On the right was a small room, evidently meant to be the parlour, just big enough to hold a few chairs, a small table, and a stand by the window on which to place a flower-pot, or rest a book. Here, at night, Sean read and worked, stretched out flat on his belly, with an oil-lamp beside his head, a practice that gave him a bad lump on his elbow, caused by the hard floor's friction, which gave a lot of trouble before it disappeared. At the back of the half-hall was the tiny kitchen where all cooking was done on an oil-stove, for the cottage had neither gas nor electricity; to the right of the kitchen, stairs, as steep as a ladder, led to a loft which took the place of a bedroom, where the boy, his mother, and nannie slept; outside of this room, along a narrow passage, was a cubby-hole big enough for a stretcher-bed, and here Sean slept stuffily, for there was no window in it; opposite was another cubby-hole in which was a bath so big that one wondered how it got in. Oil-lamp and candle had to say let there be light when the sun went down, though gas and electricity mains ran along the road but a few feet away from the garden. Chesterton would have enjoyed it a lot, and much more, if candlelight and lamp-glow had been but the glimmer of a rushlight – shades of the golden medieval age.

After some months of a bruised life, the landlord put in enough electricity for a few lights, Sean paying half the cost of installation. The rent was a pound a week, and when they had been there for a time, Sean was presented with a bill for twenty pounds, four for his own tenancy and the rest for the tenancy of the last tenant who had gone suddenly to God knows where. The landlord expected that Sean, out of kindness to landlords, would pay the amount owing cheerily-o; but Sean, in the hardness of his heart, refused. Eileen, who had a passion for cleanliness, used the bath daily for herself and night and morning for the boy, till after the fourth day's use, the bath remained full and wouldn't empty itself for anyone. It was soon shown that this would never do, for the waste water, when released, poured down into a sump-hole, and when the sub-soil became soaked, the bath stayed full, and one had to wait till the waters subsided, which might take a week or ten days. Consummate cleanliness had to stop, and a bath brightened from a monotonous certainty into an exciting hope.

The entire back of the house had no window, for it formed the gable-end of the big hothouse of the manor, making the whole house hot and stuffy on a fine day, and so a previous tenant had planted a meat-safe in the alley to the side of the house, providing a cooler place a step away from the closet. The closet itself was a simple affair, consisting of a rough seat from wall to wall, with an exposed bucket beneath the hole, and a box of sand with a shovel handy to be used discriminately after a visit had been paid to it. In the winter, a visit at night was an adventure, carrying a candle which couldn't be lighted, if a breeze blew, till the closet had been entered and the door shut.

How many miles to Babylon? Three score and ten.
Can I get there by candlelight? Yes, and back again.

A western worstern way of life. One night, groping his way along the alley, Sean slipped, and shot out a hand to the wall to save himself, immediately becoming conscious of slimy, wriggling things soiling the flesh of his hand. Lighting the candle, and shading the light with his coat, he saw the wall to be a mass of wriggling, twisting slime. Hundreds of thick-bodied snails, oozing their phosphorescent sweat out of them, and as many more corpulent slugs, were sliding damply up and down the wall; crowds of white, yellow, and pinkish worms crawled about between them; and myriads of fat woodlice and other vermin darted hither and thither when the light of the candle flame fell upon them. A Walpurgis night of vermin. A hideous, crawling, wriggling world, active in the silence and the dark. Sean turned the candlelight on to the meat-safe, and there, too, on its legs, on its sides, and probing at the perforated panels, were the snails, the slugs, and the woodlice. Sean took the light away from the animated ooze and ugliness, and stood in the darkness, shuddering, for darkness could not now hide from his eyes the sight of the mean, unwholesome medley of squirming, slimy life. Eileen and he poured pounds of chloride of lime over the detestable wall, to purify the place, but, in spite of their efforts, night after night the wall was curtained with this noiseless medley of moist rottenness, crawling and twisting about in its own unhealthy and unholy slime. He felt sick. Today, when it crosses his mind, the wriggling façade appears again, and Sean shudders.

And all this medley of wriggling dirt is part of God's creation; part, too, of Massingham's solacing and gay exhilaration of country life; part, too, of A. E.'s devotional delusion of the charming little furry things playing about in the tall grass when

Withers once more the old blue flower of day.

Sean was beginning to see even here, but nineteen miles from from London, that country life wasn't always lovely; just fields of golden corn or bearded barley; or the pungent honey-scent of haymaking; or the lark's loud song. He had come face to face for the first time with a few, out of thousands, of the farmer's enemies. And loathsome things, indeed, a lot of them were; and the fighting farmer couldn't be content, like Sean, to hide, shuddering in the dark: he had to meet them, fight them, destroy them all. These things were enemies of man; enemies of him who walked the paved cities as they were of him who walked where the elms grew and the plough, horse-led or tractor-driven, turned the furrows in readiness for the waiting seed. Later, he was to learn a lot more about the enemies of cultivation, visible and invisible, the mass-produced creations of God, boring and nibbling away the vegetable and animal wealth conjured into existence by man's animated mind and the endless energy of his toiling hands. He had heard of tubercular cattle, had seen an animal swelled and panting with anthrax, a horse twisting and stiffening with tetanus, a hen running round, gasping, its throat eaten away by the pip. Here, on the Amersham road, a farmer, before his face, had dived towards the ground, had caught a turnip-fly that had been busy with millions of its kind destroying the turnip crop.

—There's the blasted little bugger! the farmer had said, holding out the squashed speck on the ball of his thumb.

Then there was the rust in the corn, the rats in a thousand barns, the blight on the gooseberry, the mould on the apple tree. Here, and everywhere, a new exorcism was needed, and was being put into practice. A day ago, the roman catholic journal *The Universe* had reported that a boy in Washington, whose name was not given, had been, his parents said, possessed of an evil spirit, which dragged the mattress across the floor while the laddo slept on it, and sent him somersaulting out of a heavy chair whenever he sat in it. This couldn't be allowed to go on, so for thirty days a Jesuit priest, name not given, wrestled with the evil spirit, praying and fasting while he fought the evil thing, each effort bringing a violent outburst from the laddo that must have shook the windows out of houses along the street, till, at last worn out, the evil spirit went away, all witnessed by a stout protestant clergyman, name not given, who must have felt queer when he saw the demon disappearing into the stenchy curriculum of poor things damned. All broadcast from a news-service by NCWC Co, the paper said. So these dusty fables, blown about by a sour wind from the middle ages, rise like dust and blur the eyes of some, but settle again soon, to be lost in the ashes of the last stake that flamed around the last screaming heretic.

Man is busy now with a new exorcism – the expulsion of disease from man and animal and plant, defending the holy tissue of the flesh from pollution of virus and of bug; the exorcism of fear from man's way of life that he may stand up and speak out and laugh loud. Exorcism that calls for no candle, bell, or book, cassock or stole; a church where the altar is a table, the god a microscope; the ritual a bold imagination, a peering eye, a ceaseless searching mind; so that health may be sanctity, energy prayer, and the achievements of men and the play of children most acceptable praises to God.

To get rid of all that weakened or brought rot to the body; to sanction pain no more; to coffin nothing but what had lived a life to the full, a life that had no disappointed breath for a sigh at the leaving; a life that sank down, pleasantly tired, into the rest-rewarding earth. To give to the commonwealth of man the strong heart, the clear mind, the keen ear, the enduring lung, the bright eye, the stout limb, and the cunning hand – oh, Jesus, wouldn't these things be grand for man to have! Oh, Jesus, wouldn't these be achievements measuring as holy with, and higher than, Salisbury's Cathedral and Westminster Abbey!

Chalfont St Giles was almost all owned by three families, the Nashes, the Tripps, and the Lanes, all inter-connected like the interlacing of an old Keltic illumination, while in the village and on the little heights around, stretching up towards the Little Chalfonts, dwelt the notable, the less notable, and the least notable. The village and neighbourhood had three religious and three social sects: the gentry, those who thought they were gentry, and all who caught a glow from working for them, went to the dignified Anglican Church; the business people, the higher artisans, and those who worked for the business people, went to the Congregational Church; and the rest, deprived of any chance to pretensions, sought God through the Methodist impromptu prayer and the rollicking, rallying hymn.

The village of a string of cottages, a butcher's, a newsagent's, a general store, a small post office, and a chemist's, had two claims to glory: a stump of an oak tree, right in the way of traffic, where, when it was flourishing, Milton was said to have sat himself on sunny days, and the cottage where he fled to when the plague beset London. Here, it is said, he wrote *Paradise Regained*, and here in this doddering house, looking as if a sneeze would knock it down, some pens and papers, with a few pictures, were set out to bring back to shadowy life a poet long since dead. Everyone in the village knew the cottage, but Sean never met a soul who knew the man's work. Mr Nash, the business lordeen of the place, talked once of Edgar Wallace, but went silent when the name of Milton smote his ear; went silent and went away, never speaking a word to Sean again. To all the district around, it was as if Milton had ne'er been born. And no wonder, for to the poets elect of today and to those who garland these poets, Milton's name is one to be forgotten by the wisely-cultured moment. Emotion no longer minded him. The voice that sighed or shouted, the voice that sang with music, was not in a state of grace. Milton found no favour now with the Muses chattering among the cocktails, now in darkness, and with danger compassed round. Even the fine poet Eliot whispered into the ear of the embarrassed Milton, who was being silently pushed about by the quietly excited crowd – You'd better go, John, for your voice is gone and your vesture's queer. You were too prone to mix with the things poets keep away from: the voices of men throughout the wheeling years but make the present poet's ears ache; for all he worships now's the single self. England hath no longer any need of thee. They no longer serve who only stand and wait; no longer, no. I pray thee, get thee gone; get cracking, man, and go. And no one said hello; and no one asked who's he; and no one said goodbye.

After a year, they moved into a bungalow, which, though of no great shakes, at least was cleaner than the horrible cottage, and was big enough to hold the little furniture they had collected. So when they had settled in, the first question was the choice of a suitable school for Breon, now going on four, and a fine, sturdy, upstanding lad. Eileen came down at weekends from her work on the stage in London to sport with him and teach him how to read from nursery rhymes and little books she got for him – a task at which Sean was useless. The boy needed companionship, for, though Sean played a lot with him, and played well, it was a strain, and not quite satisfactory for either of them. He had played with the little girl and boy of a Cockney couple living in a cottage a few yards away, but the father went to work in a garage miles away, and so, amid many tears, the children had to say goodbye to each other. Where was the boy to go to school? Sean, who had gone nowhere and had had to seek knowledge everywhere, didn't know; didn't know anything about the method of educating a child. He left everything to Eileen, who decided on a lower-middle-class one with modern manners and cheery guidance rather than one whose rule of life was the rule of fear. But it should be a catholic school, for Eileen since her marriage had been a practising catholic. Having written for it, along came the handsome Prospectus from the Holy Cross Convent School, Gerrards Cross, for boys and girls up to ten. Fine building among trees, charming grounds, spacious rooms, good equipment, and fine fees too. And Sean's funds were very low. But Eileen was very confident; never mind; the nuns would be glad, when they heard the father was an author, to take a reduced fee till a play of his got going on a stage. They would be anxious that the boy should be brought up in the faith, seeing that his father hadn't been born into it, and had never caught it to himself; and such a fine little lad, too; you'll see, Sean. But Sean stayed doubtful. Eileen had been brought up in the lap of faith, and had learned all she had forgotten from what was taught in the Ursuline Convent, Burgess Hill. Taught primarily to repress the natural vivacity beaming from her nature, an active, imaginative, and humorous mind hidden in a silly repressive gentility, till she escaped their consecrated clutches, and found a fuller life in the theatre. All these precious convents did the same service to their pupils; you must grow up into a ladylike person at all costs; refined, reticent, ignorant of life, of its valour and its vehemence. But Eileen was quickly coming to herself: she was developing the rash and lovely confidence which the nuns had dulled; she had a bright eye for paintings; she was at home and hilarious with children; she hadn't the faintest smudge of the snobbery so sedulously plastered over the souls of the pupils in the higher-class convents; she saw through people, and her humorous penetration often burst into a cascade of laughter at the follies of men and the antics of women. She had a ready ear for conversation, and she was becoming a good judge of plays. But Sean still remained doubtful about the nuns being willing to think of a soul before a fee.

The appointment was made. Eileen dolled herself up and little Breon wore his best tucker and bib, all shrouded over with mackintoshes, for the rain was falling furiously. The bus came, and off they went, three in one and one in three – for the Convent; Breon excited, Eileen cool and confident, Sean trying to look hopeful. He was to remain outside; he might disturb things if he came in; say something to rattle the sweet sisters.

Spoil it all. Sean could see by the furrows gathering on Eileen's pretty brow that she was thinking out what to say to the same sweet sisters, potent help of Christians. Here they were out to bring the boy up in the way he should go. Which way was that, now? The catholic way, Genevan way, Mahommedan way, or the Buddhist way? These were but a few of the hundred ways carved out under the feet of every stepper-in to life. Eileen chose the catholic way; a way as good or as bad as any of the others. Sean hoped that when the boy grew up he'd take and make his own way. The right way to Sean was the desire to see life, to hear life, to feel life, and to use life; to engender in oneself the insistent and unbreakable patience to remove any obstacle life chanced to place in its own way. The way of the world; the way of all flesh: no one could show Breon the way through these ways; he would have to find a way for himself. Life's way of yesterday wasn't life's way today; and life's way today couldn't be life's way tomorrow; so neither Sean's way nor Eileen's way, nor Swann's way, could ever be Breon's.

The bus stopped, and they stepped out of it. Here was the Convent of the Holy Cross surrounded by a wall; a fairly high one, too. Private residence of the potential saints. A big black iron gate, semicircular bars topping it, within the semicircle the name of Holy Cross Convent in large letters of gold, with all the ironwork and the name crowned by a golden cross: barriers to keep out the Fluther Goods. Hardwood and ironwork without and within.

> Open your gates and let us through,
> Not without a beck and a boo;
> There's the beck, there's the boo;
> Open your gates and let us through.

Fine grounds, too, now serenaded by the sough of towering pines as their wide tops were sent swinging to and fro by a strong wind; the serenading sough accompanied harshly by a bass droning discord of cawing rooks darkening the soothing sough of the wind-swept trees; while, from the sodden, hodden-grey sky, the rain fell with a rapid drum-beat on leaf, on grass, on pavement, lulling the earth and all that grew there into activity and freshness.

Eileen opened the heavy gate, and passed through, and the

gate closed behind her with a clang. Sean watched the mother, through the bars, going up the rain-soaked drive, taking her boy to look indifferently at the cunning light in Christian eyes, and the tightened lips of divinity in man when money was in question: taking another step towards the glowing tedium of life's quick-march; then he hurried to a telephone booth twenty yards away from the Convent gate, pushed the door open, and went in to shelter from the teeming rain. From a side window, he still saw the stout wall, the iron gate, and the golden cross on top of it. A strong enclosure; fortified place; *ein' feste Burg.* How these important Christians fence themselves in! The whole appearance of this Convent called out, Come in with circumspection, and well clad; or keep out. One couldn't come in to the presence of a bishop of a community of nuns with a song as you could to God. Imagine Fluther Good, if he happened to be a father, going up this drive, his heavy hand holding the light one of his son; Fluther's shoulders squared, his walk a swagger, his lips forming the words of *The Wedding o' Glencree*; on his way to interview the reverend mother.

—How much, ma'am, for this little fella? How much? Jasus, ma'am, that's a lot to charge a chiselur for his first few lessons, an' makin' him into an ordinary, ordherly Christian man.

No; the little sons and daughters of the Fluther Goods were a long way from the Convents that flourished a golden cross; a long, long trail from the catholic way of this catholic Convent. The catholic way? Is there a widening way to wider thought there; is there the fearless peering into life; is there the loving, immeasurable sweep of the imagination in art, science, and literature in the catholic way? No, there isn't; not according to Newman, Acton, Duchesne, Dr McDonald of Maynooth, and many more eminent men who suffered and were abused for standing up to truth, giving her honour, and making this daughter of Time their dear sister. The catholic popular Press is so shamelessly pietistic that no youngster honoured with a little intelligence would be caught dead reading it. In one of their journals there is a weekly sprig of verse so dismally silly, so sentimental, so amazingly kiddish, that even *Casabianca* would look superb beside it. Their libraries seem to find few places for works on art, literature, or science. This is shown in a letter written by Mabel Jones, Librarian, Catholic Truth

Society, Liverpool, who says: 'Apart from the classics (which are not in great demand unless a film popularizes it) the bulk of novels by non-catholics, which are fit for distribution among catholics, are of ephemeral interest, and are likely to be left dead on the shelves unless great care is taken in their selection. Generally speaking, most of the writers of more serious novels nowadays hold a false philosophy of life, and a dangerous unchristian theory of morals. Thus, with some exceptions, the catholic library is reduced to mystery tales, adventure tales, and love stories of the lighter kind.' Mystery tales, detective fiction, and light stories of love, are, then, the high and holy books most catholics read, bar an odd classic when it has been suitably prepared for them by the film magnates.

Present-day Christians seem to be curiously attached to the detective story. Indeed, it is odd how even some of the theological lights among them aid the common catholic in his quest. G. K. Chesterton was their fiery godfather in this respect, and made a little, moon-faced catholic cleric a prime spyer-out of crime. The moment moonface began to beat his head, one knew, at once, that the criminal was as bad as caught. Then there's Monsignor Ronald Knox spending some of this spare time with a corpse in a culvert; and the quasi-theologian, Miss Dorothy Sayers, making the Lord Peter Whimsie into a noddle policeman, catching criminals as a good cat catches mice; and Dr Alington, Dean of Durham. Then there is another gentleman of detective fiction, a collegian, who has used his detection talent to harmonize the gospels. He might have spared himself, for a scholarly catholic cleric told Sean that Ronald Knox's essay on *Watson of Watsonia* 'was written as a skit on the compilers of the Higher Criticism of the Bible', whose efforts to prove that the Bible was written, not by one, but by many, were shown to be baloney by Knox, for the discrepancies in Doyle's books were as blatant and as many as those in the Bible, so that it could be proved that Doyle's stories were written, not by one man, but by many. Maybe by thousands. So we can all rest easy, now, when we read the Bible. Knox has made it all quite clear by having a little fun with it, though the Monsignor seems to forget that Doyle claimed no divinity to be hedging in every word he wrote. Indeed, Monsignor's thesis seems to have in it a hint of hiding himself. There seems to come from it, what, if someone else, other than a catholic, had written it, might be a glint of irreverence, making God out to be something of an absent-minded beggar. By implication, it seems to give a picture of the deity trying to remember what had been done, and when it had been done, a couple of million years before. Let me see now: What date was it now when the world was shaped from chaos? Come out, come on, come up here. Were Adam and Eve moulded by hand or made by a *deus ex machina*? There certainly were men in the world before Adam, says the catholic *Universe*, but they had no souls. When did they begin to get them? On one Hallow Eve or on a bright May morning? We do not know because we are not told. Biblical criticism, the turning tapsalteerio of testaments that had been divine authority for centuries, is no joke, and To be, or not to be, is a serious thought. There is pathos in the Christian's praying to Him whom he thinks his Saviour to deliver him from the pains of eternal death; in the Brahmin's praying to the purple-tinted God, O Shiva, grant that I may never be born again; and in the poet-tent-maker's wistful farewell, Where I made one – turn down an empty glass.

They were a damned long time in the Convent, thought Sean, for he was beginning to feel cold. The damp came through into the telephone booth. Looking out of a window on to the world. The rain still fell in sheets, racing down the glass windows of the booth as if the glass itself was melting. There wasn't a soul in sight, and the little common in front of him was desolate and deserted. A bench on the common, looking as if none were alive to sit on it, seemed to be sensing that the world was dead, and that never again would there be a lover and his lass alive to come and rest there. The trees bent over swiftly in the windy gusts, struggling back to their upright pose with labour and great creaking when the gust subsided, ceaselessly chanting the song of their soughing. Only an odd crow, heavily flapping its wings through the wind and the rain, lightened the hodden-grey sky, as it cawed resentfully, and winged a clumsy way to the rooky wood, looking like one of the nuns, caught up by a divine wind, and getting carried to heaven without her consent. Indeed, when in their black habits, the nuns looked like a flock of crows, cawing carelessly, too; for they all hummed the same tune in the one key, on the one note, throughout time, in the hope that they might hum the same tune, in the same key, on the same note, throughout eternity.

Thinking a way out of the world to heaven. The city of God. No mean city, by all accounts. O Paradise, O Paradise, who doth not long for rest: so the roman catholic and the protestant sing together, No one does really; certainly not for the rest death brings. All are ready to stick it out here as long as they can. The Christians aren't quite sure about the place above. No one has yet succeeded in suiting the manner of after-existence to man's nature. The Christian conception of it is neither pleasant nor inspiring: a dreadful monotony of eternal praise was more than one would wish to inherit. Such a never-ending job would make of immortality a life not worth living. It is said that eternal praise, eternal contemplation, was what God had in store for the saved. Had he? How come? Was it some conceited cardinal, some conceited bishop, or even some conceited saint, who, making God out in his own image, thought out this way as the way of God?

What did Sean really want of any after-life to take the place of the robe, the harp, the crown, and the eternal confinement in a prison of praise? Well, for a beginning, he'd like a thousand years of life to get to know the peoples of the world so as to be able to enter deeply into their sorrow and their joy, and to encircle them with his arms like a girdle encircling the waist of a motherly woman; and as a step beyond a beginning, another thousand years to study and enjoy the world's plant panorama from the lichens clinging to the deadening wall to the towering redwood trees of California.

The dampness was beginning to circulate through his blood, and stamp his feet how he would, they grew more clammy and numb. He opened the booth door and went out into the teeming rain to stroll, stamping, to the Convent gate. He looked up the drive but saw nothing but the rain dancing about the neatly-gravelled paths; then, when the rain was streaming down him, he saw them, heads bent, running down the drive, the little fellow laughing as he stretched out his legs to keep pace with his mother.

—Let's hurry, said Eileen, when she came up with Sean — I'm dying for a cup of tea.

The little bus swept them away from the holy Convent, redolent of God's passionate plan for man and the history of the pound note, the secluded building canopied by cawing crows, a dear little, sweet little rookery nook; Eileen chatting away excitedly to Breon, her shapely little mouth clenching into tightness whenever she claimed a pause to rest in silence. That night, when Breon lay in a cosy corner of sleep, Eileen told him all that had happened: the nuns had encircled them smiling, beguiling, giving a welcome to mother and child; welcome as the flowers in May; come into the parlour, dears; stormy weather. Oh, sacred charms of childhood, unto Christ so dear; and, if you bring a proper fee, there's nothing left to fear. Not a thing. One and twenty welcomes to the little lad. A sturdy little fellow. He would be a charming addition to their school, a nun said. And an interesting one, too, considering his father to be a writer, said another nun. Under God, children are the one surety of God's Church continuing, said a third nun, laying a partly-blessing hand on Breon's head. You both must stay for tea, murmured the reverend mother, both stay for tea, murmured a nun behind the mother, stay for tea, murmured another behind the nun. Polly put the kettle on, we'll all have tea. Thank God for tea! What could the world do without it? How did it exist without it? Nobody knows.

I'm sure he'll be happy here, said Eileen, if we can only manage about the fees. Just now we have to ask you to let them down a little, only for the time being; for less than a year at most, perhaps but for a month or two, till a play his father's written struts the stage. The cock-robin confidence died down at once. The sisters grew silent as those who had stood on a peak in Darien. Their hearts stood still. Oh, no; no, Johnny, no. The hands patting the child's head hid away under the folds of the black habit. The good nuns, and they were all good, receded to a safe distance; on retreat. No, no. There was nothing to do but go. An old nun led the mother and child to the door, and bade them a curt goodbye; a never-ending goodbye now. Shut the gate after you! Clang!

While the prudent nuns went on measuring the worth of minds by the fees they brought, Breon took his first step towards organized community life in Longdene School, owned by a young quakeress, a green-shirt of the Social Credit Party, the little lad unconscious of any educational gain or loss, with Sean sure he was better where conditions placed him. And if it were a loss,

His loss may shine yet goodlier than their gain
When Time and God give judgement.

Here in the midst of Jordans, where William Penn lies
buried, in the heart of the country where religion paraded the
sombre black suit and the steeple-crowned hat, a part of England rich in the dust of those odd quakers famous in their
longing for the grace of God and good business; here, quietly,
unmolested by either heaven or hell, Breon passed through five
energetic years, growing daily in the grace of boyhood and
yearly in the wisdom of the oncoming man, learning by experience that the clang of a closing gate is but the clang of another
one opening.

A FRIAR BY THE FIRESIDE

AWAY in a house in the deep green country, Sean nodded in his chair set near to a flaming fire, for the night was cold, and even the air of the room felt frosty. Midnight had passed by, and he was sleepy, but he knew that if he went to bed, sleep would go, for his mind was too tired to sink deep into it. Besides, the bed was far off and the bed was cold, while the spot by the fire was seductively warm, inducing a condition of wakefulness that was halfway towards sleep. He had extinguished the lamp, for the oil had wasted and the light had flickered; but the brilliant flaming of the fire gave enough light to show everything in it resting quietly among their own shadows. The whole house was asleep, and he was halfway towards it, nodding sleepily by the flaming fire.

> We're all nodding, nod, nod, nodding,
> Yes, we're all nodding good years of life away.

Father Clematis of the Cuneiform Order of Unimpassionate Canons Irregular had been to tea and supper, and had left a few minutes before twelve to give him time to mutter his Office before the last midnight chime had struck. A pleasant, chatty young man, ordinary though, whose main distinction was the habit he wore. His company was no gain, for he had entered the Order young, before life had had time to give him kiss or clout. No humour either; not a single spiritual or temporal laugh within him. Sean had seen hundreds like him in Maynooth – ordered and priested before life could give clout or kiss. Still, the lad seemed lonely, and, as he had evidently enjoyed his visit, Sean forbore to question his own foolishness in wasting time that might have been given to thought for work in progress. He was reluctant to say anything that might hurt the young friar's feelings when matters touching religion came up between them, so Sean had to keep the flag of conversation flying at half-mast; and so his mind had grown tired thinking of what not to say. And there was another reason for keeping away from anything likely to disturb the friar's mind: Sean could easily see that he wasn't made of sterner stuff; that though he might think of things, even be agitated, he would never have the gusto, the determination, to demand an answer from perplexing thoughts in his own mind, or questions put forward by the keener mind of others. Sean had known another mind like this one, but a much keener mind, that of a catholic layman, who, for a long time, had been a laughing absentee from Mass, who had expressed very liberal opinions, and had often quizzingly rejected both the theory and practice of the Church; but had neither the depth nor the resilience to carry the freedom of not knowing where life led when death came; not full enough to go on bearing the occasional foolishness and risky hilarity of humanity without a monthly assurance from a confessor that his sins had been forgiven, and that he was mounting monthly nearer to God; though, maybe, remaining as foolish, more foolish, in a harsher way, in sanctioning things and beliefs more ridiculous than had before given him any laughing pause.

For the first few visits, Father Clematis had worn the ordinary dress of a secular priest, but, afterwards, came in his rust-red habit and girdle of blue. Though to Sean the uniform didn't hide the man, to the roman catholic the habit was a grand uniform of vocational grace; the man was hidden in it, a tweedy carapace confining passion, pride, and all other characteristics, good and bad, of the common man. Sean couldn't help feeling that in its wearing on these occasions, there was something of the show-off in the young rust-red friar. A show-off, a show-off, a show–

Oh, we're all nodding, nod, nod, nodding–

A tap on the window-pane from a stem of the black-blossomed climber, Sartre resartus pedicularis, roused Sean with a start from his nodding. Curtains had not been drawn, and he could see the sky, thrilled with a multitude of frosty stars. Stare at the stars. 'These priests and Religious Orders, monks and nuns, are the Stars', says Mister Bing Crosby. What is the stars, Joxer, what is the stars? These is the stars, man – the priests and the religious orders. 'These', says Bing Crosby, 'are the real makers of history', says he. 'The rest of us run a business and make some money,' says he, 'and after a while we're gone, and the money's gone', says he; 'but', he says, 'they are building kingdoms of spiritual values, that are going to rule and influence generations years and years away', he says. And make some money along with the spiritual values, too, I says. 'Day after day they work patiently, shaping the characters', he says, 'of girls and boys, who will be the mainstays of this good American way of life of ours, which is founded on a belief in God. Look at any American coin,' says he – 'In God We Trust: on each and all of them', says Mister Bing Crosby. 'The Father O'Malleys and the Sister Benedicts are the stars in the film of real life', says Bing. The Bing Boys and the Bing Girls. And yet, I says, the highest percentage of crime among boys and girls, here in England, is among those who go to the roman catholic schools, and the lowest among those who go to the secular ones. And, I says, since our ideal in life seems to be in 'founding a little business, and making some money', then, it is a wise thing, I says, to put a spiritual slogan on the coins. We can depend on coins; they'll never let us down, and there's great value in a pious ejaculation on a coin, so there is, now. A week's holiday, without pay, from forced labour in Purgatory, maybe. Holy Night gives place to the Holy Nickel. Outside the blue-black birdies sang.

> Holy nickel, sanctified cent,
> Bless each proper lady and gent
> In every city and every clime,
> Now, tomorrow, or any damn time;
> Bless them all without reason or rhyme,
> Holy dollar and dime!

Well, there had been a Religious, a Star, sitting at Sean's fireside, a star that had a very dim twinkle. He pretended: he dismissed as nonsense what appeared in the weekly roman catholic Press, which he said, he never read, couldn't read, and wouldn't read – nearly adding so help him God (as other clerics did, too); but Sean knew that if challenged to say this openly in the pulpit, or print it in the Press, the young friar would slink off and hide where no challenger could find him. The young hand waved aside all of what he called the long-

forgotten animûs of ecclesiastical authority to punish spiritually and corporally any schism and every heresy; forgetting, or
hiding, that the canon laws regarding these conditions of
thought, flowering in the middle ages, were as fully in flower
as canon laws in the Church of today. The young waving
hand went on to decorate the voice saying, We rule and are
authoritative only in matters concerning faith and morals;
hiding the fact, or forgetting it, that roman catholic moral
philosophy covers everything a reasonable man may think
about. There is no important, and hardly any unimportant,
activity of daily life that it doesn't grip, direct, or try to choke.
'It is notorious', says G. G. Coulton, the Cambridge professor,
quoting Schulte's *Ueber Kirchenstrafen*, 'that even voting at a
political election has often been treated as a question of morals
by the Church' (*and didn't Sean know it!*). Recently, Cardinal
Griffin seems to have added mathematics; and a letter from a
roman catholic in the *Spectator*, 1902, said quite gaily and off-
hand, 'The real reason why religious persecution is unpopular
today is that nobody is strong enough to persecute'. Still, the
Church tries it on by condemnation in its Press, and by refusals
to allow any defence from an attack; by inducing its more
ignorant members to shout reports of blasphemy and obscenity
in novel or poem they have never read, or play they have never
seen; doing all they can to endanger the livelihood of anyone
daring, even implicitly, to criticize anything they have said or
done.

Our Community got where we are now, Friar Clematis had
said, settling himself comfortably in the armchair by the blazing wood fire, got it through the goodness of God and the
intercession of Holy Saint Joseph. We needed a centre of
spiritual force somewhere in this district, a place not to be too
big, but to have a generous chance for expansion; and a place
not to be too dear. A retired officer owned it; he was provoked
into putting all he had into a bogus company by a rogue of a
company gambler. The end was a pistol shot; the house was
said to be haunted, was offered for a small sum, and the Community bought it.

—An easy cop, said Sean, unconcerned in how they had got
it, or what they had given; for his mind was tired, and he was
full of sleep.

—Oh, no, not easy, said the friar complacently; we had

indeed a long search, and it was only through the intercession of our Patron, St Joseph, that we found our home at last. We must have trudged a hundred miles before we set eyes on the haven we hold now. Then he had gone, leaving Sean nodding, a nod knocking the walls away, letting the country roads flood into the room; and the fire become the rising sun at morn and the setting sun at night.

And it was as if Sean had been with them when they went forth on their journey to find a home. Out they set with a concerted sign of the cross behind them, the Prior, Father Auricula; Father Campanula, carrying a veiled image of St Joseph; Brother Bugloss, and Father Clematis; seeking a place here, seeking one there, but finding none that would do. They wandered far and wide while the winter was on, cold winds sending the skirts of their habits flapping around their legs; along the road, sometimes hardfelt with frost, with never a bird in the sky or the sound of a bird song from the empty hedges; finding no spot to suitably honour St Joseph, ever praying him to help in finding, somewhere, something their scanty means could furnish.

Through the spring they journeyed, buds in the hedges and on the trees, singing a song of a summer to come, but they found no shelter for the saint's indwelling; the days shortened into the sudden hush of autumn at her own leaves falling, as the friars trudged up the road and down the lane, seeking to the right, to the left, a sojourning place for the image of St Joseph, and finding none; journeying till backs were bent, feet went forward sore and aching, and thigh-pits flamed red with the friction of sweat; down road and up lane they trudged, around this house, that garden, without one drink at an inn to soften their dust-dried tongues, with hardly a word spoken, so that time wouldn't be lost for prayer to be said; sometimes thinking fearfully in their sinking hearts that Saint Joseph wasn't listening, or that he had decided to let the poor people sway along in their own perverted, pagan way. Then, one day of an opulent summer, they circled a house and they circled a garden till they came to a gateway, and, as the Prior's hand stretched out to open it, they felt that their journeyings had ended, and that St Joseph had brought them home at last.

—This is where we come in, said Father Auricula.

The place was in the heart of a dark wood of Mauriaceni

pines infested with original sins that burrowed under every-thing. At night one could hear the barking of excommuni-camuses, the sharp chirruping of nihil obstats, and the shrill squeals of the greyem-green birds, silenced only now and then by the baying of protestans britannicuses which had their lairs everywhere: a dreadful medley and confusion, though all said it was all part of God's curious Kingdom.

It was dusk, and the garden darkened as they stood in a bunch, ready to pump out prayers that this house might be theirs so that it could be used in the expansion of Holy Church. Here, in this group, was the lust of the Church, garn-ered into its vast psychology, day by day, for nigh two thou-sand years. And Sean was as if he were there, close by the friars in the midst of the garden where the orthoagonies and the heteragonies bloomed in the day and the dusk, where many dear little bees sucked heaven's honey from one kind, and big bastard bees sucked hell's honey from the other kind, and all was blessed and blasphemous buzzing; there Sean stood, watch-ing, listening, and hearing the sound of secret strife.

—Expose the image of St Joseph, whispered Father Auricula; and Father Campanula whipped the white veil from the image, and the Saint shone forth in his robe of glistening crimson, edged finely by fine gold, his white beard tinged into mauve by the dusk, a brown staff held forth in his right hand as when he guided his young Spouse and young Child safe into Egypt, as recorded by Luke, but by no one else, ready now to guide the Cuneiformians to a safe and lasting home.

Looka the face at an upper window of the silent house! A face so pale, a face that was twitching, a face so pale that the face formed its own flickering light, a face staring down at the shadowy friars praying among the orthoagonies and the hete-ragonies of the garden; and Sean sensed the sound of a silent strife that would make the possessor the dispossessed and the dispossessed the possessor. A deep green streak in the dusky sky gave a green glow to the window, and there in its centre shone the ghastly white face, whiter now because of the sad green light around it, with its eyes, hollow and glittering, peer-ing out into the dusk, and through the dusk to the friars hid-den in the purple peace of the garden. Looka the gaping mouth in the face at the window! But the friars looked not, but bent down lower as the gaping mouth, black in the white face in the green-lit window, gave a sigh, gave a long, sad sigh, filling the still air with a silent stir.

—Keep your thoughts on St Joseph, murmured the Prior; there are many enemies near; comtemplate the holy image: Oh, Holy Saint Joseph, Patron of the family and the home, be with us; give us what we seek and what we need and send us soon to serve thee here.

—What we seek, what we need, and send us soon to serve thee here, echoed the friars.

—Veil the image again, and let us go, said the Prior; we leave our petition with the Holy Saint: in this spot, in this place, around this house; and nowhere else; and none other house. He crossed himself, and added, Let us go!

The friars turned about, went out by the gate, and took to the road again, a sharp, sudden pistol-shot echoing loud at their heels, following their footsteps pattering purely along, away, away, a woe away; and Sean watched them go, their rust-red habits black now, as the friars, sheltering close together, forged into the purple dusk of the late evening, hugging the image of St Joseph away from any evil that might be there; for

> Self-slain soul, in vain thy sighing:
> Self-slain, who shall make thee whole?
> Vain the clamour of thy crying;
> Toll, bell, toll.

Then the door of the house flashed open, and a maid came rushing out, calling; calling; she ran through the garden, calling for help, and ran out by the gate and down by the road, calling. She had looked in at the doorway, and had seen it lying there; her heart had tightened with fear, and she had run from the house, calling. And in his mind's eye, Sean had seen it, too, lying there, coffined in its own clay for evermore; stretched out in the curious way the dead lie who leave life violently; but twist themselves in their agony or their fear how they may, they lie the same way in the sad solidarity of death. There it lay amid solid and respectable furniture, well made, lasting, rudely sneering at the lighter and more imaginative furniture of the age; christianly comfortable, made for life next to everlasting, full of the pride of permanency. The deathly face seen at the window was a face no longer, for it had become

a white mask of hardening clay, dwindling into indifference as
the maid ran along down the road, calling, and the bunch of
friars went pit-a-pat through the purple glow to where they
waited, a day's march nearer home, till St Joseph had rung the
bell, lit the candle, read from the book, and made the place fit
for the friars to live in. And so the dead stayed where it was
till uniformed brothers came to see, to connect the wound with
the gun, and both with the hand that fired it; till other brothers
came to lift it up and carry it off and hide it in the bosom of
that mother who never denies a child, but willingly shelters all
away from the heat o' the sun and the furious winter's rages. A
pistol-shot pronounced a blessing.

—So the Community got the place cheap, had murmured the
young friar; St Joseph didn't fail us, a happy thing for us.
Quam bonus Israel!

—A happy thing for them, murmured Sean, in his own mind,
wondering why this young fellow had such an odd idea of
heavenly aid, and why he never once ventured a word of sympathy for the stretched-out figure that had brought such fair
fortune to the Cuneiformians by rushing out of the world in a
wrong, wild way. He had peered at the friar, looking past the
habit to the man within: a man to whom all life and history
must be explained by a collection of dogmatic decrees, 'which',
according to Leo the XIII, 'impose themselves upon all catholics, and which no man is permitted to call in doubt'. Embedded in a decree, like a caterpillar in his cocoon. And the
bishops drum their way about, denouncing doom on all who
disagree, or venture a doubt.

Fat bucks of bishops in a barrel-roofed room,
Yell'd out, roar'd out threats of doom –
Bell, book, and candlelight standing on a table –
Pounded with their croziers in a frenzy of fume,
Hard as they were able,
Boom boom boom.

Excommunicamus, if you dare presume,
Bell, book, and candlelight will bring you what is due,
Bring you what is due and hoodoo you,
If you dare presume,
Doomday doomday doomday doom!

After two thousand years of thought, discussion, super-natural grace, and pious practice, all they can do to save man is to bind him tightly into one chair, and to bind God rigidly into one throne. Here by the fire, in a rust-red habit, with its blue girdle, sat a laddo who believed that he carried authority of life and death wherever his body happened to go; an ordinary mortal, who, because of what was called the laying-on of hands, pointed out the way of thought and action to everyone else, as if born to it as he was bred to it; with little knowledge of the way of thought himself, timidly obedient to every convention, every custom, honoured by common brethren, within and without his own community of faith. Sean had met many men in various walks of life who had assumed authority while in actual service – the doctor at the bedside, the scientist in laboratory or lecture hall, the foreman watching the rise or fall of a crane's jib: all these become common men in the give and take, the ebb and flow, of social life; but not the priest: he alone had a crystallized sense of authority that he carried with him everywhere, from the altar into all the odds and ends of social life. Pretend as he would, in casual talk, in quip, in serious conversation, the sense of rigorous, ritualistic authority over all life and all things clung to the priest, so that he could never be at one with the common man. Perhaps the one fire-side beside which a priest might feel fairly free was the fireside of an agnostic, for here he needed neither sense nor show of his grace-engrafted authority; here was equality, here man spoke to man. Here the clerical pursuivant of grace abounding found he had no claim on anything but his own wit, know-ledge, and geniality; here he was safe from any false honour.

Ritualistic grace seemed to have emptied everything else out of the young friar. He took no notice of pictures or print on the wall, never looked at the books on the shelves, never tried, or even asked anyone else, even to tinkle a simple song on the piano. Even primitive man, wrestling with life in a smoky darkness, painted pictures on the rugged walls of his cave. Sean tried to lead him to book, picture, folk-tune, but the friar leaned back from them all. They were all dangerous, a snare in each of them, though the friar loved the movies. But a thought outside the thought of the Community would leave him almost lost. It is a most dolorous sight to see a timid priest acting the bravo, providing for entertainment a quip, as innocent as a cowslip's bloom, about a bishop; knowing well that if he advanced any opposition to a bishop's or abbot's will, he would feel an episcopal fist striking his snot; and, if that didn't learn him, a crack from a crozier would lay him low. Crooks are no longer for rescue, but for authority; to thrust down rather than to pull up a soul to safety.

Nor any kindling thought for children. No light in the friar's eyes for a child. The brevity of life should be brought within the child's vision at an early age. Death should be forced up close to the young and encouraged to stay there. And the cane to guide them, to flail them into a fear of hell, lest worse befall them. In the priest's ear was the echo of the tale of how a little one, guilty of some 'mortal sin', was roasting in a red-hot oven in hell, the youngster turning and twisting itself about in the fire, screaming to get out; beating its head against the roof of the red-hot oven; stamping the little feet on the floor of the red-hot oven. A bad child, but God had been very good to it. He saw that it would probably get worse, would never repent, and would have to be punished much more in hell. So God in his mercy took it out of the world in its early childhood so that it would suffer nothing more painful than eternal imprisonment in a red-hot oven. A most gentle way of doing things. This is a fragrant roman catholic storiette, quoted by Dr. G. G. Coulton in his *Infant Perdition in the Middle Ages*, taken from number ten of Books for Children, this one named *The Sight of Hell*, written by a Father Furniss, CSSR, with the dewy *Permissu Superiorum* on its cover, and published by Duffy, Dublin, around the time when Sean's mother was a young woman about to be married. Its echo is heard still in the cry of the clerics yelling for the whip and cane to be used with precision and power to keep young hearts in the knowledge and love of God and of his son, Jesus Christ, their Lord. Gentle and kind is he. Oh, Father Furnace, how well you warn each young one of a personal *dies irae*. Here, now, was a young rust-red friar, sitting by Sean's fireside, talking about the boy, and asking why Sean and Eileen were so anxious to keep their lad healthy; why bother about what is mortal – the body? Why, indeed? Why trouble overmuch about a child's health when all that care has done may, in a moment, be a mangled mass under a passing car? And Eileen listened with wide-open and disapproving eyes by the corner of the fireside.

A raven suddenly perched on the roof of the Priory; and an evil bee of love invaded the Prior's cowl and then buzzed about in his bosom. He paused to pluck a rose as he passed, and the gay petticoat of an Annabel Lee fluttered Father Auricula into an indiscretion. A heart too soon made glad. The moth's kiss, first; the bee's kiss, now. The Community hung silent on the hook of consternation. The two primitive ladies who had given their best room for a chapel went frantic for fear of a scandal. Hush! The Prior was brought back to Headquarters for judgement, and, it was said, Father Clematis had been ordered to join a Mission in China. The silence lengthened, and the O'Casey fireside knew the rust-red friar no more. Hush, hush.

Where are you, Walter McDonald? You're needed now. They're making a show of everything, of everything; making a show:

> And we're all nodding, nod, nod, nodding;
> We're all nodding at work or when we pray.

STAR OF THE COUNTY DOWN

WHEN all was dismal, through the good and generous help of George Jean Nathan, the famous American drama critic, a contract was signed for a New York production of Sean's play *Within the Gates,* with an order to come to the United States – all expenses paid – to help in the rehearsals. Just before, he had had an invitation to come to Mount Stewart, the Irish home of Lord and Lady Londonderry, and stay a week there. So off he set from Heysham, straight for Belfast, from there in a boat dipping and rising a lot in a three-quarter gale, with two women in the next cabin far gone in seasickness, their wails and their abuse of each other preventing him from sinking into a satisfying sleep.

—Jasus, Annie, said a wailing voice, I'm in a bad way. I know it; I'm in a bad way, really – are you listenin'?

—Oh, shut your big mouth! came back an answer in a louder voice, an' let me concenthrate on me own disthress. You would insist on comin' to Belfast to slip down to Dublin to see Mr De Valera. You made your voice a buzz in me ear of sayin' I must see De Valera before I die so often that I was thricked into bein' spellbound. Who the hell's De Valera that anyone would want to see him!

—It was you yourself, Annie Fitzsimons, that persuaded me I must see De Valera before I was a day oldher, an' all because you wanted to see him yourself. I'm near dyin' this minute. I'll let you know, Annie Fitzsimons, that my intherests aren't your intherests. De Valera's led me into a nice quandary of jumpin' up an' dippin' down. If we dip down a little too far, what's goin' to happen?

—You went sailin' in an' came sailin' out, said the loud voice, afther buyin' th' tickets without a single thought of askin' them responsible if the like of this might happen, knowin' that neither of us was ever on the sea before. Sacred Heart, isn't this terrible!

—It was you yourself led me into this, said the wailing voice;

an' I'll hold you responsible, Teresa Tierney, with your De Valera's the one for Ireland; a holy man, a thrue pathriot. Well, now you know th' kind he is, an' you can have him all to yourself for Annie Fitzsimons. If I live to land, will I slip down to Dublin, to see him? I will not. Jesus, Mary, an' Joseph, amn't I to be pitied this night!

—It's meself doesn't give a damn whether you go down to Dublin or not, said the louder voice, for it was you was always sayin' you'd set foot on the land of Eireann before you'd die to lighten th' misfortune of bein' born on a foreign sthrand. Didn't you numb me ear with your ceaseless, ceaseless registration of De Valera as th' genius of the Gael? Now, looka where your lordly ideas have landed us! An' if we do strike land, what are we goin' to do when we think of havin' to go back again? To go through the same again. Have y' any answer to that one, Teresa Tierney? I wish you well of your wish! Amn't I convulsed thryin' to prevent me organs from shootin' outa me like a jet from a fountain! Stewardess! Oh, when I go back, if I ever do, what'll I say to me poor husband when he sees the state I'm in!

—An' I asked the sailor comin' aboard how'd it be, an' he said that I'd feel no more than a gentle rockin' of a cradle. What way can they be sailin' th' ship with its hoppin' up an' jumpin' down! In God's name, call th' stewardess, Annie Fitzsimons. It's plain that life's only a sideline on this ship.

—I'm tired callin' her, said the louder voice, though I'm sinkin' fasther than yourself. Call her you. Rockin' like a cradle! Why hadn't you th' sense to cross-question th' sailorfella about th' manner o' rockin' he meant?

—For God's sake, don't ask questions, for I'm feelin' near th' end of things! Annie Fitzsimons, between the waves of agony goin' over me, I ask you what'll happen if we foundher?

—We're both well foundhered already. Ask your great De Valera what'll happen if we foundher! Curse o' God on the persuasion that got me into this disasther! Stewardess!

—Stewardess! echoed the wail as Sean, between the whistling of the wind and the pitching of the ship, slipped into a slumber that silenced the voices, waking only when the siren blew on entering Belfast Lough, giving him time to put on his best shirt and jersey, have a fine breakfast in the ship's restaurant, before the elegant car slid on to the wharf to take him through

Newtonwards and along the margin of Strangford Lough to the home of his hostess, Mount Stewart, in building, the star of the County Down.

There it was, lovely and languid, embossed by beautiful gardens, sheltered by many trees, fading into hilly lands and hollow lands, fringed in the distance away south by the blue peaks of the Mourne Mountains sweeping down to the sea. Wide grounds so extensive that it seemed that to cover them it would take, even on a horse, a full day's journey. For those who walked, there were peaceful huts of a restful shape here and there, the floors and walls tiled with broken pieces of chinaware, some a rich blue, some more modestly so, others lightly coloured, and more still tending to whiteness, but tinged with the blue of their brothers. These pieces formed the floors, cunningly woven together, and on the walls were panels showing portraits of old Keltic saints, each done with the same pieces of blue chinaware, each piece of a different shade of blue from the rich, dark, full blue to a faint flush of it in those pieces tending towards whiteness, and woven more cunningly together than the tiling of the floors. In this summer-house was a panel silhouetting in blue the figure of St Columkille, in that one the figure of St Bridget, in another, maybe, that of St Aidan, the time the Keltic Church preferred Glendalough's seven churches to the clamorous call of Rome, seeding itself in the mind of the popes. Chinaware patrons of places in Eirinn and guardians of Mount Stewart and the Londonderry arms, lovely to look at; but guardians no more, for their prayers, so long effective, were potent no more since God's ear was now cocked to hear the slogans and songs of the marching peoples.

> The Communes are comin', oho, oho,
> The Communes are comin', oho, oho.
> Who still are asleep, let them lep outa bed,
> An' run to catch up with the columns ahead,
> There's the richest of wine an' the whitest of bread,
> For the Communes are comin', oho, oho!

The Communes are comin', and the Big Houses are in the way of their march. The Big Houses must go with the times. The People are debouching from the public roads into private property; the vassals and serfs are clattering into the marble halls; plucking flowers from elaborate gardens to put into vases of their own; writing their common names in the big Visitors' Book on the big mahogany table in the big manor hall: Tom, Dick, and Harry, Annie and Sue. A miner sits on a gilded chair; a cotton-spinner plays boogie-woogie on the grand piano, prelude to Beethoven's Symphony in C or Mozart's Clarinet Concerto in A major. Clap your hands over your ears. What was a feast is becoming a famine; what was a famine is becoming a feast. All heraldry, simple, quartered, or cross-quartered, has merged itself into one field of crimson, and has become a red flag. A new age is here. Christ stepping down from a spurious kingship has become a carpenter again. God save you merry, working men, let nothing you dismay. Rejoice and be glad that this day is our day; this year, our year; the future is ours for ever.

And Mount Stewart was one of the Big Houses forced to flee the new and robust life. They were the triumphs of vast wealth and withering poverty. Then, all the wealth was gathered in by the few and the only wealth the worker had was the spittle he spat on his hands to give him a firmer grip of spade or hoe. Mount a hill and look around and fail to see where Mount Stewart ended. Here were meadow and farm, orchard and garden, majestic trees and thick-set shrubbery; lowing of cattle, bleating of sheep, neighing of horses, high-stepping animals as handsomely endowed as the family that owned them; and a mighty wolf-dog cantering from hillock to valley, through the gardens, into the big house one way in and out of it another; massive in body and so gentle in manner; a shaggy beauty that sometimes tempered man's nobility to a seemlier modesty. Here were flowers from many families; roses that one would wish could turn to marble and stay for ever; many flowers Sean knew well already, and many more he met for the first time, never to learn their names; antirrhinums, mazed with their own colouring, defending the house from evil spirits; purple and crimson fuchsias that would make gorgeous fringes for a high-priest's fullest vestments; all the browns and yellows of France's marigolds and England's too; begonias in great masses, decking the ground with pink, orange, and crimson rugs, looking like magic carpets of the East that had grown tired of sky-travelling, and were having a rest on the duller earth, their elephant-like ears ribbed through the green with the colours of the flowers themselves. The spacious gardens were packed with a chorus of blossoms that found no place for the gentle murmur of the primrose, which, earlier on, had clothed the hedge and bank with a carelessly thrown-on yellow gown of spring; and in the garden's centre, a great gathering of crimson flowers formed the firm red hand of Ulster, defiant and sullen, but looking pathetic in its glowing loneliness. Rich dark-yellow apricots dangled in hundreds from the sunnier walls of the big house; apricots

> which, like unruly children, make their sire
> Stoop with oppression of their prodigal weight;

apricots so luscious that their delicate savour would make any Duchess of Malfi sigh for a helping of the dangling fruit. Farther on, long and deep thickets of hydrangeas bordered the Lough, the blue of their blossoms echoing the blue of the sky above them, while on a paved courtyard, in huge green-painted tubs, orange trees grew with fruit the Irish sun couldn't coax to a size much bigger than a crab-apple, but whose tiny golden globes gave a twinkle to the bitterness of the black north. Not so bitter either, for the north was bitter only when the north wind blew. The whins could be golden in Ulster, and the hawthorn blossom heavy; the thrush's song could be merry and the blackbird's could be loud, and purple heather could clothe a clumsy hill with cloth of glory, each tiny bell of the mass formation offering a fairy flagon of honey for the prodding bee; ay, and more, for Alfred, the Saxon King of Northumbria, said of Ulster,

> I found in Ulster, from hill to glen,
> Hardy warriors, resolute men:
> Beauty that bloomed when youth was gone,
> And strength transmitted from sire to son.

But protestant Ulstermen have failed to fuse the past with the present. As soon as they are out of earshot of the hammering of the shipyards, the rhythmic clacking of the spinning-mills, or away from the sowing and reaping of the fields, they see the cannon-smoke and hear the musket-shots of Boyne's

battle. The god-confident protestant David is always going
forth to fight boastful catholic Goliath, and, indeed, the wee
sling and a few wee stones are part of the rites used in initiat-
ing a newcomer into the Orange Order.

Down to the south lies the spot where St Patrick is said to lie
buried, and, a little to the north, is Saul, where, it is said, he
said his first official Mass in Ireland – two sacred places that
no one cares a damn about, though one might think that many
a miracle would be hopping round here quietly. France's
Bernadette and Italy's Anthony are honoured more by the
Irish than their own St Patrick. His grave is said to be covered
with bramble and briar by any occasional traveller accidentally
coming to it; and hardly a hand in Ulster, or in any of the
other three beautifields of Ireland, has ever planted as much as
a primrose on the spot where Patrick's buried. No one goes
near it, though thousands parade to the grave of Wolfe Tone;
and Downpatrick is better known as the place that saw the
hanging of *The Man from God Knows Where*, rather than the
burial-place of the land's apostle. The whole county reeks of
ecclesiological memories that have been long forgotten. The
town of Newry in the twelfth century saw a horde of kings and
chiefs giving a charter to the Cistercians by which they got
half the county from the king, McLoughlin, as his own proper
gift for the health of his soul, and that he might be partaker of
the benefits of masses, hours, and prayers that were to be
offered in the monastery till the end of time. The end of time
came quicker than they then thought; but the gifts made a long
list of the people's lands and their riches to the holy brother-
hood: the lands of O'Cormac with its lands, woods, and
waters; Enachratha with its lands, woods, and waters; Crum-
gleann with its lands, woods, and waters; Caselanagan with its
lands, woods, and waters; Lisinelle, Croa Druimfornact, Letri,
Corcrach, Fidglassayn, Tirmorgonnean, Connocul, and many
more places with all their lands, woods, waters went away
from the people to the monks in honour of the Blessed Virgin,
St Patrick, and St Benedict, given by the King of all Ireland,
who also said that with the lands he threw in the mills as well;
and added pointedly, I WILL also that, as the kings of Iveagh
and of Oriel may wish to confer certain lands upon the
Monastery, for the health of their souls, they may do so in my
lifetime, that I may know what and how much of my Earthly

Kingdom the King of Heaven may possess for the use of his poor monks; while Giolla MacLiag, Archbishop of Armagh, with the *Staff of Jesus in his hand*, which was the Crozier of St Patrick, nodded approbation, with a pleased grin on his gob; and all the nobles, with their tongues in their cheeks, of Dufferin, Racavan, Lecale, Donnegor, Kinnelaerty, and others, signed the assessment, or clapped their hands, and cursed silently and severely the circumstances that had made them give up so much of what they wanted to hold; Giolla Odar O'Casey, the Abbot of Downpatrick, gave a congratulatory blessing to those who had provided such a nice and decent chance for God to get up early to enjoy the freshness of a morning, or walk about at his ease in the cool of the evening through the lands and the woods and by the waters that a holy king had given to the poor monks. Not a damn word about the poor people.

Where are all these lads, so manly, so imposing centuries ago? Gone. Even the dust they became has vanished from the sight of men. Basil Brooke is now, not only chief of Down, but lord of Ulster, co-adjutor with Churchill and Atlee in the affairs of the Realm.

Where now are Cuchullan and his brothers of the Red Branch? Gone, too; gone into dust ages ago. Not altogether gone to dust: their heroism is told still, and their great names are listed in a lot of memories, though the clang of their bronze chariots galloping by has gone into the clang of the hammers in Belfast shipyards; the handsome women in the sunny place of the clan's household, busy embroidering, turning the spinning-wheel, are changed to the clacking of the spindles in the many-windowed mill; and all is embossed, all is ordered by the blustering brilliance of the orange lily. But these in the mills and those in the shipyards are the clansmen and clanswomen of Lecale, of Iveagh, and of Oriel, as Irish as the O'Casey, Abbot of Downpatrick, or as the O'Loughlin, Archbishop of Armagh, with a grin on his gob as the woods, the lands, and the waters of the people passed away to the monks. And clans of mill and shipyard will have their own again.

Now a cry has gone forth to save the broken turrets of the Big Houses, restore the towers that are dropping their stones, replace the wide gates that are hanging loose, scrape away the damp mosses clinging to the weakening walls, and give back a lacquered life to the gentry who live in them. Let them become the pensioners of the State; tax the workers so that the gentry may be there for the workers to go and see how they live; and come away civilized. Many of them have been gracious and charming, but these are but the glittering scales of civilization, easily scraped away. Civilization goes far deeper down than either grace, or charm, or big house. There isn't much in the well-made silken gown or well-pressed suit, the stately walk, or the delicate handling of silver spoon and costly cup and saucer. Easy to be charming, even to be courageous, where these are plentiful; but their charm cannot come near the dignity and the courage so often found with the earthern floor, the vulgar earthenware, and the ragged skirt and trousers. 'A building', says an architects' Journal, 'is part of a way of living.' A building to the many is a home, and a home is more than a part of a way of living; and it is these buildings called homes that must be made gracious, comfortable, and enduring. Apart from these homes, the public buildings, the school, the factory, the hospital, the store, the theatre, and the church, owned by all, used by all, will manifest the temporal and spiritual march of the people, all participating in design and form of the newer shape of civilization; each national community preserving in them the essences of their own racial utterances in art, from the pile-dwelling days to the day of the steel-boned building, the jet-plane, the motor-car and motor-coach.

The revolt against the Big Houses has come even into the hearts and minds of the younger members of the grandee families. Those who have any outlook on life, any intelligence, no longer want to breakfast in a room big as a concert hall; no longer want to be ruled by a string of servants; no longer wish to sup soup from a golden plate; no longer desire the many inconveniences of being chained to a big estate. When life began to answer them back, and they couldn't give a clear account of why they lived in this burdensome way, they began to look like things lost in a museum; the house and the things in the house themselves had become objects of a life that had passed away for ever: there was to them a touch of ridicule, with aspect laughingly pathetic, like a sedan chair borne seriously round Oxford Circus, or a hansom cab tinkling through the streets of New York city. Gone and almost forgotten, too.

And what was under, always under, this graciousness and

charm, seeding and fruiting in the Big Houses of the land?
The very commonplace things of worldly goods and worldly
power. The first anxiety of the gracious charm of the Lords of
the State was, as Dickens says, 'the safety of the preserves of
the loaves and fishes'. With all their grandeur flaming, the
elegant crowd were out after, as they had to be, as the workers
were, their 'bread and cheese'. 'Not heaven or any of its delights were the incentives of the peasants of the Middle Ages,
but, as always and everywhere, for a sufficiency of bread and
cheese', says Coulton, in his *Five Centuries of Religion*: and
in all the manorial houses the richly-dressed, stately-mannered
persons were after the same lowly fare, though disguised and
garnished under ornate dish, soup-tureen, and sauce-boat. And
what a base of misery kept up this lacquered superstructure of
charm and graciousness! The misery of millions in every land,
of black and white men moaning. Sean had seen much of it
himself in Ireland, though the worst of the evil had been then
broken by the people, headed by the noble-hearted leader, himself a landlord, Charles Stewart Parnell. Misery conjured up
among the millions was everywhere, in every land. One of
their own class, General Gordon, of a great Scots clan, one of
whose ladies gave an immortal regiment to the British Nation,
says of the robbery of Egypt by the English rich, 'Duke of This
wants steamer – say six hundred pounds; Duke of That wants
house, etc; all the time the poor people are ground down to get
money for all this. If God wills, I will shake all this in some
way not clear to me now.' And again, 'They weigh the actions
of ignorant natives, Zulus, Kaffirs, and Pondos, after one and
their own code, they act towards the natives after the native
code, which recognizes the right of the stronger to pillage a
neighbour. Oh! I am sick of these people. It is they, and not
the blacks, who need civilization!' A rather shocking indictment of the charming lords and ladies who poised those
charms on the heads of poor people, black and white. 'Punish
the natives if they don't act in the most civilized manner, but if
it comes to a question of our action, then follow the custom of
the natives – viz, recognize plunder as no offence whatever.'
Gordon's actual words. Is this the reason why Gordon's name
is never mentioned? Was this why he was left alone to disappear from life in faraway Khartoum? Do the charming
ladies and gentlemen recognize themselves in this mirror held

up in the hand of Gordon? No, of course not; why should they? If they do, they swiftly turn their faces to a curtained glass. But the natives are recognizing them for what they are – from China to Peru. And not only black men, for Gordon asserts that few anywhere suffer the conditions endured by the Irish peasants. So shocking were the sights he saw there, that he drew up a plan for compulsory purchase of the land from the landlords, warning the Government that 'no half-measured Acts which left the landlords with any say to the tenantry of these portions of Ireland will be of any use, for the state of our fellow countrymen in Ireland is worse than that of any people in the world, let alone Europe'. And General Sir William Butler adds, 'These were terrible words, coming from such an authority, coming from one whose knowledge of human misery was unquestionably greater than that of any living man, but they fell on ears that wouldn't listen'. The gracious ones, the charming ones wouldn't listen; and didn't listen till they were made to listen. And as it was in Ireland, so it is every-where else: the charming ones, the gracious ones won't listen till they are made to listen. To preserve all they have they would be content to make of the world a commonwealth of woe. But not all then; not all now: Shaftesbury is a name worthy of a place on a people's banner when the children march; Disraeli, for all his hatred of Ireland, thought of the people; and Gordon; and now there are young and warm-hearted Tories asking why so many should have so little, so few so much.

But now these selfish ones are being challenged as never before; by those who have never gone to Lyonesse, but who have magic in their eyes; by a truth far greater than any share of truth they may have had in the beginning; by a dignity no less than theirs; by a kindliness that makes each man and woman, through labour, a golden digit in the sum of man. Jesus of the life that rayed out courage and new thought, gal-lant Mahommed, pensive and holy Buddha, help us to skip aside from the danger of having too much!

Sean himself belonged to the generation that had looked up to class privilege as God-begotten in a natural law, ordained to stay put for ever; honoured and almost worshipped by the quiet people. The rich and noble lay safe in the sweet shade of the green bushes, fed and attended by their true love, the quiet people. But they have lost their love. So confident beside the green bushes they never saw, never felt, her go, and woke up one morning to find the dear one gone.

When he came there, and found that his true love was gone,
He stood like a lambkin that was all quite forlorn;
She's gone with some other, and forsaken me,
So adieu the green bushes for ever, said he.

But now Sean had to turn aside from higher thoughts, and bend low over his own affairs (how quick the austere mind lands down on a lower level when faced with need of bread and cheese!). The last penny was leaving the bank, and he had nothing now. Lord and Lady Londonderry had generously given a guarantee to Sean's bank on his behalf for two hundred pounds to let him go to America with an easy mind. Nothing was given out on the guarantee, for Sean began to get American largesse in the shape of royalties before Eileen had parted with the last of her fifteen pounds; but that fact took nothing away from the kindness of his two friends. Indeed, it might well have been that when they gave the guarantee, they bid goodbye to the sum it guaranteed, for things of this sort are often quickly used, and as quickly forgotten by those who have benefited by them.

Goodbye to the Keltic saints reposing so snug in their pretty summer-houses; to the ripening peaches on their sunny wall; to the Red Hand of scarlet flowers in the garden's centre; goodbye to his generous Irish friends; goodbye to the serene face of Strangford Lough, for he was off to Philadelphia in the morning. The people of America held his destiny tight in their hands. If they failed him, he was a goner. They needed bread and cheese, too; but if they didn't give him, Eileen, and the baby she was soon to have, a share of what they had, he, Eileen, the boy, and the baby would be goners go bragh. The Americans had to work themselves for their bread and cheese, and he couldn't expect them to weep or work for him; yet his one hope now was that America might stretch out a helping hand to an O'Casey. America's busy, teeming, intricate whirl – shut not your doors to him. A penny for the young guy.

SHIP IN FULL SAIL

BOUND for New York, for the Manhattan of Whitman! A huge ship, unwieldy-looking, seeming too massive to move, rising up from the Mersey like a futuristic town, with her short masts – really derricks – her big-bellied funnels, wider than many of the English roads to take buses and lorries along, her sides peppered with port-holes; the whole aspect of her shouted to all who looked that she had a mighty confidence in herself, her broad sides and sturdy bow asking what wave on God's ocean could topple her over. Like the world at large, she was divided into classes – steerage, tourist class, and cabin-passengers. The last – which shall be first – had two decks to themselves on which to promenade and play; the tourist class had more than half of a deck below, and the steerage had the bit that remained. Yet the steerage travellers numbered a huddled hundred to each of the other's ten; so, even here, passengers were divided into the nice sheep, rougher sheep, and the goats. The white-coated stewards, dashing about with the smoothing-iron, were running up and down the gangways, silent, in rubber-soled feet, settling the passengers into their cabins, thinking out the tips they'd get at the journey's end. Sean had been warned that the chief steward must get two guineas, his own steward a pound, the waiter at his table another one, with other tips, suiting the amount of work done, to him who provided a deck-chair, to him who handed out books from the library, to the barman who served the drinks, and to the quartermaster supervising the deck-sports. It seemed to Sean that he should have taken the fifteen pounds and left the five with Eileen. No deck-chair, no book, no drink for him; nothing beyond the bare necessaries bringing him safe to New York City. He must have been the poorest cabin-passenger that had ever set foot on a White Star liner. A record established, never to be broken. He was amazed at the quantity of luggage brought aboard by the passengers; some had a ton of it. The men dressed differently six times a day, and the women seven

times, or more. A friendly steward showed him the cabin of a
couple when they were rushing around in shorts on the sports-
deck, playing deck-tennis: clothes were flung about everywhere, across chairs, on the floor, over the beds; good clothes,
too, much of them costly, flung about like litter left behind on
a camping field. Enough of it to clothe a slum family for years.
These self-busy ones never asked a single question about the
stuff in the steerage; never once thought of them. Occasionally, a few cabin-passengers stared down at the deck where the
tourist class paraded the limited space provided, but none gave
the tribute of a look to where the steerage mammals prowled
about their closely caged-in quarters: they were but part of the
cargo.

The stewards slipped along the corridors in their snow-white
jackets and black trousers, half ghosts, half men, hiding themselves under the passengers' orders, rarely giving themselves a
glimpse of the sea, inhaling the testy smell of the cabins from
port to port, answering all questions, asking none, linked to
the bodies of the passengers but not to their souls; their whole
life upon the ship the waiting upon a wish. Once only had
Sean caught a steward looking over the ship's side at the swell
of a subsiding gale, and heard him say, with a shudder, Deep
troughs, sir; must be thirty feet down; seem to want to coax a
man down to them; and shuddering again, slide through a
doorway back into the ship to be safe with the will of the
passengers. The friendly steward brought Sean stealthily down
to their quarters, down very low in the ship's belly, where the
top of the ocean was but a foot or two below the lower rim of
the port-hole, so that, even in a light swell, the port-hole had to
be closed, or the sea would come pouring in on top of them;
almost airless, too, with tiers of bunks leaving but a head's
space in which to preen themselves into the natty, white-coated
figures one saw gliding around the ship.

The liner made a curving cut up Cork Harbour, going slow,
for there were shallow banks on either side that might ground
the big ship. Sean looked about for Spike Island, where John
Mitchel had been as a treason-felony prisoner on his way to
the convict settlement of Bermuda, and where he had met the
gentle, scholarly Edward Walsh who taught the convicts. Walsh
was a harper and a Gaelic scholar wasting his sensitive life
away teaching the convicts how to add two and two together,

his golden hair grey, his beloved harp dusty, his heart hanging hazily on to life, working that he might have bread and water with a taste of meat on Sunday. Out came the tender carrying another crowd away from the western holy land to The New Island, as the United States was called by the Gaelic speakers. They streamed into the ship, and but two, who were priests, came to the cabin-class passengers; the rest were lost, a few to the tourist class and a crowd to the steerage. Away round the cliffs of Kerry to Galway for another crowd, a 'great port' which the people had made with their own hands out of their pipe-dreams. It was dark night now, and the tender came with a green light and a red light sparkling on port and starboard. Again the gangway fell; Galway passengers came aboard, three priests, a bishop, and a solicitor to join the cabin-passengers, a few others joining the tourists, and the crowd again pouring into the steerage. All the descendants of the clans were streaming like silent sheep into the steerage of the White Star liner.

> Goodbye, acushla, goodbye, me darlin',
> I can no longer stay.
> The good ship she is waitin',
>   Grief must be abatin';
> Goodbye, me darlin',
> I'm off for Amerikay!

American soil is rich with the dust of the descendants of Irish king, chief, tanist, poet, bard, and artificer. Many and many a son of Conn, and many a blue eye of Clan Colman, lie deep in the earth of New York, of Indiana, Butte of Montana, and Texas in the deeper south; forgotten. And more go freely. Let the singers who stay chant how they may about the lure of Ireland, the brown of the bog, purple of heather, blue of lake, red of fuchsia, white of lily, the gold of the whins; the goers will go timidly or go galloping to where they think the corn to be nearer to the groping hand. The few among the tourist class, the fewer among the cabin-passengers, may return; but the ones in the steerage have muttered a kiss-me-arse goodbye to Banba of the Streams.

Flying from history, too; from fine history lapping Ireland round in greatness, with many a remembrance giving glory even to that which has none; glory not needed with Burren of the kings, Tir Fhiachrach Aidhne; Gaura in Meath, where Oscar fell and the Fianna were broken; the cromlech covering Aideen's grave, Oscar's sweetheart, on the head of Howth; Tara and Emain Macha, and Cong where Ireland's last king lies stretched;

> *Peace and holy gloom possess him,*
> *Last of Gaelic monarchs of the Gael,*
> *Slumbering by the young, eternal*
> *River-voices of the western vale.*

And what is Rory O'Connor, dead these many hundred years, to those hurrying into the steerage, or to the better places of the ship; what is he to them, or they to him? Nothing.

> *Clear as air, the western waters*
> *Evermore their sweet, unchanging song*
> *Murmur in their stony channels*
> *Round O'Connor's sepulchre in Cong.*

Galway itself, while stout William of Orange, helped by his stouter officers, was shoving Ireland into England's bag, sheltered the Irish Tirconnell and the French Lauzun who had fled from Limerick, laughing at Sarsfield when he said he would hold the town; Lauzun telling him the town walls could be battered down with roasted apples. There, shrunken into saviours of themselves, glittering in their rich uniforms, they paddled in the sea when the sun shone, and played bagatelle when the rain fell; while Sarsfield fought with the men, the women, and the children of Limerick; fought so heartily that William was thrust back, who, disillusioned, packed his troubles in his new kit-bag, and returned to England, leaving General Ginkel to carry on, which he did, right worthily, by packing up too, and getting as far away as he could from Limerick, while Lauzun and Tirconnell paddled away in the sea round Galway. So, signs of Irish regard for Sarsfield's gallantry, Patrick became a common name for the boys born in Ireland from that day forth. But Churchill, later Marlborough, greatest grandfather of the present one, battered down the walls of Cork, and took the city, forcing the Irish to abandon the fight for the Stuart King, who left them to recover from the war in the worst way they could. Christ, Ireland has had a rough time with God and Man!

The big ship swung round, and set her course for Boston, in a calm sea, with the Aran Islands fading away into dark dots, then vanishing from ken, leaving the men of Aran behind among their tiny homes, their patient cattle, their pitiful potato patches made from handfuls of earth pilfered from grasping crevices in the brine-soaked rocks and from kelp gathered dripping from the sea, and carried home on their backs to fertilize futility – a suitable life of austerity for the workers in the heaven-loved Aran of the saints.

The passengers settled down, some to play .shuffle-board, some deck-tennis, others parading round the promenade deck and around, at a great pace, while the crowd stretched themselves stiff on to deck-couches, covering themselves with thick rugs, so that the ship seemed to be on the way to Lourdes:

> There they lay all the day
> On the broad Atlantic low;
> Long they pray – keep thy sway
> Gentle, mighty ocean O!

On the first evening of the voyage, the chief steward had asked Sean if he would like to have his meals at a table presided over by an officer, or would he prefer a place less conspicuous, and Sean had bewildered the steward by asking him if he could have them with the crew. Less than a hundred miles from the Irish coast, the sky darkened and the wind blew, setting the ship to a jauntier motion on the sea's surface. Sean noticed the crew taking things from the main deck, tarpaulining the hatches, and fastening loose things firmly. There was a scurrying among the ones reclining, who flung their rugs away, and hurried off to their cabins, and the hardier promenaders walked the deck no more. Sean found that but he, a priest, and a ship's officer remained on deck watching the rise of the sea and listening to the gathering howl of the wind. The deck he stood on was forty feet above the sea, and was surrounded by thick glass so that the wind gave no feeling of its strength, the breaking sea not strong enough to smash the glass, so he could face it all, and enjoy it all, with acclamation at the wonder of its fierceness. As far as the eye could reach, wave after wave, in close battalions, came rushing towards the ship, the waves following those about to strike her pushing the ones in front, as if in a desperate hurry to strike the ship themselves. The cleaving prow of the huge vessel cut through the surge of the piled-up mass of agitated waters, which, after a ponderous pause, roared over the deck, everything on it disappearing under the swell of the green-and-white tumble of waters, so that Sean seemed to be standing in a glass-house tossed about in a surging greenery of waves, the tops of them shattering asunder to slash viciously against the thick glass through which Sean looked, often now but a screen of streaming water between him and the tumult outside. Then, as the stream rushed its hasty way down the glass, and vision came again, he saw the deck below buried under a passionate surge of wave for a few moments, till the ship rose out of the trough, and the waters poured away through the scuppers down to the leaping sea again.

Hour after hour, Sean watched the waves and listened to the wind, feeling a thrill whenever a mountainous wave rose up level with the upper deck, poised itself for a moment, and then fell, like fronds of a horrifying fern, in a downfall on the main deck, hiding everything below from all watching eyes under a tumbling millrace of wriggling, rushing, greenwide waters.

What crowds of glimmering ghosts floated aimlessly about underneath all these waters, from the years of the famine to years of the First World War! How many of the Irish, fleeing the famine in the coffin-ships, fell into their keen, cold, undulating grip, and found their never-ending silence there! Swing him over the gunnel – one, two, three, while some storm-along tried to mutter a prayer he couldn't remember. Now! And down went McGinty to the bottom of the sea. Many an old man, old woman, chattering child; many a lusty youth, handsome maiden went down engulfed in the proud, pouring toss of the billows. Billows? Somewhere in a letter, the fine poet, W. B. Yeats, rebukes a poet for calling a wave a billow, adding the news that another fine poet, T. S. Eliot, wouldn't permit the word billow to enter *The Criterion* for fear of smearing its odorous and austere integrity. But these seething masses of waters, rearing up, with menace in their aspect, before they came tumbling down on the quivering ship, were more than mere waves. These bulging breasts of sea, gigantic and fierce, as the eye searched into their smothering depths, made the nerves thrill and the body shudder, for in them was no rest, even for the tossed-down dead. Each oncoming mass had in itself its own half-hidden tempest. It was within these sly, green billows that many a soul went tumbling, scrambling down through the fierce ebb and flow and sway of the deep green sea. Many a lass whose name was Mary; many a blue-eyed Irish boy; many a Nora creena, many a larboard watch ahoy. Many a frantic lad saw, for the last time, his true-love's gasping, last farewell: Adieu! she cried, and waved her lily hand. Sean could see sweet faces, fair forms lunging round, helpless in the swelling sway of the tumbling sea: Propertius' Cynthia; Yeats' Dectora, sadly mingling with the common ones outside the longing, lasting memory of verse.

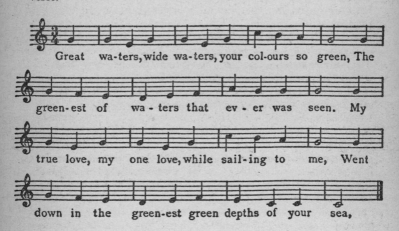

Great wa-ters, wide wa-ters, your col-ours so green, The
green-est of wa-ters that ev-er was seen. My
true love, my one love, while sail-ing to me, Went
down in the green-est green depths of your sea,

I'm coming, quite fast, on a ship sailing south,
To print all my love with a kiss on your mouth,
She murmur'd; I heard her, and waited in glee;
But the ship and my true love sank in the green sea.

She lies fathoms down, lapp'd in mother-o'-pearl,
Lies quiet that once was my high-hearted girl;
And over her all the wide, green billows roll,
Chanting a green keen for her sea-shrouded soul.

Sean noticed a heavy iron door, grimly bolted and locked, in one of the lobbies. A door leading to the steerage, through which cabin-passengers weren't allowed to pass, though Sean saw none making an effort to try. He did; a steward left it open for him, and down he went, like another Dante touring Inferno, with the circles growing hotter as he descended. Down to the steerage. The corridors were crowded, the little lounge was packed. The throb of the engines here was palpable, pant pant pant, and the place quivered with their movements. No privacy here, no room to stretch away a bit of boredom. Here were Galway, Mayo, Roscommon, Cork, and Tipperary, standing, squatting in the stairs, crouching on the floors, wedged together, while Sean, crouched on the floor, too, talked to some of them. Sean surmised the many miseries that must have fruited here while the storm was on; and no priest from the cabin-passengers came here to share the discomforts of this part of their flock. No; comfort was the priests' guardian angel, poker their amusement. Squeeze people closer, cram them together, make a herd of them, so that neither soul nor body has room, and then bellow about the sacred rights of the individual!

Along the coast of Newfoundland through a thick fog the ship crawled, with Sean on the deck all night, listening to a sailor calling out the soundings, while an officer took them down in a log-book, the siren shrilling shudders through Sean at regular intervals. The passengers, paralysed by the storm, slept peacefully through the dangers of the fog, unafraid of a greater danger. Sean, chilled to the bone, remained throughout the night ready to leap for his life-belt if any crash came; for he could see the officer was anxious, even telling him that a captain sleeps neither long nor well when there's a fog round his ship. Slow, slow through the fog the ship crawled, breaking out at last into a dreamy sky of slowly-drifting clouds, and the steady sea was dotted with boats, some puffing steam from them, others spreading a wide sail. The passengers came pouring out from the saloon, hurrying over to the gunnels to peer away into the misty distance.

—There she is, said a puffed-out man, staring through a pair of binoculars; there she is, at last, stout and taut as ever.

—What is it? ventured Sean; what do you see?

—Statue of Liberty, said the puffed-out man.

America's Lady of the Lamp. He couldn't see her, but he
knew the golden words she nourished on her lap:

> *Give me your tired, your poor,*
> *Your huddled masses yearning to breathe free,*
> *The wretched refuse of your teeming shore.*
> *Send these, the homeless, tempest-tossed to me:*
> *I lift my lamp beside the golden door.*

Little sparkle in the words now; well worn and nearly
rubbed away; the refugees musta worn their welcome out.
America now had huddled masses and homeless of her own,
and there were a lot more than a hundred most deserving cases
of poverty in the United States; thousands of very poor, unhappy souls. The words on Miss Liberty's apron had lost their
meaning. But wait a minute, think a little, boy. Wasn't he, in a
lot of ways, a refugee himself, coming to the United States out
of necessity rather than out of love? He was already half
homeless, and would be homeless altogether, if he didn't succeed in getting American dollars to carry home with him.
There was no denying of it. Like a budding hero, he carried a
drama with him as a banner, hoping to astonish the Americans with a work of art; but down in his heart he knew he was
here to collect funds. He was a refugee, for Ireland had cast
him forth, England couldn't afford to keep him, so he depended on America now to provide him with a sufficiency to
keep him and his family for another year or two. An unpleasant fact, but a solid, sober one.

Sweet Miss Liberty, Belle of New York, and Man of Manhattan, hear my prayer, and let my cry come unto ye!

A new land, honoured nowhere with a Greek temple or a
Roman road; no medieval monastery showing itself off as a
tasty heap of ruins; no Norman castle to let us fancy seeing
bowmen from the walls shooting arrows into the bowels of
people living round it; no Ides of March, or anything else like
them, to remember. Here, instead, were the cloisters of Emerson, the limitless habitat of Walt Whitman, the battlefields of
Washington, and the rush and rendezvous of modern mechan-
ics; all the lure of freshness and of power. They were enough,
and had in them many miracles for the future.

He would meet new people, and see new things. He would

see the Hudson River, Grant's tomb, Bunker's Hill, maybe, and Brooklyn, the camp of the dead brigade; for the first time he would set a foot on foreign soil, though for him no land was a foreign one, since all were peopled by the same human family. But it was like the squirrel meeting the mountain, and having words with him. Well, if a squirrel couldn't carry forests on his back, neither could the mountain crack a nut.

IN NEW YORK NOW

As the great ship was being tugged to the dockside, Sean felt so agitated by what was before him and what he had left behind him, that he was a little giddy, and his heart beat so that he pressed a hand to his side to steady it. Here he was on the fringe of New York with but a few pounds in his pocket, while Eileen at home, expecting a baby in two months' time, was moving to Battersea with fewer pounds in her pocket, if there were any left there now. He was about to descend on to the land of Babbitt, the go-getter, land of the rush and roar of business, with a gangster at the corner of every street, according to the films. He had read a volume of Mencken's *Americana*, and knew there were strange men and things north and south of the Mason–Dixon line; but he knew, too, that there were odd men and things east and west of the place where the River Shannon flows; so Americana didn't frighten him.

But he felt very lonely. In spite of the close connexions between the USA and Eire, he knew little about the fullness of American life. He knew why the Flag had its stars and its stripes; knew some of her past; had heard of the Pilgrims, of the Covered Wagon, the Ride of Paul Revere, of Pocahontas, of Johnny Appleseed, and of Daniel Boone; and, of course, he had read of the last stand made by General Custer. He knew something of Washington and a lot about Stonewall Jackson, whose Life he had read, for his admiration had first gone to the South for no other reason than that John Mitchel, the Irish rebel, had stood by the men in grey, and had sent his sons to battle for them. He had been suckled on American culture, for the first fine book from which he had taught himself had been fashioned in New York; an old book, called *The Comprehensive Summary*, for use in American schools, containing flashes from science, mythology, and biography, with paragraphs of history from that of the Medes and Persians, down to Bunker's Hill, Yorktown, and Saratoga; and in its broad bosom lay a fair and full copy of the American Constitution. A kid's book that he had learned by heart, leading him a little way into the past and present knowledge of life; a book he had kept close to him till it had fallen away, page by page, with the dint of use. It had been a godsend. He wondered was there any record, any remembrance even, of it in America today? He would love to hear·it was still alive in some American memory.

He had heard the names of Harvard and Yale, which had but a faraway sound of Oxford and Cambridge. He had read some American literature, past and present, and had contributed a few things to *The American Spectator,* a magazine that had told him there were minds in America that were flushed with courage, with wit, and an unreluctant will to show up political hypocrisy and intellectual sin. He knew something about Nathan's American theatre by what the critic had written about it. It was a brave and dignified theatre. No one was asked, for all its grandeur, to take his shoes from off his feet when entering, nor obliged to genuflect, nor even to salaam; but each had to behave himself. Here thought went back to the past, and here thought stretched forth to the future. Here Edmund Kean and Coquelin had laid different tributes on the same altar, and Shakespeare's and Molière's shadows coloured the glass of the windows gay. Here was heard often the hush of awe, but the hush of awe was always fringed by the silvery bells of laughter, for here the jester laughed beside the man about to die saluting Caesar.

During all his life Sean had spoken to but four Americans – John Anderson, a drama critic, who had come on a visit when on a holiday in Europe; John Tuerk and George Bushar Markell, the two men responsible for putting on his play in New York; and Claire Luce, an actress and a very lovely lass. Going down the gangway, he felt very lonely, not knowing whether he was about to enter an indifferent maw, or going down to rest on a friendly arm. Not for long, though: in the Customs' shed, two men were waiting for him – Dick Madden, Sean's American agent, and George Jean Nathan, the famous drama critic, waiting for him with hands outstretched.

Nathan standing in the huge Customs' shed full of flurried passengers teasing white-coated stewards with anxiety and question, who were busy bearing bundles and cases from the ship to the shed, so that they looked like swarms of varied-coloured fowl cluttering and cackling around white-plumaged cocks, indifferent to their outcry. Here, among the great boxes, the corpulent trunks, the elegant suitcases, among the chattering passengers, the cold-worded Customs Officers, keen in their readiness to poise and pounce, Nathan stood looking at nothing, seeing everything, his luminous, wine-coloured eyes glancing at Sean, to see, maybe, if there was a chance of him being something more than a bore; and Sean thinking what in the name of God he would say to this famous critic now standing before him, a soft slouch hat on his finely formed head, set safely on a thick crop of dark hair, slightly tinged with grey here and there; a greatcoat, so full in the shoulders that it fell round him capewise down below his knees, a curving wrinkle of humour, now in repose, trimming the corners of a full, sensuous, handsome mouth.

Nathan in his cape-coat reminded Sean of Augustus John standing calm in Victoria Station, where Sean had gone to wish the great artist god-speed to France; standing there within a throng of excited passengers running hither and thither, porters hurrying this way, that way, laden with luggage, a slow voice from a loud-speaker directing passengers where they were to go, accompanied by the hissing of steam or the shrill yell from the siren of a train departing: there the painter stood, straight and pensive as if he stood thoughtful beside deep waters of a standing pool, his searching eyes dividing nature's cruder patterns into finer forms, her reckless colours into lovely tones and tints on road, in tree, flower, jug; or in figure at play, resting by a sea, or working close to a caravan. As John stood then, so Nathan stands now, half adream in the agitated crowd; almost motionless, his one wakefulness, maybe, a hope that this O'Casey will be something more than just bearable company, standing there, with the surge of two thousand years of drama forming the kingdom of heaven within him; watching with anchorite concentration, week after week, cascades of theatrical fireworks, pale or brilliant, rising over the New York stage, and breaking out into ephemeral brightness under the battens, watching in the hope that out of the falling, fading lights, a lasting star may at last shine out from the falling dust, and mount higher to hang itself in the heavens.

Beside Nathan stood Dick Madden, handsome, tall, able,

and eager, a pouncer to set any client well before the public *belle vieu*; smartly dressed, and proud to have attached Sean's *Within the Gates* to the great wheel of the theatre, now praying that the play would be a New York hit.

Sean enjoyed himself and Sean saw many things, though his visit to the States was but as a lightning-flash graciously lingering just a few seconds longer. The streets were deep and Dantesque, dizzying the mind when one looked up to the top of the buildings, towering up as if they sought a way to the blue sky and the sun ashine therein; and the whole city in its aspect and its agitated life grew into a rosy, comfortable, and majestic inferno; life so busy and stimulating that all but the sick in soul and very sick in body forgot the time they would come to dust in the cool of the tombs: a grander-patterned background than many of the grand ones Sean had threaded in his hasty way through life.

The wide wonder of Broadway is disconsolate in the daytime; but gaudily glorious at night, with a milling crowd filling sidewalk and roadway, silent, going up, going down, between upstanding banks of brilliant lights, each building braided and embossed with glowing, many-coloured bulbs of man-rayed luminance. A glowing valley of the shadow of life. The strolling crowd went slowly by through the kinematically divine thoroughfare of New York, each of them like as if he were a child in a daydream, wandering, open-eyed, through a city conjured into a gem-encrusted glow by the genie of Aladdin's wonderful lamp. Veneration for the god of the kinema, who, by day, slept under the drabbest coverlet man could make, a naked tangle of wiry web over the doxy-minded god; and, at night, stood up in a robe of scintillating jewels for all to see and to admire. Honolulu, honolulu! Lost Angeles has come to town, and glory whines around. Honolulu! And names of the demi-gods of the films hang in the gigantic glitter, their faces, too, silently calling on the millions to come and splash about into the ecstasy of seeing themselves in the amazing magnified mirror of the lady of shallow, and worship the lord gaud of Sobbaoth.

What is the great crowd seeking, the young, mostly courting couples, prowling so aimlessly, yet so steadily, along the Great White Way? They seek the Muses, though they know it not, for these restive lights are to them

a bank whereon the wild thyme blows,
Where oxlips and the nodding violet grows.

They straggle along seeking beauty which is yet a shrinking
seed within them. They seek for what they know not, though
they feel their need of it, and sometimes sense a twinge of near
arrival within this blaze of bastard culture. Roman catholic and
protestant mingle and mate with the uncomplaining, muted
midgets caught in the glare of the Great White Way, unaware
that outside its dazzling destitution, away in the darkness
ahead, shine faint, enkindling rays from the stars of art,
literature, and science. They have been told and yet they do not
know; for the tale came too late, or it was told too low for
them to catch the whisper. They have had no help to get away
from the fairy tales of infancy, lovely in their day, but turning
slyly silly when men reach the age of misunderstanding. But
many of the common people are now making for something
more than the savage contentment with coloured bead and
strip of coloured calico. They ask for something better than
these things no higher than flimsy rhyme and fainting fairy
tale, without the shrewd jingle of the one or the longing beauty
of the other. Even this gaudiness, blaspheming light, wherein
they wander webbed, is an outward sign of inner seeking all
they feel they need. The people are beginning to realize the
longing for good shaping of things; in the streets they pass
through; in the buildings banking the streets they pass through;
in tablecloth and crockery ware; in the homes they have to
have; in pictures they see, music they hear, the simple vessels
they handle; in all things whatsoever which mingle man with
life: a share in all the greatest the community can imagine, in
all the greatest the community can do.

Many are getting rid of the dismal daydream that the good
in life is something similar to Christmas in Killarney with all
the folks at home. First, they are seeking and fighting to keep
taut and even that umbilical cord stringing all men together –
the bread line. They have long prayed for their bread, now they
fight for it. May Jesus Christ be praised! They are organizing
to alter the mad method of life among them and bring it into
order, as Lycurgus did in Sparta in the old time before them:
'Where the State was overloaded with a multitude of indigent
and necessitous persons, while the whole wealth of the land

had centred upon a few. To the end, therefore, that he might expel from the State luxury and crime, and those yet more inveterate diseases of want and superfluity, he got them to consent to a new division of land, so that they should all live together on an equal footing; merit to be the only road to eminence, and the disgrace of evil, and credit of worthy acts, their one measure of difference between man and man.' There's a lot in this, my people, a lot in it.

Whenever Sean got a chance of sliding aside from a daytime rehearsal, he wandered through the streets of the city, looking up, ahead, behind, left and right, looking everywhere his eyes could go. He thought curiously of the Dublin guttersnipe stitching himself into the gay and hurrying pattern of New York city. A figure with a lean and hungry look threading himself through the streets, so firmly, maybe, that he might be there for ever. Far easier to weave oneself within New York's life than within that of London, for this city's life is too sloven, too outspread, and too voluminous to weave any conforming pattern a human mind could frame; the world-weaving activities here created but a bewildering tangle in London's life. Even the poets and prelates reposing in Westminster Abbey are buried out of sight in the impenetrable, smothering tapestry of London city. So he went around New York watching, wishing he could spend a decade with the life and its background around him. Once, on Thanksgiving Day, he was caught in a great crowd in Times Square that had watched a procession of bands and contingents carrying gigantantic effigies made of blown-out balloons; and this great crowd was now crossing east, crossing west, great flocks of people, whenever the tremendous traffic paused and seemed to present them with a chance of moving. In the street's centre stood a huge policeman shepherding them this way, that way, so that they might go in safety. He was perspiring and impatient, waving the people across with angry gestures. Once, when a flock wanting to cross hesitated to answer his impatient gesture, Sean was astonished to hear his voice roaring out in the rich and lilting accents of an Irish Civic Guard:

—Christ! Are yez goin' to cross over, or are yez goin' to lay down there, an' die!

One thing that struck Sean hard as he scanned the streets, on the level and high up, was the fading away in New York –

more than in other cities, far more than in Moscow – of the
orthodox, institutional conception of the Divine Idea. There
had been too many mitres planted on too many musty heads.
Here, the churches seemed to shrink away into eroding
corners. They seem to have ceased to be essential parts of
American life. They no longer give life. It is the huge buildings
of commerce and trade which now align the people to attention. These in their massive manner of steel and stone say,
Come unto me all ye who labour, and we will give you work.
Work! Labour the *aspergas me* of life; the one great sacra-
ment of humanity from which all other things flow – security,
leisure, joy, art, literature, even divinity itself. Passing through
the bustling streets, it seemed to Sean that the churches
crouched silently into solitude, thrust aside by the bigger buildings, standing erect, monumental pride in their height and
form, coldly ordering any church within their view to Get
away, old woman, you have had the time of your life, and
have no more interest for the beautiful people. No use of you
yelling out now, 'Hello, out there; if your heart's in the lowlands, this is where you will find comfort, sucker, and care';
for the passers-by hear you not, or, if they do, heed you less.

The newcomer to New York City, American or foreigner,
doesn't spend a glance on St John's of Morningside Heights,
or on St Patrick's in Fifth Avenue, or on the Russian Basilica
on Fourth Avenue, or thereabouts; but makes for Rockefeller
Center, where he can get an eyeful worth seeing; he comes to
gape at man's newer magnificence in building, a newer Babel,
significant of order instead of confusion; the fuller fruit of
Stonehenge. New York's mother-church of commerce and
trade, not honoured by the head bending, for here the head
must be thrown back to sink within the cavity between the
shoulder-blades to see its summit. Here the visitors come, here
the visitors go; and even New Yorkers themselves, having seen
the building day after day, still glance up at its wonder as they
hurry by. Many times Sean wandered round it, finding its back
parts as well proportioned as its front face, flashing with the
clean austerity of stone and glass. In the midst of the crowds
going in, coming out, the lifts going up, coming down, the
never-ending groups of sightseers, the building stands aloof, as
chill and as lovely as an Alpine glacier, as sparkling, too, when
the sunshine glints on its glass, imposing a sense of cold awe

on every soul who sees it. There it stands, majestic, with the brassy figure of Prometheus, having snatched fire from heaven, lying at its base, like a tawdry brooch which the building, resenting an attempt to disfigure it, had shaken from its breast to the indifferent pavement below. And Sean sat down on a bench to brood.

He bent his thought on the difference between this strident, confident building and the languorous loveliness of Westminster Abbey, or Salisbury Cathedral that Constable painted from the midst of the luscious meadows around it; built first on a hill, where winds blew constant and boisterous, and the lord of the adjoining castle owned the one well, and charged the clergy so much a bucket for its waters; the wind and the water so plaguing the bishop that he appealed to the Pope, and got leave to change to the valley, where few winds blew and where water was plentiful. As one hefty bishop said to the Chapter's Dean, after they had come down from the windy hill of Old Sarum to the sheltered valley – 'A body would need a brassy bottom to stand the wind there.' A different wind, but a keener one, indifference, blows around their bottoms now. And so the bishop hied him down to where the big cathedral stands today, lingering out a life that the castle had lost centuries ago. There was Salisbury Cathedral, here was Rockefeller Center. Here is life; busy and often very vulgar in its entertainment, thrust out over the people by broadcast, cinema, and theatre; but it is life, and always capable of growth. But death always glosses the cathedral with gloom: the tomb of this bishop or lord, that poet, thon statesman, meet you as you walk the way of the aisle or nave. Sculptured tombs, once gay with armorial colouring and dizened with royal gilt; but with the colours gone now, and the gilt grown rusty. In a book about the Cathedral we are told that: 'Here the first Earl of Salisbury is buried. Here the effigy of the warrior lies wrapped in chain armour, his head exquisitely turned to the right [an earl's head would hardly be turned exquisitely to the left], his left arm bearing his shield, lovely with the six golden leopards of Anjou, his right arm fallen by his side, the heavy armour fallen from it; more wonderful than the life. Nothing in the world is grander or more touching than this exquisite statue; there is nothing in the world to surpass it, and little to equal it.'

More touching! A mother suckling her babe, for one thing,

is far more touching than this memorial to this fellow, probably a bloody ruffian who won his 'golden leopards of Anjou' by slaying as many people as he could. And Angelo's David is a far, far finer figure than this one. Odd how, even in this day, some wanderers through life swoon into a mad praise over chantry, tomb, and cloister. A dead idea that nothing new can be as grand as anything old; souls who live their leisurely dreams, supine, in the 'twilight of grey gothic things', moss-grown and mouse-ridden. Cathedrals in which is shown no tomb of those who built them with their labour, or who furnished the wherewithal to build them in the sweat of their face toiling from sunrise to sunset, their hard lot a massed measure of wealth for lord, lady, abbot, and bishop, to whom, always, the steel tip of a lance was more fervently sweet in the sight of God than the steel tip of the plough. A few shattered pieces of glass, saved from a heap left lying on the ground by the puritan destroying angels, have been gathered into the big west window, and there one can see the shield of Gilbert of Clare (whoever he was) was its three red chevrons on a gold field; and the blue one scattered over with the golden fleurs-de-lis of St Louis of France, the crusader, brother of Henry the Third; and the red one figuring the three golden leopards of Henry the Third himself. Not far away, stretched out stiff, embalmed in marble, lies the giant Cheyney, standard-bearer to the bold Richmond, whom the crooked-back Richard, in the battle of Bosworth, sent spinning from his horse with a thrust from his lance; so that from what can be seen in the windows, on the floor, and all around, one is assured that the kingdumb of heaven admits no one lower than the rank of knight; now, not even knights, for them were the days when knights were bold.

Out in the cloisters the footsteps of Sean and of his younger son rang hollow as they strolled along, while heavy rain fell beyond their shelter, copiously soaking the green of the cloister garth. Here the canons of the Chapter used to seek refreshment, reading their pious books, so that they might be the better able to arrange the life of the world by the method of theological legend and divine myth. Behind them, on the cloister walls, decaying wooden crosses, brought from the graves of Englishmen who fell in the First World War, were hanging dolefully, to associate, in some magic way, the souls of the dead with the reputed holiness of the place. The names and ranks of the fallen were painted on the wooden trinkets of woe: all officers; the graves of the well-known warriors; the rank and file and all that appertaineth to them could go on lying where they first fell. Grey stone, green grass, grey rain, and an old man with a young one walking on the grey-blue pavements of the cloister, some of the slabs covering the long-ago canons of the cathedral. Lonely and slow, the two paced the cloisters, a man of seventy and a lad of fifteen; slow, each thinking his own thoughts. Did the old canons here ever bother to say Anima Christi, sanctifica me. Corpus Christi, Salve me. Sanguis Christi, inebria me? Ignatius Loyola's aspirations – far less musical, less courageous, less penetrating than the Deer's Cry, the appeal put up by whomsoever, under the name of Patrick, went down the slopes of Meath to face the Irish pagans. A lad of fifteen and a man of seventy; the old picturing in his mind the old, forgotten life led here, dead down now; the young lad curious, consciously indifferent, his grade of life separating him for ever from it and casting it away.

And many more, too, of the old and the young. A roman catholic, writing of this cathedral of Salisbury, says: 'On a market day, the city of Salisbury is at its best; but it is curious that the lively English crowd, so cheerful and yet so sober withal, altogether avoids the cathedral, which is then, as always, in its magical if icy silence. In the fifteenth century the cathedral would have been thronged, the shrine of St Osmund all surrounded with worshippers, the lofty nave filled with a multitude that gave it all its meaning. The Wiltshireman does not tread the aisles, he avoids the place, it frightens him. It seems to belong to the gentry, and though the doors stand open wide, never will he enter in.'

Seems, sir? Nay, it does, and always did, belong to the gentry. Though the gentry and the churchmen fought each other, they always united to keep the common people down. How low we've fallen, implies this crier after long-forgotten things; how high, with all our faults, we've risen from it all, thinks Sean in his searching heart. In the heyday of these ecclesiastical activities, how did the Peter the Ploughmen, their wives, and children live? While the lesser sons and daughters of the gentry entered nunnery and monastery to have a good time with wine and women and bawdy song, Peter the Plough-men toiled on ceaselessly, poverty their whole being and

misery their companion, with death and the black plague ply-
ing their bulldozer spades to make graves for tens of thousands
of them within sight of their own poor doorways.

No cathedral equalled this building of New York in its
height, its cool beauty, its significance for the present world –
not even Wren's St Paul's or Angelo's St Peter's. It was the
new displacing the old; the old that had lost its meaning and
its use. Within, it had the means of flooding the people in
stupid song, stupid story. It could send out a message, saying,
over the wireless: 'By the courtesy of the Louisiana loo loo
Motor Corporation, you are about to listen to the Voice of
God'; and then some pip-squeak of a cleric would minimize
God to his own conceit of himself, mangling even the terse
beauty of biblical phrases in a dreadful disdain of the divinity
of man's diction and thought; but, still, through the rowdy con-
ceits of cleric, of crooner, of clown without wit or verve, came
pushing forth the voice of God through the words of eminent
men of science, of drama, and in the sounds of Beethoven's
and Mozart's music.

Sean sat on the bench, and thought how lively, how lovely
the place looked: a warm and brilliant sun shining on the
gigantic façade of the building, turned the glass to gleaming
crystal. Some rectangular pools, curbed by stone, ruffled by
tiny but restive waves, gave out a minor gurgling song; like lily
pools they were, with waters too restive to allow the growth of
the lotus or languorous lily; and a vivid blue sky hung over all
– blue and grey, grey-green and silver, giving a grand picture of
colour and tone to the receptive mind. Secular serenity as serene
as any ecclesiastical church or cathedral. Once, all the stately
buildings in a town were church and monastery; here all the
stately buildings are secular – the Empire State Building, the
Chrysler Building, the Singer Company's Building, and the
railway stations, whose booking-halls are as lofty and fine as a
cathedral nave, and much more useful. It is better so? Are we
brighter, safer, merrier, having wider minds and greater knowledge than we had when the Churches and their Canon Laws
constricted life within the terms of their congealing catechism?
Yes, a lot merrier, safer, having greater knowledge and wider
minds, with an amazing chance of splendid development in the
future. God wants to be with us now.

It is odd – mostly entertained by roman catholic apologists

for their own reasons – how many prate of the days when the Church ruled the roost, as if then all was jollity, sweetness, and effulgent light; whereas, in fact, those days were riddled and ruined with venomous puritanism; hatred of dancing, of music, of painting, of sculpture (except the sculpture of saintly figures and the sculpture of the tomb), and of any natural beauty in woman. Hilaire Belloc in his *Europe and the Faith*, says: 'Two notes mark the thirteenth century for anyone who is acquainted with its building, its letters, and its wars; a note of youth and a note of content'. Again, dealing with the effects of the three hundred years following the Reformation, he says: 'With all these, of course, we have had a universal mark – the progressive extension of despair'. Even the English *Church Times* said a few years ago: 'Medieval spring, summer, and autumn had many delights when the church's holidays were holidays; when the people not only worked hard, but prayed hard, and played hard'. There were, then, says G. G. Coulson, a hundred holydays in the year; on these the people could do no servile work; the landlords, lord and abbot, refused to divide, and so the holydays were dark indeed to the workers. As for 'playing', almost all of it was done under a shower of denunciations from the clerics. St Jerome, with his lion, an authority quoted throughout those times, bawled out against all the frolics and joys that flesh is heir to; and St John of the Cross warned us that 'the spiritual Christian ought to suppress all joy in created things, because it is offensive in the sight of God'. The sea, the rock, tree, fern, and flower, offensive in the sight of God! Oh, lord! But there's worse than these; oh, ay. The whole period's frantic with the abuse of woman, who, to the clerics, was far more dangerous than the American blue-tailed fly. Odo of Cluny, a big-shot Benedictine in those days, says: 'Looka, boys, though girls have no power to add to their looks, they powder and puff and dye their faces, or fiddle their hair into fanciness, give the glad eye, and vary their dress by divers other far-fetched methods; how much better it would be, all this while, if they were intent upon the upkeep of their souls!'

Ha, ha, ladies of *Vogue*, who go contrary, and how does your garden grow? Are you looking after the garden of the body rather than the garden of the soul? Know ye who sit on a cushion and sew a fine seam, and feed upon strawberries, sugar, and cream, that beauty is but skin deep. So says this great Benedictine of Luny, adding that: 'If men could see below the skin, as the lynxes of Boeotia are said to see into the inward parts, then the sight of a woman would be nauseous to them. All that beauty consisteth but in phlegm and blood and humours and gall. If a man considers that which is hidden within the nose, the throat, and the belly, he will find filth everywhere; and, if we cannot bring ourselves, even with the tip of our fingers, to touch dung, wherefore do we desire to embrace this bag of filth?' Why indeed? God only knows. Not a very amiable fellow, this. Yet there is fire in dung, and tremendous energy that gives rich sap to the corn and to the fruit tree. Sean had fearlessly handled it himself in the freeing of choked drains, in the cleansing of septic tanks; and many a delicately-handed surgeon removes rottenness, giving health again to a body racked before with pain and illness. Odo's thought is not a godly, but an inhuman one. Odd that Belloc and Chesterton never seem to have known the sweetness and light of their own authorities. Odo wasn't a bird alone; there were thousands of little Odos saying the same thing. Much better than the man from Luny is Solomon's Song of a lad for his lass and a lass for her lad: 'Thou art all fair, my love; there is no spot in thee. Thy two breasts are like two young roes that are twins, which feed among the lilies.' Or the nursery rhyme of What's a little girl made of, what's a little girl made of? Of sugar and spice and everything nice – that's what a little girl's made of. Poor, pitiable men groan and agree. It seems men can't help hugging them, whether men like it or no. Men are like the hermit student brought up in the desert, who, when he walked to the town with his abbot, and saw women dancing, asked the old man what they were; geese, replied the abbot. When they returned the young hermit fell into a flood of tears, refused to eat, and when asked what can the matter be, what can the matter be, shouted out so that all in the monastery could hear, I want to eat of the geese I saw in the city!

It is laughable to think of Chesterton's or Belloc's vision of medieval days as a happy time of 'Dance, and Provençal song, and sunburnt mirth!' A time of plush and Christian perfume. And how! Even today, in the *Catholic Encyclopaedia*, a writer on dancing is in a funk about what he should say concerning the vicious denunciation of the sport in the meddle ages by the clerics. He hems and haws it off by saying that: 'Undoubtedly, old national dances in which the performers stand apart, hardly, if at all, holding the partner's hand, fall under the ethical censure scarcely more than any other kind of social intercourse'. Hedging. Speak your mind, speak your mind! Come unto these yellow sands, but don't touch hands. Keep your distance, Harry. Don't let trousers touch the skirt, or there might be trouble. This is an Alice, where art thou dance!

> Oh, what shall I do, love, and what shall I say?
> Shall I tumble down flat, shall I hold you at bay?
> I'm frighten'd a lot of that buzzing, big bee
> In your impudent bonnet of bonnie dundee!
>
> I've lost sense of time and I've lost sense of date,
> I can't tell even now if its early or late;
> I'm longing to hug you, while anxious to flee
> From the sight of your bonnet of bonnie dundee!
>
> Be cooler, be calmer – don't clutch me so tight;
> If you want to do things, learn to do the things right.
> Oh, I've tumbl'd; take care – you'll do damage to me,
> With that impudent bonnet of bonnie dundee!

All these old boyos dreaded the dance – St Augustine, Salimbene, Aquinas, even Abelard, and many others. In the *Summa Angelica* rules are laid down for wholesome dancing: No one must dance for a considerable time. The dance must be of an honest kind. The dancer's intention must be good. St Antonino can think up no case where a dance can be free from sin; and G. G. Coulson says Antonino was a good chap, full of the milk of human kindness. 'Chesterton wrote an article in *The Dublin Review*', Coulson goes on, 'defending the attitude of the meddle-ages' clerics on sports, basing his arguments entirely upon a single passage from St Thomas Aquinas, which he has evidently not sufficient Latin to construe correctly. It is odd that the Editor of the *Review* or some theological friend should not have intervened to save him from such a blunder. I have appealed to him in the *Review of the Churches* to name a single orthodox writer from St Thomas Aquinas

to the year eighteen hundred who understood St Thomas
in the sense required by Chesterton's argument; but Chesterton
reserved his defence with a dead and dumb silence.' Even
Sean's own St Patrick's Purgatory gave a friar a vision of 'a
great thick circle of iron set with needle-pointed nails on which
a group danced while a rain of red-hot coals and sulphur fell
on their naked bodies, dragons gnawing at their bowels'.
Happy-minded fellows these, weren't they! Even Petrarch,
even he, immersed in the puritanism of the medieval Church,
denounced dancing too. Even he, a poet! Says he, 'From
dancing we get nothing but a libidinous and empty spectacle,
hateful to honest eyes and unworthy of a man; take lust away,
and you will have removed the dance also'. No

> Swing your Kate, swing your Sue,
> Swing your girl and she'll swing you,

for Petrarch. Apart from one Pope and Bernard – who permitted it on a stout string – and St Francis, who is said to have
loved the troubadours, they all dreaded and denounced dancing. Music, too; oh, yes, music, too, just the same. The medieval clerics couldn't stick it; couldn't stick 'the rush of the
bellows, the clashing of cymbals, and the harmony of the
pipes'. Even were it not Mozart at his best, it must have had
funny moments, and fun didn't glorify God. Surely God must
have been amused; or is it a ukase from the clerics that God
must go without a laugh from one end of eternity to the
other? In one of Dunbar's poems there is the big idea that God
can laugh, for he tells of a gay goodwife's sly slide past Peter
into heaven when Peter's back was turned;

> And God lookéd and saw her lettin in, and laughed his sides
> sore.

Many young girls were amongst those who circled around
Sean, coming to see the great Metropolitan Church of New
York's secular buildings. Many of them were pretty in figure
and face, a number of them delightfully so. In a younger state
of life, if they had let him, Sean would gladly have swung with
any one of them in any round or square-dance, and violently
risked hell as a consequence. As for ugliness under the skin,

man had as much of it as any woman; as Sean's own doctor said once, laughingly, 'We all carry a cesspool about with us wherever we go'. We do that, but we won't despise each other because God has been pleased or contented to make us just in that way. If Church prelates, past or present, had even an inkling of physiology they'd realize that what they term this inner ugliness creates and nourishes the hearing ear, the seeing eye, the active mind, the energetic body of man and woman, in the same way that dirt and dung at the roots give the plant its delicate leaves and its full-blown rose. This outlook on woman, as strong among the clerics of today as it was in the middle ages (unaware of it as he sat on the bench, Sean, because of his play, was to suffer a deluge of it from the clerics a little later on), is just sinisterly silly. The woman, for a start, is half the human race; and a woman's hand, however bawdy in its touch it may sometimes be, can salve a wound, cool a fever, and bring courage again to a disconsolate man. The swish of a skirt in this world is more useful, more encouraging to life than the swish of an angel's wing.

All of these young lassies, passing by, were probably in jobs; working-girls; most of them gracefully dressed, each with a splash of colour on dress or bodice or hat, made brighter by the brilliant sun shining. Colour: a sign of the changing of time. Not now were the workers all dressed in the law-imposed drabness of russet clothing, as in the earlier days, up to, and far beyond the time of England's queen, Elizabeth; when colour was the ornamental benefice of the noble and the gent. In spite of the darkness in America yet; in spite of the poverty there; of the sad things happening in the South; in spite of the deep depression that F. D. Roosevelt and the people were trying to fight away through a fair deal, life was moving in all the forty-eight States of the Union.

The theatre, too; oh, yes, the theatre too: the House of Satan to the clerics. To this day, in his own diocese, no priest is permitted to attend a performance in a theatre. He can go to the kinema as he will to enjoy there the many succulent shows of sex, garnished with tendentious words, and leave the place elated. But the theatre is taboo. A great, if earlier divine, and a powerful preacher, Massillon, says: 'You ask me if theatres are innocent amusements for Christians: In return I have but one question to ask you. Are they the works of Satan or of Jesus Christ? There can be no medium in religion. You have but to decide whether you can connect the glory of Jesus Christ with the pleasures of a theatre. Could Jesus Christ preside in assemblies of sin, where everything we hear weakens his doctrines? Where the poison enters the soul by all the senses. Every Christian should keep away from them.' The theatre is neither the work of Satan nor of Jesus Christ: It is the glorious creation of Man. Does that frighten you? Where have we left to go to? Only the kinema. From the earliest days, up through the monks and friars, down through Gerson and Massillon, and so to the *Roman Catholic Encyclopaedia,* the clerics shake their fists at the tavern, at music, at any fairness in woman, in any brightness they add to their dress, and at the theatre. Are we to live like white bones scattered under a juniper tree, without even the song at or as the white bones sang in Eliot's poem? Shall we close our eyes so that we may not see a lady on a white horse, rings on her fingers and bells on her toes? Shall we close our ears so as to fail to hear the music that follows her wherever she goes? Aw, hell! And Sean rose from the bench and went his way, as the dusk fell and the evening came quick.

On that same calm evening, when the moon rode high, George Jean Nathan guided him towards the one hansom cab left living in the world. There it stood, wisting not of the new world's ways, cab, horse, and driver, embedded in time that had stood still for them; close to the kerb of a sidewalk in a measureless street running past a threatening towering hotel, racing on ahead of life, and pushing its way out of the past of a year ago. There they waited, an *ill penseroso* of forgotten days; jarred in a jellied time within the surrounding epic of living steel, concrete, and stone. A dreaming ghost of Fergus Hume's *Mystery of a Hansom Cab*. The serious critic and the serious dramatist, the man from Indiana and the man from Dublin, climbed into the cab for a jaunt through a park in the moonlight. Away they went through Central Park to the tune of clop-cloppety-clop of the hansom's horse, valiantly keeping his tail up; the beetling buildings surrounding them looking like stony titans watching two of their titan children taking an evening airing in a huge old-fashioned pram with its big hood up like the horsey's tail; the buildings, ebony where the moon-

light shone not, quietly candescent with a primrose silver
shade where the moonlight fell; cloppety-clop now through a
patch of gloom, then through a glade marred delightfully by a
crop of rugged rock spurting up through the delicate grass,
glazed over with soft moonlight and sad, shining like a light
from a lantern carried by a god looking for a lost and lovely
goddess.

The horse, the cab, and the driver sent ghosts of the past
sidling up to Sean; shadows of the time when men's eyes
sought the jutting bustle, and whose ears listened for the frou-
frou of the trailing skirt; when the inverness cape was set on
their shoulders and the double-peaked cap was set on their
heads; when men rode bicycles that could be mounted only if
one had the spring of a leopard; when Madame Patti sang
Home, Sweet Home under the gas-light glitter, and when Sherlock Holmes stole through the streets to solve some mystery;
time of the transformation scene and the harlequinade, of
roses from Picardy, and the Martini-Henry rifle; with two old
children enjoying it all; a joyous jingling hour of life; a big, red
berry on life's tree. A joy-ride: the pair of them were young
again, and heaven was all around them.

WITHIN THE GATES

THERE is nothing in life so dusty and dismal as a curtainless, gaping stage yawning out at those sitting down in front of it, and to those treading about within the poverty of its boastful emptiness, during the harassing transports of a rehearsal. In one of these dark places, within a first-class New York theatre, the rehearsal of *Within the Gates* went on under the guidance of Melville Douglas, a stalwart chap, handsome and able, and, after many struggles, began to show itself off from among the dusty shadows. These times are very harassing to all, but most so to a dramatist whose conscience ranges a little outside of himself and his own interest. He has to think (though he tries not to) of the actors who work so hard for weeks, and yet may walk about idle again, after performing for a few nights, even, maybe, for one night only; and of him who furnishes the money for the play's production, however wealthy the man may be; but especially if the producer be one who has just managed to scrape enough dollars together to lift the play to the stage. Grey hairs grow fast during the rehearsal of a play, brazen with imagination and experiment, on the commercial, or any other kind of stage. And the finer the production the greater the anxiety, for, in a bad production, the dramatist is almost assured from the start that the play will be a failure. So Lillian Gish, Moffat Johnston, and Bramwell Fletcher, with many others, were busy on the play's behalf; went on gaining ground over difficulties, till, at the dress rehearsal, it broke out into an unsteady but glowing cascade of speech, movement, colour, and song. Sean was glad; let it succeed, let it fail; at least the play would justify its full and defiant appearance.

During the whole period between emptiness and dusty posturing, in dull working-kit, to the breaking out of the play into colour and song, there was but one disturbing incident. One day, Moffat Johnston, who was playing the bishop, came to Sean, very worried, to say that the designer had arranged the crucifix he was to wear so that it would dangle, not upon his breast, but at the base of his belly. The amiable actor was very uncomfortable, and many others of the company were distressed, too. Sean assured him that the symbol was meant to hang on the bishop's chest, and there and nowhere else it would be worn. He went to the designer, Irish by descent, and, by all accounts, a roman catholic, and told him so. The designer angrily said he had so designed the symbol to hang between the legs, and there it was to hang, or he'd have nothing more to do with the production. Sean said the symbol would hang in the place where the script had placed it, but he was told that the design was more important than the play; Sean, responding to the angry face glaring at him, said, The play was the living body and soul and the clothes that covered them, while the designing added coloured buttons, braid on the sleeves, and, maybe, epaulettes on the shoulders; but however important and lovely these things might be, and often were, without the play they couldn't be summoned even into existence. The script says the symbol is to hang on the bishop's breast, and there it will lie till the play comes off; and, in a high rage, the designer ran from the theatre, and they saw him no more.

At intervals, or whenever he could sneak away from rehearsals, Sean sauntered the New York streets, trying, in a once-over, to get some idea of what New York was like. The great city is indeed an animated place; a glittering go-boy, with a grace and dignified strength that makes the go-boy grand. Many have said that the city is a place of confounding noise, and some have said that its clatter kept them from even one decent night's sleep during their stay in it. Sean slept there as serenely, more serenely, than he sleeps now among the quiet hills and valleys of Devon. The road to Plymouth running outside his house, with the sounds of its passing lorries, vans, private cars, varied three times a day by the more musical tumult of noisy children just let loose from school, makes more noise than any Sean heard, even adding the siren-calls of the rushing police-cars, in the abiding places of New York City. Then, in summer, all the day, and on into the evening, ears are entangled in the ceaseless calls of the cuckoo cuckoo; and, later on, when the cuckoo has got tired, there's the bark of a dog here, there, and over yon, crow after crow from many a cock; and, in the night, the eerie squeal of the screech-owl out on the prowl for prey. Again, in the first freshness of morning, when all but the farmers sleep on, the chant of competitive birds shrills out as soon as the sun sends his first finger of light into the low sky; and sleep, except for the hardy, becomes a contest in a restive bed. A countryman soon gets used to a town; a townsman finds it harder to get used to the country.

The first natural thing Sean enjoyed in New York was the sparkling blue sky overhead, giving a clear and buoyant air in which to breathe alertly. The desecration came along some of the Avenues, from the sombre, crudely woven steel and timber of the Elevated Railway, running from one end of Manhattan to the other. The trolley-cars came swift behind it. Sean watched for well over an hour one night these strange-looking cars swinging around Fortieth Street, or one nearby; watched them clanking along, clod-like on their iron rails, bringing home to his ears sounds common on the quayside of Dublin's docks. Long and low, solidly framed, doorway and body, dull-coloured, borne heavily along on cumbersome swivel and wheel. It might almost be that, out of this one, clumsily clanking around the corner, Walt Whitman would step down jauntily, lilting one of his many songs of Manhattan.

The New York subway in harmony of structure, comfort of use, or brightness of aspect, limps a long way behind the London Underground, and a longer way behind its remarkable cousin in Moscow; and the pale, mauve lights, indicating a station, show all the apologetic timidity of a poor relation to the prouder and more opulent activities of the city. So, too, are the buses running along Fifth Avenue, looking like expanded perambulators carrying the family as well as the baby. It is the taxi which commands the streets of New York; fleets of them, like gay-plumaged swallow flocks, red, yellow, green, brown, white, and black, ground-bound birds skimming along the road's surface as if swiftness were all; a thrust-forward tension in each of them, even when they come to rest; a sway upward and forward as the lights suddenly call a halt to the swift going, an agitated purr of an engine delayed; and, as the shadow of green appears in the lights, a slim, sliding spring ahead, and the eager bird is on the swift wing again. It seemed to Sean that the American taxi, in its indolently slim form, is a daughter of the gondola transfigured into the muse of energy, while the English taxi, in its stiff, box-like stand, is the son of the sedan chair.

One day, he sped in one of these swift cars to a great synagogue, the Temple of Rudolph Sholem, if he remembers aright, whose pastor was Rabbi Newman, a young man with a pretty wife, three children, and a passionate love for plays and literature. He had invited Sean to come to speak to his people when they had gathered together for a Sabbath Service in a building so long and wide that a microphone stood by the rails of what Sean thought to be the chancel. After the chanting of psalms, led by the Cantor (identical with Caintaire in Gaelic, signifying a singer or chanter), the Rabbi spoke a few words of introduction, and Sean, greatly harassed by shyness, found himself speaking to a great crowd of Jewish people. There was no conceit in his stand, for he would far rather have been down among them, speaking to this man, that woman, as time and strength allowed. Conceit is a mother of many evils. Oh, Jesus, Oh, Buddha, Oh, Krishna, let a core of humility be in every conceit of energy necessary to life or dear to the heart of man!

Sean spoke about the curious resemblances existing between the Jews and the Irish – apart from the wild legends of the Irish being the descendants of the lost Ten Tribes, or that the first to land on an uninhabited Ireland were a granddaughter of Noah, her husband, Fintan, who lived for five thousand years, and fifty companions, who came there to try to escape death from the flood. The Irish were always eager to make themselves out to be as old a race as the Jews. Maybe they are, too. But, apart from these, there are many points in which the two resemble each other. There is a likeness between the old Gaelic poetry, in rhythm, emotion, and manner, and the poetic literature of the Jews; the Irish country people like bright, even gaudy, colours (Sean had a gradh for them himself); the one power of the Irish was their wit and nimbleness of mind, like the Jews; and, like the Jews again, the Irish were a scattered race, and had suffered great persecutions in their time. Spenser, the Elizabethan poet, gives an appalling picture of Ireland in his day; and, later on, in 1846–7, famine swept millions into the grave and millions more to the kindlier shore of America. So Sean went on, probably the first Irishman who had publicly spoken in a synagogue.

When the service ended, Rabbi Newman told him there were

many Irish men and Irish women there who wished to go by Sean, shaking his hand as they passed him; so for a long time Sean stood astonished, shaking hands with an Irish woman married to a Jewish man, or an Irish man married to a Jewish woman. He heard the name of almost every county Ireland had, including Connemara and his own Dublin, so that by the time his hand began to ache, all Ireland had paraded before him. Greatly – perhaps foolishly – moved, Sean had to murmur in his heart that the world's best blessings would swarm round the Shield of David and the Harp of Eireann.

The play was presented to a large audience, went well, though reviews the following morning were sharply divided; some were hot in their praise, others cold and caustic. It was a beautiful production in every way, and any fault shown on the stage was in the play itself. No voice, clerical or lay, was raised against its mood or its manner, and after a number of weeks' run, a tour of the play was planned, beginning at Boston. While the play was on in New York, coming up to Christmas, Sean left New York for home to be with his wife who was soon to have the other child. Two children now for them, but the tour was almost bound to bring Sean enough to make one more year reliable. Hurrah! Silence for a while, then the news that the Bostonian clerics were out in force against the play, and that the Mayor had banned it. Sean was being tossed about once more in the old sturm of style. Oh, God, here it is again! Wesleyan and Jesuit had joined hands to down the play.

'While I was in Maine', said the Wesleyan bishop, Charles Wesley Burns, 'my preachers in Boston held a meeting, and, when I got back, I was told they had voted to protest against the play because of what they had been told by Father Sullivan; and so I added my name to the protest.' The coo of the Wesleyan pigeon was aligned with the croak of the Jesuit raven. Point counter Point. Keep the kingdom of heaven respectable, please. So a bishop of a big church, eminent in the great city of Boston, decided a question of art and morals, not on first-hand news, not even on second-hand news, but on third-hand evidence: he decided to protest because of what his preachers told him of what Father Sullivan had said. Father Sullivan, SJ, representing the Boston College of Roman Catholic Organizations and Head of the Legion of Decency, followed the bishop with, 'Any religious affiliations [curious phrase – religious affiliations] would protest against the sympathetic portrayal of immorality, and all right-minded citizens, too, would protest against these things described in the play, and even more so the setting forth of the utter futility of religion as an effective force in meeting the problems of the world.' Sweet Jesus, will you listen to this! He thinks the futility of bishop or priest is equal to the futility of religion. Do not the thoughts of this Jesuit themselves show how ineffective his part in religion is, anyhow, in meeting the problems of the world? Is it immoral for a young woman to desire motherhood? Or to want to earn a living without having to prostitute herself to her boss? Or even to go away with a young man who loves her, and who was the one who showed understanding and regard for charm and vivacity? Isn't the whole play a cry for courage, decency, and vitality in life? Is it any more an act of immorality for a man and a woman to come together without a permissive chit from a priest than to make golden corn a flaming martyr before the eyes of hungry people that profits may be kept steady and sincere? Bum priests blathering.

Sullivan was joined by a brother Jesuit, the Rev Terence Connelly, SJ, the 'noted dramatic critic'. Worse and worse. Here he is starting – he's off: 'The whole play is drenched with sex. The love-song in the play is but a lyric of lust and a symbol of death. O'Casey has written on immoral subjects frequently in the past, but in art, as in life, the end does not justify the means. There are degenerates who delight in looking at raw human flesh, and in art there are those who demand life in the raw. But normal human beings swoon at the sight of human flesh exposed. They require the silken curtain of the skin to tone down the sight, and give the human flesh the normal colour that is the symbol of life. O'Casey has often written on immoral subjects. It appears first in the incident of the betrayal of Mary Boyle in *Juno and the Paycock*.' Even Juno; even she! Never a word, never a public word about the well-known and very able roman catholic writer Graham Greene's *Brighton Rock*, in which Brighton becomes a city of darkest night and darkest morn, too; in which everything and everyone seems to be on the road of evil. Talk of James Joyce! Joyce had humour, Greene has none; and in the darkest parts of Joyce there are always bright flashes of light; here the very light itself is rotten. Even the blessed sun 'slid off the sea and like a cuttlefish shot into the sky with the stain of agonies and endurance'. Here the roman catholic girl of sixteen and the boy of seventeen, respectively, are the most stupid and evil mortals a man's mind could imagine. One more quotation, and, if the clerics want to stick their noses deeper, let them get the book: 'She was good, but he'd got her like you got God in the Eucharist – in the guts. God couldn't escape the evil mouth which chose to eat its own damnation'.

Stand up there, now, Terence Connelly, stole and all on, if you want to wear it, till O'Casey has a word with you; a word he wanted to say when the row was on, but couldn't, because influences were used to prevent its printing. Isn't it amazing that such things should be said but a few years after a war had flung millions of men out of life and had so mangled millions more that they had just enough life left in them to hang on to it for a few years longer! Just as they did in the middle ages, so they do now, like this lord high admirable crichton of morals and art, going about to damn any who see and hear better than they; damning all as if they were bosses of the universe, cosmopolitans of the cosmos, dukes of divinity, and blights of the world, with the right to decide what man shall think, say, do, and imagine at all times, even to the time and the manner in which and by which any man or woman whatsoever shall proceed in slow motion to the hymeneal bed, or, in perversity, shall, on the other hand, fling themselves, as it were suddenly, with ravening speed, on to a couch without prim and purposeful preparation for the roister-doistering deed of love. It's funny, when one thinks of it, that a permissive chit from a cleric makes all the difference in the world, presenting those who get it with what Bernard Shaw said was 'the maximum amount of temptation with the maximum amount of opportunity'. Aw, let them blather! Neither life nor art cares in its creations a damn about them. Look at the God-laurelled ghosts in literature hovering about and laughing at these black-clad figures spitting on the musky petals of the rose – Tristan and Iseult, Abélard and Héloïse, Romeo and Juliet, Paolo and Francesca, Parnell and Kitty O'Shea, Jennifer and Dubedat. Let them rave: the musk of love will ever cling to the rose of life.

'The curtain of the skin has been put there by God to tone

down the horrors beneath' – as another cleric said: By God, it hasn't! It has been said that the skin – far from being there to save man's feelings – is there to protect the delicate and vital tissues beneath it; not one, but two of them to make assurance double sure. Whoever created the human skin (or any other kind), or however it came to be evolved, it didn't come into existence to save man an emotional shock, but to save him from a physical one; to protect the amazing network of vein and artery and tissue beneath it, which the poet Osbert Sitwell so poetically (and so rationally, too) calls *The Scarlet Tree*.

And here's a frill to the stupid remarks of the learned Jesuit: 'Normal people swoon at the sight of human flesh exposed'. Wouldn't it indeed be a hapless thing when man was plunged into an accident on rail or road, in factory or in mine, or in the deliberate mangling of the battlefield, if normal fellow beings, running to help and deliver, swooned down dead at the sight of flowing blood or human flesh exposed by the lacerating infliction of an accident, or the deliberately-imposed injuries of the battlefield! Or, again, wouldn't it be frightening if a surgeon about to separate flesh from quivering flesh so as to take away some poisonous interference with healthy life, fell flat in a swoon when he caught sight of what he was doing! Salute to Florence Nightingale and all true nursing sisters who nurse men out of plague and fever, and bind up wounds with courage and with skill. Silliest idea of all is that of God plastering silken skin over a body to enable normal people to live in harmony away from the sight of all that throbs beneath it. A comical association of a theological aspect of the biological reason of protection. And, anyway, who are Fathers Sullivan and Connelly to denounce the body when God Himself found it good enoughsky? D'ye call dis religion? No, no. D'ye call dis religion? No, no. D'ye call dis religion? No, No-o! What is it, then? Dope! Is it any wonder Bernard Shaw wrote down that he had 'never yet met an intelligent Jesuit'?

But the Wesleyan bishop and the Jesuit priests didn't quite get it all their own way. The students of Harvard stood by the play, as did those of Radcliffe, Wellesley, and Tufts Colleges. A letter to Sean from Richard C. Boys of Lowell House E-42, Cambridge, Massachusetts, said: 'We are in the midst of the furor created by the banning of your play in Boston by Mayor Mansfield. Realizing the stupidity of such an action, we have circulated petitions to the prominent colleges of the Boston area, and the response has been great, and in two hours last night four hundred signatures were obtained in Harvard alone [Atta Boys!]. Part of the Petition runs, "We protest that the action of Mayor Mansfield in banning *Within the Gates* on grounds of immorality and irreligion is not warranted ... and we urge a reconsideration of the Mayor's decision. If religion today has not developed in its many adherents a moral and religious attitude capable of withstanding the 'insidious attack' allegedly made in this play, it is a criticism, not of the play, but of the religion, which should be able to stand against the gates of hell. It would appear, furthermore, that the play does not attack the essence of religion, but only those external and ossified fripperies, which, in the play, as so often in life, are presented to the communicant as true religion."' (Atta Boys, again!) But the Jesuit janissaries had their way, and the play was banned. The lads and lassies from Harvard, Radcliffe, Wellesley, and Tufts Colleges came in special trains to see the play performed in New York City. Other places, frightened, followed Boston, banning the play, disrupting the plan of the tour so that it had to be abandoned, and so Sean's additional reliable year went vanishing into the stuff that dreams are made on. Abandoning the crackling fire around the figure tied to the stake, the clerics do things now in a more refined way. Cunning boys!

Apart from the Wesleyan bishop Burns, and Fathers Sullivan and Connelly, who are most honourable, very learned, and fit to stand, heads up, among first-rate men; let us look at the average and a half of the roman catholic clerics who walk the world, teach in the seminaries (as described by their own Dr McDonald, for forty years Professor of Theology in Maynooth College, Eire), or sit by their fireside in their presbyteries as parish priests or as catholic curates; those who set themselves up as anointed authorities on what should be read in a book, or what should be seen and heard in the activity of the theatre. Looka that chap walking along before us – just like ourselves. As a young fellow, he has gone (probably) to Maynooth where he has read 'a bulk of books' – à la tra la Cardinal McRory – listened to lectures, tried to crook himself away from the touch of any passing skirt; till, finally, he has said certain things in front of a bishop and the bishop has said certain things in front of him; then with many gestures, touches, and genuflections, he receives the authority to serve the sacraments to the faithful, which, even in the rigidity of his own limited community, doesn't give him the authority or the education to be an authority on the art of the theatre. Thousands of these laddos swarm the world, having gone through a systemized ceremony, filled their minds with a smattering of Latin (and in the matter of Latin, not only parish priests and their curates, but the starlit scarlet cardinals of Rome; for, as Dr McDonald, so long Professor of Theology in Maynooth, tells us, when a petition or document in Latin goes to Rome, the first thing done is to translate it into decent Italian so as to make it easy for the Curia to read); and then scatter over the world, to settle down and inflict their infallible awethority on men concerning literature, art, drama, science, morals, height of bodice, length of skirt, politics, and God wot else; if there weren't spirits near enough and capable enough to keep them in their small corners. It's a big beneficium clergicorum they are after; and not only that, but curselorum, too, ay, and ratolorum as well. They had them all once; but man's wiser now; and the venomous denunciation of *Within the Gates* brought no restoration nearer.

What splashed from the play over the Jesuits wasn't filth in any form, but hyssop, purifying hyssop, though the clerics didn't like the sting of its cleansing criticism. There is no more of venomous vice in the young woman of the play than there was in the young woman, Katerína Maslova, of Tolstoy's *Resurrection*; a book which, probably, the Jesuits never read, though a reading of it would do them more good than the reading of their Breviariums. But to a lot of clerics, as Tolstoy said, 'What they consider sacred and important are their own devices for wielding power over their fellow men'. They tried to wield this power over Sean by making it more difficult for him to live; but dark difficulties have often proved to be brighter angels, and, in this instance, he doesn't grudge the throe, for their enmity towards the play has made them, not more, but less, and him it has made, not less, but more.

PENNSYLVANIAN VISIT

SEAN went on a weekend visit to the Pennsylvanian home of the play's backer, George Bushar Markell, a descendant of the Dutch colonists, accompanied by the play's producer, John Tuerk; good-natured and amiable men, putting themselves out a lot to make things pleasant for the foreigner. It was a great trip in Markell's swift-moving motor, away up to the hills first cousins to the Appalachian range. The car swept by fields full of Indian corn, woods, and pasture lands, and for a time along the bank of a river in spate, but Sean could only now and again snatch a glance at the new and gigantic country through which the car was speeding. Never before, save once when strolling through the wood of Burnham Beeches, in Buckinghamshire, in late October, had he seen such a tapestry of autumn tints in field and wood, a wild and drunken display of summer's fading. Nature in a desperate and colourful song, setting aside for a moment the surety of death. Such a display could be equalled only by the tabard worn by a herald from the king of kings, lord of lords, and only ruler of princes; a mantle given by the Fall, and that the Fall would shortly take away, leaving the trees in a patient, penitent nakedness that would quicken again in the spring, to swing into a revel when the summer comes icumen in again.

When the car had climbed for a long time, they came to a simple and cosy house set in the shoulder of a hill. It was fitted in front with a Dutch porch where a huge telescope stood on a tripod, which brought the farther hills and the valleys around them close to the gazer's nose. At the door to meet him and give him welcome was Mrs Markell, a woman something over thirty, very handsome and lively in her manner and her movements. Before a meal had ended she was calling him Sean and he was calling her Gertrude – certainly a very amiable one-way manner in the American way of life. After the meal, Sean was brought down through a long and wide garden to see the swimming-pool; a very practical one, wide, deep, and long enough for an honest swim. It was a plain pool lined and banked by concrete, with concrete huts in which to dress and undress when the sun made swimming desirable. It had nothing Hollywoodian about it; it was there for use and not for show. The garden that led to the pool shocked Sean. They walked through a garden of tremendous growing tomatoes; tens of thousands of them, ripe, luscious, and full of goodness; thousands dying, too, within a tangled mass of leaf, blossom, and fruit, each as big as a full-blown grapefruit; some of them in the full scarlet flush of maturity, some others a day or two away from it, touched still with a golden yellow; but most of them slinking into a pulpy decay to hide from man's refusal to make a kindly use of them. So hard to come by at home; as plentiful here as blackberries on a bramble-covered English common. Here they were, lost, their richness trickling sulkily away into the indifferent ground. So many that Sean's boots crushed their crimson as he went along; so many, and all lost to the mouths of men; so many, yet not even a Jack Cade starving here to meddle with and munch one.

That it may please Thee to give and to preserve to our use the kindly fruits of the earth, so that in due time we may enjoy them. They are here, they are here, O Lord, but we do not enjoy them: a glorious pride of edible wealth wincing here and vanishing. Look down, look down, O Lord, and tell what you think about it. Fruit here in multitudes, and no man here to pluck them; no man; though Bushar Markell no more than Sean himself could do a thing about it.

The hospitality of the house was gentle and full-hearted. Roosevelt, the President, was to give a fireside chat over the wireless in a national hook-up the evening of Sean's arrival, and he, full of the New Deal and of what it might mean to America, and, indeed, to the world, was very eager to hear what the President would say, ignorantly assuming that every American loved the man and his Fair Deal. He asked if he could hear it, and promptly the wireless was tuned in for the President's speech. Sean listened eagerly, said Hear Hear and Clapped Hands at several points made in the speech, never noticing the sombre silence of his friends. Weeks afterwards, when he had gone back to New York, he found out that his friends' feelings towards their President were anything but friendly. They had been staunch Republicans all their lives, dreaded the New Deal, yet no one of them had shown a sign beyond a simulation of interest in what the American President was saying to Sean's fascination and delight. It was a quiet and grand gesture of courtesy, giving silent sanction to a chat they nearly hated, so as to cause no embarrassment to a favoured stranger.

A remarkable thing, one that made him wonder, a thing he had never seen before, was a miniature waterfall pouring down the chimney of the sitting-room. There it was, in the midst of a painted background, with real plants backing its reality, cascading down in silvery streams, real water tinkling through stones, and vanishing away, with a melodious gurgle, through the bottom of the grate. It was unfamiliar, funny, and attractive, for within the chat of the evening one heard the tinkle of falling water and its gentle gurgle saying goodbye going away; but it never caused discomfort to the ear, nor did it disconnect in any way the easy flow of conversation. There was method in the madness, too, for when the sun was strong, the cascade kept the room adorned with a cooling sense of breeziness; and, if the weather suddenly changed to coldness, the waterfall could be made to disappear by the pushing of a button.

Another wonder worked more usefully in a basement, where a mechanical-stoker kept a furnace going with rhythm and precision. A huge hopper was filled with coal; when ash accumulated, a raker started to rake all superfluous ash away, and when the fire sank the hopper mechanically refilled the furnace, so while the household chatted, took their meals, or slept at night, the robot boyo in the basement kept working away, keeping up an even and comfortable glow that suffused the house with a soothing and satisfying warmth.

In the sitting-room was a lovely mahogany or walnut cabinet over which stretched a bright steel rod. This was called, if he remembers aright, a theremin. By placing the hands near the rod, drawing them away to certain distances, bringing them nearer again, various tunes could be played on it; and Sean's host, with rapid and graceful movements of his hands, played *Home, Sweet Home* and *The Star-spangled Banner* for him. In a basement room was a workshop in which Sean's host did many things; he painted pictures, and made things from wood and metal; but, apparently, got tired after a while at whatever he happened to be doing, and so the place was strewn with lost achievements. Bushar Markell had been born into wealth, and there was no need for him to take life seriously. A great pity, for many things he had done showed him very clever with his hands, and, had necessity forced him to work for improvement of his talents, he might have done many good things in wood-work or in metals. Sean had noticed this detention of talent in a number of persons who had been born into a comfortable allowance. While the sensation of a new effort was fresh, they enjoyed themselves, but knowing no necessity to be thorough, the monotony of practice tired them out, and they abandoned any chance of profound or even competent workmanship for an easy-chair, a book, a girl, or a game of bridge. Wealth often takes away chances from men as well as poverty. There is none to tell the rich man to go on striving, for a rich man makes the law that hallows and hollows his own life.

The second day of Sean's visit was one of shelter from a flooding curtain of rain, that came pouring down in broad sheets stretching away far farther than any eye could reach; so heavy, so constant, that the splashing of it over valley and hill gave forth a melodious, watery hum, and all around, tree, hill, house, seemed to be aswim and asway in a flooded world. There was no thunder, ne'er a flash of lightning, no breeze blew; only the rain teemed down silently save for its own sound; falling as if it had begun when the world started, and would go on to the world's end. A heavy, grey sky leaned sullenly on the tips of the hills; never a sparkle appeared in the pouring rain to chasten its steady gloom, and, looking through the telescope, Sean saw slaty floods chasing madly down the mountain roads. He had never seen anything like it before, save once, many years ago, in Dublin, standing beside Jim Larkin, the Irish Labour Leader, under the portals of Liberty Hall, headquarters of the Irish workers' militant movement, the movement that had stitched a red flash for ever into the green, white, and orange of the Irish Tricolour. Throughout the night they had stood there, in the open doorway, watching the rain, the lightning, and listening to God's concertina, the thunder, in full play. The square in front of them was lit from end to end with vivid, rapid-following flashes of lightning, so vivid, so frequent, that it seemed there were many mingling and whipping through each other, like a weave and warp of furious streaks of bluish light, knitting themselves together

throughout the sky at the same moment; flashing the great
Customs House before them in a sea of flickering light; farther
off to the right, the thick and thinner masts of the ships
moored to the dockside, sticking up and wavering in the bluish
glow, like conductors' batons guiding the rhythms of the
storm. Only for a few brief seconds, and at long intervals, did a
sudden darkness ease their eyes, to give way again to the flash
and the flow of the fervid lightning; so expansive as if light
were enveloping darkness, and filling the firmament with lumi-
nant aggression. And through it all the rain falling, falling,
diminishing at times to a heavy shower, then rushing down
again with vehement speed, slashing itself even into the portal
where the two of them stood: watching God having a little
play-about in the streets of Dublin. Jim Larkin, Sean, and the
big Barney Conway, big-bodied, big-hearted; barely able to read
and write, but a grand talker, a fine story-teller, who, had he
had a suitable education, would have been one of Ireland's
great men; the three of them stood, silent there, watching a
storm in Dublin, as he stood now with two other friends, on the
side of a Pennsylvanian hill, watching another one, watching
the rain, silently falling, save for its own sounds, flooding the
valleys, tumbling down steadily from the low, dark-grey sky
through the disheartened air, saturating everything that stood
or crouched without a shelter, bending the trees with persistent
pressure, having and holding the visible world within its splashing power.

So Sean stood, so many years ago, within the doorway of
Liberty Hall between two friends, Larkin and Conway, watching a Dublin storm, just as he stood now with two new
friends, within the portals of a house in the Pennsylvanian hills,
watching the fall of the pelting, blinding Pennsylvanian rain,
bringing to his mind a night-long vigil, in the throes of a great
lock-out, through a storm of lightning and of rain, standing between two great comrades in the doorway of Liberty Hall: life
staring back at him again, reminding him of old and happy,
far-off things, and battles long ago: far away and long ago.

WILD LIFE IN NEW AMSTERDAM

DURING rehearsals Sean became acquainted through Dr Pat McCartan (who, years after, came to Ireland, and stood against Sean T. O'Kelly for the Presidency of Eire, making a great fight, but losing, which was a great pity), then carrying on the profession of physician in New York, with a Judge Lynch, who, for some curious reason, had a liking for Sean's plays, and had showed his effusive admiration by embracing Sean when they met for the first time. This Judge Lynch and Dr McCartan had a friend living in a residential suburb on the fringe of New York City. This family group consisted of husband, wife, and one living son. They invited Judge Lynch and Dr McCartan to dinner with them one night, and kindly extended the same invitation to Sean, again through Dr McCartan; and he, falling for the warmth and kindliness of Lynch and McCartan, agreed to go. After Judge Lynch had received therapeutic treatment from Dr McCartan for a stiff neck and painful shoulders, in the Doctor's surgery, the three of them popped into the Doctor's car, and shot off to visit the friend. A swift journey in a swift car through the darkness to a big house in the midst of many dark shapes which Sean's peering eyes took to be trees, and they sauntered into the brilliantly lighted home of the host, the wife, and the one son. A quick introduction, a quick lowering of a glass of rich-coloured sherry within a murmur of informal phrases, and then to dinner in a big room, resplendent with a wild display of walnut and mahogany reflecting the gleam of glass and the glitter of silver; thick carpets embedded boots at every step; candles lighted the outspread magnificence of the table, flanked with flowers and spired with many slender, tapering bottles of differing wines. A rich household, redolent of plenty, developing into a warehouse of rich and selected goods. A residence fit for Arnold Bennett rather than a home for Walt Whitman. Courtesy here, touched with a taint of vulgar grandeur. The host was a portly man, shrewd-faced, with a round head, bald, ornamented with

a few tufts of hair; he hadn't very much to say, though he
surveyed those present with a look of Aha, I'm here, see, while
a pudgy hand fiddled and diddled with a fine watch-chain
crossing his superior belly. His wife, too, was stout, taller than
he, and had, for all her gallant dress and genteel manner, a
half-hidden look of a mother about her. An Artegall changed
into a bourgeois gentilhomme with a lady Britomart revelling
in reduced circumstances, according belaccoyle to strangers.
Dunged deep with a complacent regard of themselves. Sure of
themselves, they silently pointed out to the visitors that they
were in the presence; that they were surrounded, hemmed in,
by substantial things in which the family had its being. They
sat down in the midst of good things; they could raise their
eyes, and see plenty before them, circumspect, costly, and
thoroughly polished. The five guests sat at the round table with
the family, the son on his mother's left, Judge Lynch on her
right; Sean next to the Judge, then the spearman; the father sat
opposite the mother, either at an end of the table; Dr McCartan sat on the right of his host, then a man, a stout protestant,
from the County Down, bringing the circle to the son again.
The spearman was an American whose livelihood began by the
hunting and killing of big cats (jaguars and panthers) with a
spear having a ten-foot shaft and a one-and-a-half-foot blade,
then advanced into the job of bringing out the sons of rich
parents, wild with a lust for adventure, to do the same thing,
but more safely with a rifle. Ahunting we will go, and ahunting
we will go! He was a rather short man, but trim and hefty,
with twittering eyes, a somewhat restless manner when spoken
to, and a brown pointed beard gave a sharp look to his face. He
had chaperoned the host's young lad on a safari through weeks
of prowling and probing in a jungle of South America, pushing
through tanglewood tales, so that the led lad could possess for
ever within his Id the idiotic ecstasy of having killed one of the
world's big cats; so, heads down, noses pointed forward, eyes
left, eyes right, through the dangle of the orchids and the
tangle of hibiscus, one day, the growling came into their ears,
the jungle jangle parted, and the beast leapt. Puff! And when
the smoke cleared, there was the laddo, rampant, behind the
body, one hand resting on his hip hip hurrah, the other holding
the rifle, the butt alongside the lad's right foot resting on

the dark and tawny stripes of the snuffed-out animal. And so to bed.

Sean gazed at the coloured photograph showing the lad with his foot on the tiger, the spearman standing by to look respectfully over his shoulder, the lad at the other side of Sean asway on his feet, so dizzy was he with the pride quivering within him; the mother a little way off, smiling towards her raptured son, the spearman murmuring, He got his cat, right enough; first shot, too, plumb in the head; good hunting. So, for evermore, the lad would have something to weary his comrades with; something within setting him aside from ordinary folk: a one who shot a great cat in the tales of tanglewood. Rather a weedy lad, something over twenty-one, a gentle grin showing his weak nature, and his whole aspect showing that the glow of his limited mind was almost too much for him. Sick with ecstasy at others getting to know of his astonishing achievement. Hardly able to eat, so full of himself. Sean saw that the father knew it and felt it by the assertive way he ignored the lad, and kept his attention on his guests; he was disappointed in his son. The mother, nearer to charity, tried to shield the boy from being discovered, and, while pretending to listen to the table-talk, would, at times, swiftly bend towards the boy to whisper something to him to bring him within the circle of diners; and Sean saw the boyish, grinning face change to a foolish gravity and the head give a cursory nod, as if the hunter was acknowledging a trivial remark from a timid, trying woman. The civilized tigress watching over her civilized cub: we aren't very far from the animals. Oh, the wild wish to see our children shine! The curse of money begetting the force to put a life where its power is in the way of a larger life. Taking up time and thought needed for finer things. How high the cost of equipment, the big fee for the hunter-charman, the expense of carting this lad to a faraway jungle and of bringing him safely back a wriggling hero, with a picture of himself, his right foot stamping unsteadily the lovely body of a big dead cat; his mind remaining a mind that would never peer into anything higher than a boy's annual. It was odd; the father knowing what his son was not, but tolerating the idea of a special worthiness, though in fear that strangers saw through the contradiction, puffed out his own importance, as if to assure himself that his own impressiveness was more than equal to his own importance and his son's defects. The mother seeing the sham in her heart, silvering it over, as the oyster iridescently nacres an irritation, with a sham of her own, accepting the myth, and decorating it with gravity and praise. The spearman complacently assuring himself that he had lifted the limited lad into an eminence, deeply doping the lad with a ridiculous glory, and affording the parents a chance to take a tormenting interest in a son never to be so clever as his father.

All wore dinner-jackets, save Sean and the spearman, who was dressed in rough, wide tweed trousers and a rougher tweed coat, befitting a man whose important part of life was joined to the jungle. The dinner was eaten within a radiant sparkle of all things; sparkle of glass and silver, of mahogany and walnut, with the more graceful glamour of snowy tablecloth and richly laced table-mat and napkin; and the sparkle of vivid conversation carried on between Judge Lynch, Dr McCartan, and the man from God knows where in Ulster; talk of things that had happened to them, of things they had heard, mostly incidents from colloquial history, sprinkled tartly with stories about Yeats, the poet and the man; the host at the table's head nodding knowingly, the hostess, at the other end, sending simmering smiles around when the others laughed, the spearman trying to enter into it all, and the laddo content to remain drunkenly alone in his daring achievement of killing the cat: all within the gleam and glitter of glass, of silver, of walnut and mahogany. They talked away, the host nodded approval, and his wife accomplished many a smile of amusement, when Sean was startled by hearing the Ulsterman say slowly and sharply: 'The Irish wud be a grund people but for the inseedious releegion of the romun catholic church ruining thum'.

Sean saw an uneasy look flash over the lean, almost ascetic face of McCartan, and a murmuring Hush hush; oh, hush, came from the gleam and the glitter of glass, silver, walnut, and mahogany.

—That's a matter of diversified opinion, came from Judge Lynch, in a conciliatory murmur; as a matter of fact, the catholic faith has never put any obstacle in the way of an Irishman's advancement.

—I'm tulling you different, said the voice from Ulster; it brings puverty and eegnorance everywhure it fastens on the minds of people. Thure's one thing stupping the Irish, one thing only: the clinging of thum tae what hus no wurrunt from the mind of mon, or the ravelations of holy scriptures.

—That's a debatable question, came in a sharper murmur from the Judge.

—It's no' a debatable question, I'm tulling ye! It's the prime on' pure truth! Ulster's voice was loud now and the face was flushed. On', looksee, St Puthrick, himself, was eegnorant of three-quarters of the beliefs common to romun catholics the day; on' thut's no' a debatable question with ony open mind, either.

—So protestants say who don't know a word of historical truth; and the Judge's voice, too, was louder as he thrust his stiff neck forward over the table towards the Ulsterman. Will you deny that St Patrick did penance for the Irish on the cold, windy top of Croagh Pathrick, and that he got his holy mission from Rome?

—Looksee, that's only two of the old wives' fables you Romanusts use to strungle God's truth! Croagh Pathrick! If he wasna' a fule, what for would he want to climb to the tup of a wild ond windy hill to say a prayer when he could do it better in his own buckyard or his own frunt room? Besides, uvery mon must confuss his sins, not to a priest, but to God. If ye confuss your sins – surch the scruptures, mon.

—Oh, God, thought Sean, Connemara's Croagh Pathrick and Belfast's Cave Hill are at it again, and, of all places, in New Amsterdam!

Dr McCartan leaned back in his chair and sipped from a glass of wine uneasily. His lean face assumed a dreamy look as he murmured for all to hear, I remember one day in Dublin, when Yeats and Gogarty were going down Sackville Street—

—Wait a munnit, Pat, wait a munnit, said Ulster's voice with a note of annoyance in it, tull we suttle this question of reeleegion once fur all; thun we can listen to your blether about Yeats ond Gogarty going down Suckville Street. This question concerns truth on' mon's eturnal future, on' is not to be compurred with Gogarty on' Yeats goin' down Suckville Street. What has God's truth to do with Yeats on' Gogarty goin' down Suckville Street? Naethin', mon. But He has with this question: th' question we're suttlin' is God's own question, I'm tullin' you!

—St Peter's our man, a saint; the rock on which our church

stands. What's yours piled up on? On a shameful attachment of a despicable English king for a loose lady of his court! Judge Lynch was getting hot and bothered.

—Lussen, mon, lussen.

—I've listened to you long enough, almost shouted the Judge. Henry the Eighth and a harlot! It gets me down how any decent mind can take it. The only two saints in the protestant church, Henry the Eighth and his harlot – it makes me laugh; ha ha!

—Gentlemen, gentlemen, change the subject, please, persuaded Dr McCartan.

Hush hush, murmured the glitter and gleam of the glass and the silver, of mahogany and walnut wincing; hush, oh, please do.

—Ours is the one church that is universal, and your shouting doesn't shake it, said the Judge, shouting himself; there in the beginning, it will be there at the end; yessir :

> A great while ago, our church began,
> With a hey, ho, the wind and the rain;
> In God's all-important and permanent plan
> There's no place at all for the protestant man
> Except it be out in the wind and the rain –
> So rid yourself, Ulsther, of peppermint malice,
> Extra ecclesiam cun grano salis;
> Top of the morning's to Biddy McCue,
> There's nothing but hell-terror awaiting for you;
> Stark naked and shy and all flusthered with pain,
> A flaming soul lost in the wind and the rain!

—Och ay, ye can laugh the day, said Ulster, pushing his tumbler farther back, so he could thump the table; but wull ye laugh whon ye get tae the pearly gate – gin ye mount sae high – what wull your ain Pether say tull ye thon?

> Oh, Roman lad, you're out of date,
> You're all too early, all too late;
> Aha, the ruein of it.
> Ye didna' hulp the sawls in need;
> We ken the real plant frae the weed,
> On' scorn the blether in your creed,
> Gang off frae here, on' gang wi' speed,
> Aha, the ruein of it!

What d'ye say, O'Casey, mon? he questioned suddenly; adding, as Sean stayed silent, Go on, O'Casey, speak your mind; say the richt thing, like a mon. Go on; you know the truth as well as ony man. You're an onlightened mon, as I om. Truth is waitin' on tiptoes fur ye tae speak out.

—Oh, said Sean, trying to shuttle the argument off, the wide-open spaces are needed when a row starts between Wittenberg and Knox on the one hand, and Maynooth and the Vatican on the other. In these disputes, we are like frightened birds jostling each other in the dark.

—We're no' birds, said Ulster angrily, on' we're no' frightened; we huv our intullects, ond we're well abune the birds. Ye know the scruptures, O'Casey. Well, then, quote thum, ond you'll be nearer the murk.

—If God be what He ought to be, must be, if He be God, said Sean, then He has no time to bother about the Anglican Thirty-nine Articles, the Westminster Confession, or the Trentian Creed.

—This is no laughing mutter, O'Casey, said Ulster; we're talking now about the affairs of God ond not about affairs of mon. I want to know if God is a catholic or a protestant: onswer thot, wull ye?

—He's neither, said Sean laughingly; relationship with Him isn't sanctioned by the push-button of an opinion. He may be more than He is claimed to be: He may be but a shout in the street.

—That remark's derision! ejaculated the Judge. It wasn't right to use it. A shout in the street! What d'ye mean? What kind of a shout?

—A lomuntable remurk, O'Casey, said Ulster; on' irresponsible. Tull us what kind of a shout God could be.

—When God is a shout in the street, said Sean, the shout is never a creed.

—It must be a shout of something for a purson to believe in; a church for all ond God's world for us all untull the end, said Ulster.

—It might be a shout of people for bread, as in the French Revolution; or for the world's ownership by the people, as in the Russian Revolution; or it might just be a drunken man in the night on a deserted street, shouting out Verdi's *Oh, Leonora,* unsteadily meandering his way homewards.

—Now maybe you realize the lamentable result of denying tradition and sacred authority in order to decide for yourself? said the Judge, stretching the stiff neck farther towards Ulster across the table: God is reduced to a common shout or song in the street!

—Not common shouts or a common song, said Sean.

—I want no guessing, said Ulster irritatedly; I want the full facts of the whole truth. Thot's my faith, the releegion of a protestant: the full facts of the whole truth.

—Gentlemen, said Dr McCartan, rising, we have to go. He bowed gracefully to the hostess; thank you for a very pleasant evening. Come, gentlemen, we've a journey to go; Ulster a farther one, and the night is ageing.

They moved towards the door, the host following, McCartan between the two arguers, arguing still, muttering moodily:

—Your thochts are born out of confusion of mind, mon.

—Out of clarity of mind, you mean.

—Confusion of mind, I'm tulling ye.

—Clarity of mind.

—Confusion.

—Clarity.

Sean lingered behind hoping the Ulsterman would be gone before he got to them. He thanked his hostess, and on his way out, he stopped to look at a photograph of a clear-faced, handsome young man hanging on the wall.

—A handsome lad, he said; who may that be now?

—He was my son, said a quivering voice, my elder-born. Everyone said he was a very clever lad, and everyone liked him. He died more than a year ago of some fever, of pneumonia; oh, I don't know what – he just died on me!

Sean turned to look, and saw the plump body quivering and tears running down the rouged cheeks. She, too, had the immovable pearl of sorrow in her breast. Just as he had seen long ago Lady Gregory looking at her son's picture, while the tears ran down her face. Cover his face; mine eyes dazzle; he died young. This vulgar woman, agog with her possessions, for all the way she strutted proudly through them, would, Sean saw, willingly give up the gleam and glitter of silver, of mahogany and walnut, could she but have her son again; the son thought to be so clever, the one everyone liked. Oh, my son! Would God I had died for thee, my son; oh, my son! How many mothers have anguished the air with the same cry! His own mother over her dead Tom. It is time that this cry at least should be silenced the whole earth over.

Bring me a grain of mustard seed, said Buddha to an agonized mother who had brought her dead child to him, beseeching him to restore it to life; bring me a grain of mustard seed from any house anywhere in which those who live in it have never suffered sorrow through the death of a loved one; and I shall restore your little one to health and strength. And the woman had searched and searched for many months, but could not get a grain of mustard seed from a house that hadn't suffered through the death of a loved one.

Jesus, Buddha, Mahommed, great as each may be, their highest comfort given to the sorrowful is a cordial introduction into another's woe. Sorrow's the great community in which all men born of woman are members at one time or another. Here, the better had been taken and the lesser left. We all make mistakes at times. He took her hand, and gently pressed it, and said, My dear, dear sister, here a mother loses a son; there a son loses a mother. We are all the same when equality brings us grief.

> Oh, known and unknown of my common flesh,
> Caught in the common net of death and woe,
> And life which binds to both.

He went out to mingle with the muttering immensity of Calvin and Bellarmine disputing whether the banners borne by heaven's seraphim, cherubim, thrones, dominions, virtues, powers, principalities, archangels, and angels were the yellow and white of the Vatican or the orange and blue of protestant Nassau.

HEARTS AND CLUBS

THERE are a great number of critics and reviewers in America, and Sean got to know a lot of them in New York, Boston, and Philadelphia. Busy chaps, all; but friendly, and anxious to be good to a foreigner. No time to be formal; let's get acquainted: This is Tom, that's Harry, and here's Dick. Indeed, friendliness is the badge of the American tribe. All right by Sean. They were very different from their critic brothers in London. Nothing a foreign dramatist visiting there can do or say can push away the friendliness of the Americans. They almost hoist him up on their shoulders and carry him around everywhere. They have the happy, human quality found in critics the world over of differing casually or violently from one another; but they unite as one big man to try to make a foreign dramatist feel the warmth and good nature that is generally believed to live and flourish in a home. Every drama critic whom Sean met, those who liked his work and those who didn't, linked an arm through his, and gave him friendship. They confirmed it with a meal in this critic's home, or in that critic's club, or, more casually, but none the less heartily, with a sherry egg-flip at a busy bar. Sit ye down, and I'll trate ye decent; so they said, and so they did, too. There was one snag in all the kindliness: it hemmed one in; there was but a bitter chance of seeing the plain people of the city, or finding out how they lived, what they thought, and where they worked. Only when Sean could sneak away from the clutching hand of friendship could he go alone to wander where he listed.

This lilting kindness of American friends, especially of the drama critics, struck him the more forcibly because of the coldness and curious reserve blossoming from the frosty nature of the London critics. He had thought that this icy blandness was inevitable in the nature of criticism till he went to New York. Never had he paid a visit to a British critic's home other than Bernard Shaw's; never had he had a meal with one of them, either in restaurant or club; never had he ever even had a sherry or a small port with one of them; never had he even sipped a single cup of strong or weak tea with one of them in a Lyons corner shop. It was curious, now, when one came to think of it; for even as they did, so he, too, belonged to the theatre. It couldn't be because of the many faults within him. There were many for sure, but none that would be likely to inflict torment on the poor critics. He wasn't, he believed, a bore – the worst fault anyone could have. He had hardly been twelve days in America before he seemed to be friends with all the New York critics; he had been twelve years in England, yet had never sat opposite to one of them in a bar; never stretched a leg under a table of theirs; never had a single drink side by side with one of them; never even sat beside one of them on a bench in the park. Indeed, he has now been in England for twenty-five years, yet never a one of them has blown him a kiss or given a wave of a hand from a distant point: bar Bernard Shaw. He had had meals with him, long chats, and many good moments. They had laughed together, Shaw drinking milk, Sean lowering a modest glass of wine; good fellowship and a dear liking right to the very end; unto this last. With this one only. None of the others had ever given a knock on his door, nor had he been asked to give a knock on any door of theirs. He wondered why? Too full of himself, maybe? But he was as full of himself in New York as ever he had been in London; fuller, in fact, for there he threaded himself through and in and out of a friendly tapestry. To Sean, the London drama critics seemed to go about like reserved sacraments,

The hope only
Of empty men.

Well, goodbye, and God be wi' ye! Till we meet again. Never, now.

At a meeting in London, Mr Tom Hopkinson, ex-editor of *Picture Post*, is reported to have said, 'Anyone who has seen American films, read American books, and visited America, was aware of a streak of brutality in the American character'. Is this idea of American friendliness that had enveloped Sean, then, an illusion? Just a mirage of souls, unAmerican, and long dead? Does this 'streak of brutality' (because of what was done in Korea) run through the American nature like a tiger's stripe? No, not any wider nor more conspicuous than the streak of brutality in other peoples. All nations in tensive times and peculiar circumstances have a streak of cruelty in them. Look at the Indian Mutiny when the English fastened the rebel Sepoys to the muzzles of their cannon, touched the guns off, and filled the air with flying bits o' bodies; or – for Sean hadn't to go back far to find another example – look at the time of the Black and Tans, the Auxiliaries; and even the decent, common English soldiers, when fear assailed and assoiled them; then many an Irish nostril was stung with the cindery smell of a burning town, and many a lintel of an Irish doorway was splashed with the blood of a first-born. Just to show there's no heat here, look at the time the Black and Tans, the Auxiliaries, and the decent British soldiers were gone, hardly halfway over the sea on their way home, when the Irish Civil War began, and the catholic Irish showed in executions and torture (the gentle Yeats voting for a Flogging Bill) that they were as good as any other at rifling life and liver and all out of temples of the Holy Ghost. The indictment of one nation over another in this way is foolish, for when greed of gain or of office becomes an uppermost idea in a soul, or when the blood's afire with fear, the arm will be raised and the fist will strike, let the fist be black, yellow, brown, or a Christian white one. To Sean the Americans weren't in the remotest degree like those seen in the films, or like those read about in American books; and these very films and very books are as welcome as the flowers in May to the English and Irish cinema-goer and reader as they are to the American people. We are all tarred with the same brush. In war, judgement flees to the brutish beasts, and men just lose their reason. All men, not merely Americans. And there will always be a strain towards war, international and civil, while the lust of profits is allowed to mar the mind of man. As Nietzsche says somewhere: 'Merchant and pirate were for a long period one and the same person. Even today mercantile morality is really nothing but a refinement of piratical morality.'

And often, not even refined. The English tycoon rapes life as readily as the American tycoon. The Jolly Roger is the banner of competitive business. Free enterprise brings war to other countries, and strews poverty and disease about everywhere in its own land. But the American people, as people, are not as they represent themselves to be in their own films and their own books. To Sean, the peculiar streak in the American nature (apart from them being presidents, tycoons, judges, critics, workers, democrats, republicans, communists, or any other walk of life or mode of thought) is that of a lavish and delectable generosity. They may be cautious as critics, venal as judges, ruthless as tycoons, but, in their personalities, in their inner natures, they all have this glow-like streak of generosity in them. They seem to be unable to help themselves against it. A warm-hearted pushing crowd.

One thing only that Sean met in America frightened and harassed him: the Women's Clubs. It was a flutter of the heart to have to say yes, for the sake of the play, to an invitation to come and speak at one of the gigantic gatherings. He felt as Moses did when asked by God to go to Egypt and speak on behalf of the chosen people. But go he had to, for these Clubs bought bunches of tickets for a play, and were very powerful. Go he had to, though his head was a bulging vacancy. At one of these gatherings, two other speakers were, thank God, present; one, Mr Williams, who wrote detective fiction; and a Mr Stone who wrote a life of Van Gogh. The women came in thousands to hear the three famous fellows, and you could hardly find stir or breath. It was a monthly Club lunch, and this one happened to be a birthday number. Desperately dejected, Sean put on a cheerful and confident gob, and inwardly prayed, atavistically, that he might be given something to say to these good women. He lifted himself from his worried want of thought at a thunderous outbreak of clapping, and away in the distance he saw a giant cake, resting on a four-handled barrow, each handle resting on the shoulder of a sturdy waiter, carried into the room to be paraded about, while all present sang 'Happy Birthday to You'. It was, he was told, to be given to one of the New York hospitals. When the cake had gone, the lights suddenly went out, and at the far side of the vast room, curtains shot aside, and he beheld the American flag fluttering in a floodlight. All stood up while a woman standing beside the banner sang in a rich soprano *The Star-spangled Banner*. Emotional nonsense! He didn't know about that, now. He himself had enjoyed emotional tension at the display of romantic Ireland's green flag; later on, at the tricolour of republican Ireland, and, a little later, at the fluttering of the international red flag calling on the workers of all lands to unite together. Nationality was something deeper than even life in a man's nature. There seems to be something eternal in the feeling one has for the land in which one moves, or has moved, where one lives, or has lived, where one has, or had, one's being. Good it must be, and it will persevere, though the Roman Catholic Church cautiously regards it as a heresy, bringing about the 'deification of the state', a belief, the Church says, that sprang from the mind of Rousseau, and the higher thought of the French Revolution; though, surely, as Shaw points out, nationalism was beginning to show its mind in the lifetime of St Joan. What the Church fears is that nationality will bring a national Church into existence, as happened in England in the time of Henry the Eighth. The Pope and his cardinals wanted the Church to become another expanding universe, with the bishops sailing about on supersonic clouds guiding us in the right use of literature, science, art, contraceptives, politics, and parsing. The Welfare Church! Outside of her, all things tended towards evil. The Renaissance was a bad start. The Rev P. J. Gannon, SJ (another Jesuit), says in the roman catholic magazine, *Studies*: 'The Renaissance was followed by the most disastrous revolution in European history, though it was euphemistically called The Reformation'. And a shout from Mr Hilaire Belloc tells us 'Europe must return to the Roman Catholic Faith, or perish!' Down, down to hell, and say Belloc sent thee thither! Dither.

Yet when all Europe were of the one and only Faith, there was the same disunion, the same discords, the same murder that gentlemen say are plaguing us now. From the moment, and before, that Christianity became a consolidated force with the Pope at the head of it, seeking temporal power and crescent wealth, the holy roman catholics were stabbing at each other's powers, clawing at each other's ambitions, filling Europe with battle, murder, and sudden death. On and on and up and up it all went, so that even in 1918 they were hard at it, according to one of their own authorities. One example: Donald Attwater, author of *Catholic Eastern Churches*, tells us in *Studies* that: 'After a period of incredible confusion, Poland in the autumn of 1918 assumed sovereign authority over Galicia, lately an Austrian province. Civil war followed immediately. The war was pursued with detestable bitterness and unscrupulosity on both sides. When one reads of the rapes perpetrated by Catholic Poles in the churches, monasteries, libraries, and so on, of their fellow-Catholic Ukrainians, one can hardly be surprised if certain Ukrainian priests so far forgot their Christian duty as to preach in their sermons the extermination of the Poles, as the Polish Government, truly or not, alleged.'

Catholics destroying catholic churches, monasteries, libraries, and so on; and gutting their fellow-catholics, too! The roman catholics' delightful manifestation of the Sacred Heart all burning with fervent love for men! A contradiction in therms.

Here they were sitting down, the song sung, the fluttering flag gone again behind the heavy curtains, the lady chairman knocking with a mallet on the table for silence; *mater silentii*; and Mr Williams rising to address the audience. He spoke of detective fiction as an art, as being, at its best, on as high a plane as any other art; of its many difficulties as to plot and characterization; and that inspiration played as big a spurt in its composing and creation as it did in any poem, play, or novel. He said the nickname of Whodunnit given to detective fiction was conceived by star-crossed envy engendered in those who couldn't achieve success in the creation of convulsive consternation of the prime detective story. He remarked in passing that one of the great divisions between them and the Soviet Union was that while the detective story was an integral part of Christian western civilization, communistic Russia but held this art in very remote remembrance. He emphasized the great development of the art since the rather primitive efforts of Sherlock Holmes, adding that the art today was bursting with experiment that was sure to furnish new wonder and delectation in the time to come. He spoke as if to the manner bread, and proved that crime and murder were substantial parts of Christian conceptions, and equally so in man's place in nature. Then he sat down again, enveloped in upstanding and determined applause.

Then Mr Irving Stone got up and spoke of the labour and the research that went into the writing of the lives of great men. Something no one could imagine. The research and the creation concerned with the setting forth of an orderly story was a work of years. The reward was the making of a great man to live again. So Mr Stone furnished all present and correct with the synoptic account of the work he did in fashioning Van Gogh into life again; that odd, strange man who gave an old chair an honoured place in the universe, robed an old jar with the purple of the iris, sang a pictorial song of golden corn growing, and gave to roses the whiteness of priestly hands breaking the sacred bread.

While Sean was silently murmuring Lead kindly light, lead kindly on, and lead me outa this, he heard his name called out by the Lady in the Chair, and up he stood to enlighten the minds of America's mothers, sisters, daughters, sweethearts, and wives. He opened his mouth, and taught them, saying – but he had nothing to teach them. He expounded unto them a parable – but divil a parable Sean had to expound. Why was he uneasy at the risk of speaking badly, of boring his audience? Looking at it in the deeper way – conceit. Anxious to shine, be God! To show off, be a big fellow; hear others clapping him. At home, De Valera was preparing to withhold the land annuities from England – doing the big fellow; in England, J. H. Thomas was preparing to circumvent De Valera – doing the bigger fellow; and in Europe, the Furor, Hitler, was strutting around Germany doing the biggest fellow of all, a deed that was to deluge the whole Continent with a mangled mass of Jew and Gentile in one red burial blent.

Sean was here just because his name had appeared in the papers. Probably each woman here was as deep in life as he was himself, and knew a lot more about it. Women were nearer to the earth than men; they had their feet deeper in the soil. Men went lightly over the ground; women trod firm. They are closer to common things, and so have a more ready and lasting knowledge of life. Men shout dogmatically, they gesture, and run here, run there; women stay more still, speak more quietly, and say more in their silence.

Now, for an hour or so away from their silence, they had come to hear him because his name had appeared in the papers. He couldn't believe that many of them had gone, or would go, to see his play, and that the sale of his play-books would jump a lot after the meeting had ended. Still, he had to do it. Ay, but how? Irving Stone had talked about the apparent failure of Van Gogh, and, indeed, the great artist must have been dead tired with a sense of failure when on that memorable day he rose from his chair by his brother's side, went out, and shot himself sadly in the garden. So Sean talked of failure that might be a success, and success that might well be a failure; urging that no one should be cocky in what was declared to be a success, or despondent in what seemed to be a failure. No one, but Time, knew definitely. Time was the boyo who placed the final crown on the head, or gave the final kick in the pants. Be apprehensive always of success; never be afraid of failure. There was always honour in failure as a result of doing one's best. We can never be sure that failure isn't success in a shroud. And, anyway,

> Vivas to those who have failed,
> And to those whose war-vessels sunk in the sea,
> And to the numberless unknown heroes equal to the
>   greatest heroes known.

And Sean's flag fluttered laxly, went behind the curtain, as he sat down tired.

ONLY FIVE MINUTES MORE

With rehearsals over and the time coming to go, go back to the Rose and Crown, the tempo of Sean's running about quickened. Only a few of the dozens of invitations to go to places and speak unto the people could be accepted; mainly because he didn't feel constrained to speak to the people; mainly because he felt he had little to say to them. He wasn't one who contented himself with the Salvation Army's method of saying any kind of nonsense that floated into their minds; their building up of a beautiful life, here and hereafter, with a phrase of 'Out of self into Christ, into Glory. Simple, isn't it?' as he heard a Salvation Army officer say once. Damned simple, right enough. Turning everyone into a quick-change artist. Becoming in the twinkling of an eye guided missiles shooting into heaven. He came across a group of them on a street in Philadelphia. There they were, large as death, ensconced under a huge umbrella, coloured red, yellow, and blue; there they were spouting out their spick and spam way of eternal life. Their glory was vanishing now. Like all the bursts-out of evangelical heat, this one, too, was beginning to cool quick. Just like the energy and enthusiasm of the first friars, black, white, and grey, launching themselves among the poor to save them from the Reformation; whose love of poverty soon lay buried under a gigantic and splendidly built rubble of riches. So, too, the Wesleyan outburst of all-embracing piety to set aside the lukewarm decline of the Anglicans, fell, itself, into the same dead state; so badly that we can read in *Americana* the wail of a Wesleyan faithful few, keening:

> The Church that God through Wesley launched
> Two hundred years ago,
> Is going now beneath the waves,
> Down to eternal woe.

Piety has become a possessing pose. In one of the *Capuchin*

Annuals (1942) there's a grand picture of His Excellency, The Most Rev Paschal Robinson, OFM, Apostolic Nuncio to Eirinn, showing him in all his gallant costume of richly made undress cassock, piped and braided, with his lovely chain holding on to his jewelled pectoral cross; a gorgeously dressed cavalier of the Roman Church, and very nice, too. This gent didn't live in a slum or shack, ate things higher than pulse and beans, refused to sit and work in fireless rooms, and never roamed about in the cold with bare feet blue. None of them do. Not till they are dead. This one, this Excellency, the Papal Nuncio in Eirinn, died a year or so ago, and in his last gasps ordered that when he was dead, he was to be dressed in a coarse garb, his feet bare, and set so as to stick out from under the shroud to show there was no deception. Tramp tramp tramp, the boy is trium- phantly marching up to heaven in his bare feet. A grand ex- ample to the workers to embrace poverty for the good of their souls. Workers of all lands, don't bother about wages, don't bother about thin clothing, broken boots, scanty meals; re- member the dead Nuncio in his bare feet. Christ, how many saints would the Ireland Sean knew have given to God, if saintship rested in pinched faces, empty bellies, and bare feet!

Easy a minute; easy a minute, now: it's damn easy to go about in your bare feet when you're a day dead. And a nice change, too, when, like this excellent Nuncio, you spend all, or most, of your life well housed, well fed, and covered cordially with crimson or purple array; with handsome, rain-proof shoes for the street, and violet or scarlet satin slippers for wear when the poor feet pass over thick and soft and gay-coloured car- pets. No, Mr Monsignor; it's a bit too late for the bare-feet blues when the time comes to stick your toes up.

Hurry up, hurry up, on the way, through Connecticut and Rhode Island, all the way to Boston, in a Pullman car, sitting in a cosy armchair that can swivel round to face where one desires to look, its comfort coaxing a soul into a conscious rest; and with many choice foods to shorten the journey, a magnificent negro setting them out in front of one with skill and courtesy; all the way from Alabama; Sean asking him as he served, would he like to be back home in Alabama.

—No, suh, he said; I'se all right here. There's noding in Alabama, noding for me, suh.

This little Alabama coon didn't want to go back home to

Alabama. Nothing there for him. Nothing in Ireland for Sean; nothing for this great negro in Alabama; exiles, the pair of them. How often had he sung the song when a lad,

> Hushaby, don't you cry, mammy's little baby,
> Mammy's liddle Alabama coon.

The crosby touch when crosby was being hushaby'd himself, and just as solidly sentimental.

Only twice had Sean met souls from Alabama – this splendid negro now, and, many years later on, another; this time a white from the same State – by accident. Outside of his home, Sean was watching a long convoy of great American tanks, lorries, and guns, the lorries packed with GIs, toiling along the narrow Plymouth Road, all in a hurry to get to the front, but stopping often to squeeze through a narrower part; crawling along a way never meant for these huge thunderers of Thor. In one of the lorries, a steel-helmeted American sat astride the tail of a lorry; a young lad, who glanced about from right to left, wondering.

—Eh, boh! he shouted to Sean, where are we; what's this place called?

—Tot-nes! shouted back Sean. It's in Dev-on, in a south-west corner of England. Where do you come from?

—From Alabama! shouted back the boyish soldier.

—It's a hell of a long, long trail from here to Alabama! yelled back Sean, as the lorry jerked away.

—It sure is! came back the voice of the boyish soldier, and a sad note seemed to be in the sound.

> On the way, well on the road,
> The leaden road to Okinawa,
> To splutter in war's muddy mode,
> The soldier rode, the signposts show'd
> The leaden road to Okinawa.
>
> The call has come, I'm made obey it,
> If I knew a prayer, I'd say it,
> Along the road to Okinawa.
> Oh God! if God but only knew
> What we poor bastards tumble through,

He'd strip off all this sulky woad
From Yank and Jap, and disembode
Us from the glamour of the road,
The leaden road to Okinawa!

To lose oneself, becoming wholly
War's tatter'd, bloody roly-poly.
Farewell to arms, to legs, to seeing,
Farewell, maybe, to all my being.
No more now than a skimpy toad,
Made up in shit-like sulky woad,
I make my way along the road,
The leaden road to Okinawa.

Oh Jesus, it is only fair
That we should live as long as there
Are years to live before we're old,
And not be thrust down in the mould,
Before a grey rib stabs our hair.
But on and on I'm firmly tow'd,
To give death all I haven't ow'd
Till all my fresh, young blood has flow'd,
And laid the dust along the road,
The leaden road to Okinawa.

Two men, one a negro, anxious to keep away from the cotton fields, or from a job in Mobile; the other, a white, eager to get back once more to Alabama; and God deciding. Nothing in the State for one, everything in it for the other.

Sean passed through Boston in a taxi, seeing nothing but tall buildings whirling by, blurred in the flabby greyness of a thick fog; but remembering that here Emerson had been born, who, transcendentalist (big word) and all as he was, stretching himself up to the sky to handle what wasn't there, still kept tiptoe on the common earth beneath him; the taxi speeding on to a big hotel, where cordial Pressmen gave him a cordial dinner, talking through the hours of what was and what was to come to the theatre, little realizing what was to come to the world. On, then, in the early morning in Horace Reynolds' old grey mare of an automobile, to Cambridge, where Sean was to speak to the members of the Harvard Poetry Society on the Elizabethan

Drama as pictured in Archer's *The Old Drama and the New*, the worst book ever written about drama, new or old; and the silliest. It was to be an informal chat in a cosy little room to about fifty members of the Society, but Sean was frightened when Horace Reynolds told him in soothing bits of information, as the car rattled along, that a lot of interest had been aroused in the lecture; that many wanted to hear it; that they had to take the large Hall, and that, instead of the quiet, simple fifty, hundreds and hundreds would be there. So Sean had to give one ear to hear what Horace was saying, and the other ear to hear himself praying for deliverance. Sean, standing on the professorial rostrum, gave his lecture, and, of course, was applauded. The audience could hardly do anything else out of politeness. Indeed, one middle-aged professor told Sean afterwards, *sotto voce*, that he wished he could lecture in that way; knowing quite well, if he did, he wouldn't hold his job a week. A hurried look at the buildings, a cosy hour with the younger students in their club-room, heightened by tea and sherry, and lowered by many questions that Sean couldn't answer, but answered all the same; and a trot round the modern library, rosy-red and inviting, confidently exclaiming in its layout and attractive façade that all older universities needed knocking down so that sensible premises could take their place, more suited to the outlook and needs of our changed and more attractive and secular life. Dinner then with the amiable Horace Reynolds and his charming wife, Kay, with their two lively and handsome children, John and Peggy, looking him over, without Sean having chance or time to show them he was something of a kid himself still: both married now, and Peggy a mother. Oh, we grow old, Master Shallow, we grow old! Later on, he was to entertain in Devon several of the young students when they had grown into combatants of the war against Nazism.

Swing low, swing high up on to the train again, and off to New York, sleeping roughly in a bunk as the huge train pounded its way along, char-char-charrity-char, with a clatter across a level-crossing, a roar diving into a tunnel, and loud, sibilant hiss penetrating opposing winds as she whirled by another train going the opposite way; and into the great cathedral of the New York station at five in the morning, to hurry down to the splendid underground restaurant where a wash

and a fine breakfast armed them for another day's excitement.
Off the next day to speak at a club in Philadelphia, to meet at
an exhibition of stage designs the lass, Kitty Curling, who had
played Mollser in the Abbey Theatre production of his *The
Plough and the Stars*, and who was now an American wife and
mother of a baby. A rapid talk of an hour with a group of
Pressmen, after the lecture, and on the train and off again for
New York, chut-chut-chuttity-chut, a clatter over level-cross-
ings, and a roar of a dive into a tunnel, waste o' time waste o'
time waste o' time, chut-chut-chuttity-chut, for he had spoken
and spoken, yet had had nothing to say. Oh, God, he must
have been born to be a bishop! For once in a while he was
feeling a sense of sin. He was doing all this to swell, by one or
by two, the numbers that came to see his play; a swift-flowing,
tightening, sibilant hiss as they passed a train whirling along
the opposite way; chut-chut-chuttity-chut, waste of energy
waste of energy doing what he couldn't do well, maybe what
he couldn't do at all. A dot of Irish humanity rushing around,
carried about in taxi and train to impress itself upon the
American people. Ravelling himself out of the American fabric
by trying to knit too much of himself into it, and all for the
sale of a few more tickets that he might still go haltingly on
through life. But needs must when the devil of echonomic
memory of past poverty drives one to where one doesn't want
to go. If these speeches got him into touch with the people,
they would be grand things; but the one sure way of being
intimate with humanity is to work with them, go in bus, ele-
vator and underground with them, or sit chatting with them by
their own firesides. Lectures built up on facts should be given
by scholars and experts; by those who have the faculty for
teaching, having fitted themselves for the job; chats by those
whose imagination would turn history into a song and
theology into a ceremonial dance.

Chut-chuh-chut-chuh-chuttity-chuh, over levels, under tun-
nels, through culverts, the train steamed into New York again,
a wash, a meal, an evening's chat with George Jean Nathan, a
sleep, and off again, in a taxi this time, to the Bronx, with Dr
Herring, President of the Bronx Rotary Club, to speak to its
members. A great gathering in a big room of a big Bronx
hotel, ready for lunch. Men and their wives assembled for
their monthly meeting, gay, and in a gavotte mind, withal

taking themselves very seriously; looking upon themselves as the leaders of the Bronx people, which in a sense they were, for they were the professional men and business men of the place; the better-off inhabitants. Indeed, from *Americana* we learn that a Pennsylvanian member said of Rotarians that 'Rotary was more than a luncheon club; it was a Posture of the soul'. (Now that the Vatican has banned any priest from membership, and warned its lay members to keep out of it, it is plain that the Vatican looks on Rotary as an Imposture of the soul. Even the innocent Rotarians banished from the Civitas Dei.) Well, here he was in the midst of the Midianites, eating with them and chatting away, till lunch was over, and the birds began to sing. A big green broadsheet was handed out to everyone, splashed all over with the words of the songs. He had it before him now. In the right-hand corner were pen-sketches of heads of pretty, neatly-hatted young ladies. In the centre, the title of The Bronx Rotary Club; and to the left of this, Welcome Ladies, leading into the festivity of the Bronx Rotary Greeting Song:

> Hollo, hollo, everybody – Bronx Rotary is greeting you today,
> Hollo, hollo, everybody – we're glad you're here,
> We hope you'll like your stay.
>
> Words by Andy Keogh.

First a song, led by the men grieving at being married to the women, then a verse by the women grieving at being married to the men, to the air of *The Man on the Flying Trapeze*; the men's verse going:

> Once I was happy, but now I'm forlorn,
> Since I've been married my liberty's gone,
> No more do I go out and stay until dawn;
> Gone are the girls of my dreams.
> Oh, the dame that I wed is so stubborn,
> And I try all I can her to please,
> But I'd give all I have for the freedom
> Of the Man on the Flying Trapeze!

They gathered this way monthly to sing and eat, and, if the chance came, to sling a speech from a guest at the assembled fathers and mothers badged with the Rotary spirit. Here they were, the smaller of the bigger men of New York City, doctors, dentists, solicitors, teachers, contractors on a small scale, and shopkeepers; active, hard-working, and important people, forming a vast part of the American public opinion; very simple and courteous to their guests. None of them spoke to him about his play, and Sean was suspicious that none had gone to see it. His name had appeared in the Press, and the leaders of the Bronx social life had been eager to show him off to their comrades, much in the same way as they might go to see a strange animal in their own Zoo. They sang loud, with a rough-edged harmony, but the songs didn't seem to echo in their hearts; looked as if they had to exhibit a gaiety and a confidence the state of things denied them. Few of them, perhaps, had any sense of a secure tenure of profit, even of life. They were striving in the deep middle of a deep depression; so they sang songs that brought to them no genuine thought of love, or adventure, pain, or doubt; less than a child singing a song of sixpence. But they were determined to be gay, fixing themselves, for the moment, in the daring hilarity of a song. Here we go again, Let me suffer and let me sing:

> Dear Old Girl, the robin sings about you,
> Dear Old Girl, it speaks of how I love you,
> The blinding tears are falling,
> As I think of my lost pearl,
> And my broken heart is calling,
> Calling for you, Dear Old Girl!

Nothing in the way of poetry; little in the way of verse; but, apparently, the best they could do to emotionally speak their minds. And who is big or grand enough to say it is awful? Perhaps there were some of the men there who had shed tears over the death of a Dear Old Girl. It wasn't impossible; or some woman who mourned the loss of a Dear Old Boy. No American folk-song flitted into their singing; like that about the little black bug from Mexico – the Boll Weevil; or Some got Drunk and some got Boozy, an' all got struck on Black-eye'd Susy; or the Nova Scotia one, *The Tree in the Wood*, that Sean had so often chanted himself among national groups in his own Dublin; or *The Dying Cowboy*:

Oh beat the drums slowly,
And play the pipes lowly,
And play the Dead March as I'm carried along.
Bring me to the valley
And lay the sod on me –
The poor dying Cowboy who knows he's done wrong!

One would be too near to their inner thoughts; maybe they knew none. Gay and irrepressible chaps and lassies, but haunted all the time: with home problems, with State divisions, with the growth of the unemployed, with the state of trade. Sean couldn't help feeling that there would be less disillusionment, fewer disappointments among these decent people if they hadn't to hurry about so much in search of bread; if life were but a little more certain; if today could tell even half of tomorrow's tale.

Only five minutes more, and the great liner would swing away from the giant dock. Life had given him one more grand experience: he had touched down on American shores, and had scored a try. He had made a good few good friends who would stand to him through a trying time, though he didn't know it then. He carried away with him many desirable memories, the strangest one 'The fervent blessing of an old priest' from Dr Morgan Sheedy of Altoona, Pennsylvania; the life-long friend of Dr Walter McDonald, so long a Professor of Theology in Maynooth College. Land of riches and of poverty, farewell, in whose sky hung the purple star of generosity. A young land, a little nervous of its own power, not quite sure of what to do with it; flexible in its moods and kindly in touch to strangers.

The siren blew, warning friends of passengers to leave the ship. Sean shook hands with George Jean Nathan and his friend, the lovely, regal Mimsie Taylor. Farewell! He was tired, very tired, from the strain of speaking publicly so often, without enthusiasm, without the desire to do it; for his words were not the ready ones, but the words thought of and handled before they ventured out to speak for themselves. Yet, withal, had he not had a beloved wife and child, with another on its way, waiting for his company, he would have stayed here where Ballyvourney spoke to Kiev, Budapest to Mexico, Edinburgh to Athens, Jerusalem to Rome; where the thoughts of all lands with their differing moods commingled. Well, farewell to all of ye, and my blessing remain behind me.

The five minutes had passed, and the liner swung out into the harbour, with Sean leaning over the side watching New York drawing away from him. It was a calm day, crisply cold; the evening was falling over the city, and Sean saw it fading in the half light of the dusk, its towering buildings darkened, and a myriad lights from hill and valley of windows gleamed like friendly eyes watching him go: a city that is the outcome of many civilizations – of Stonehenge, of Peru, of Mexico, medieval Europe; melted down, remoulded, and cast out into the modern America; before all men, with all its faults, tremendous, terrible, inspiring. Many thoughts about many he had met were embedded in his memory for ever: the long, lean figure of Eugene O'Neill in the latest of Daks, with a warm, welcoming smile softening his sombre face, the deep-set eyes of the great dramatist burning with a light like what would glow in the eyes of a battle-scarred crusader staring from a rocky, sun-browned hill at the distant city of Jerusalem; his wife, Carlotta, caring for him, a dark flame of loveliness; the clever, voluble Sinclair Lewis praising the goodness of the corncob; the sturdy Elmer Rice quivering with rage at the thought of what Nazism would do to the world; Richard Watts calmly raking through heaps of sandy stagecraft in the hope of finding a nugget, or, at least, enough gold dust to make a ring for a lady's finger; Lillian Gish growing younger as the rest grew old; Brooks Atkinson talking of Roscius and roses, or rushing from the theatre at curtain-fall to send a review skimming on to the prattling printing-press, his charming wife easing his impatience while setting elegant and comfortable hospitality before a guest; the open door of George Nathan's hotel home, and the cosy armchair within waiting to seat Sean safely; the kindly and bustling workers behind the scenes with whom Sean often had tea below the stage; and many more, and all. All fading into a sea mist now. Oh, Honey, fare thee well, fare thee well! Is America a land of God where saints abide for ever? Where golden fields spread fair and broad, where flows the crystal river? Certainly not flush with saints, and a good thing, too, for the saints sent buzzing into man's ken now are but poor-mouthed ecclesiastical film stars and cliché-shouting publicity agents,

Their little knowledge bringing them nearer to their
 ignorance,
Ignorance bringing them nearer to death,
But nearness to death no nearer to God.

Nor to man, either. Golden fields would spread fair and broad
when all men were one; spread fair and broad in all lands; and
saintship would be left to private enterprise. America, like all
other lands, was a land for men and women and children, and
that was enough for Sean; for where the people are is the land
that never hath an ending, that never hath an ending, that
never hath an ending.

The buildings now were but faint silhouettes, fading into the
lights of multitudinous windows; soon all these, too, would go,
and there would be nothing but a sullen sky above and a grey
and choppy sea below to keep him gloomy company.

Hail and farewell, America! It was unlikely he would ever
walk the streets of her cities again; so an Irish blessing and an
Irish goodbye to America's people who shall never have an
ending, never have an ending, never have an ending.